ADRIAN

What Ha

To Simon
Best wishes
Adri

ANOTHER SMALL PRESS
No.5

Copyright © Adrian Bean 2024
All rights reserved

ISBN 978-0-9957127-5-1

Published in Great Britain by Another Small Press, 2024

www.anothersmallpress.net
Cover design by Fine Fine Lines

Adrian Bean was born in Cardiff and grew up in Nottinghamshire. He has worked as a director and writer in theatre, radio and television for over forty years, and has always been fascinated by aeroplanes. In 1995 he directed the BBC's acclaimed and groundbreaking radio drama *BOMBER*, adapted from the novel by Len Deighton, broadcast in real time on Radio 4. He is a member of the Fosseway Writers based in Newark where he now lives. In 2023 Another Small Press published his first book *L For Lanc*, a collection of short stories. *What Happened* is his second book.

Contents

Author's Note	7
What Happened	11
Acknowledgments	343
Bibliography	345

Author's Note

This book is based on actual events. It is not a history of Bomber Command, nor of 305 Bomber Squadron or 2SFTS but the personal stories of people who were brought together by their service in those organisations. It is also not intended to be a definitive account of what happened over a Nottinghamshire village on Thursday June 12th, 1941.

Although I have tried to ensure the accuracy of the facts, there are some that will never be known for certain. Where historical fact has failed to provide the details, I have turned to the writings and testimony of others who had similar experiences, and of course, to my imagination.

Where possible, I have tried to rationalise punctuation and the spellings of names, places and ranks, which vary widely over time and distance. I sincerely apologise for any linguistic or typographical errors as well as for any imaginative liberties I may have taken with people and characters, living and dead.

Adrian Bean
May 2024

For my mother

One

'Look - RAF Syerston. That's where your uncle George's brother died.'

It is a warm, sunny afternoon in early May, 2022. I am driving Mum home from Newark, where we have spent a pleasant couple of hours chatting over Sunday lunch in the Prince Rupert, when we pass a road sign for RAF Syerston.

'During the war?' I ask, glancing at the sign.

'Yes,' she says. 'He was stationed there when he was killed.'

'Oh,' I say, immediately interested. 'What happened?'

'I don't really know,' she replies. 'George probably told me, but I've forgotten.'

I'm intrigued. 'Was he flying? Was he aircrew?'

'I don't know,' she says. 'I should have written it down.'

'What was his name?'

'I don't know...' Mum stares into the middle distance, trying to remember the dead man's name. 'I did know, but I've forgotten.'

I think for a moment. 'Syerston was a bomber station. They flew Lancasters from there.'

'Oh no,' she says. 'I don't think he was a pilot. But I'm sure George said it was an accident.'

'Maybe it was a collision, a crash, or an explosion at a bomb dump,' I say. 'If he was ground crew, he could have been involved in something like that, those things were quite common during the war.'

'I don't know,' she says. 'You don't think about it at the time, but when you're older you wish you'd asked more questions, and George is dead now, and my sister Ann, so the story's gone, I suppose.'

I'm surprised. Although in her early nineties now, Mum is always pretty hot on details about the family, relatives and places. It's odd that she doesn't remember the name of George's dead brother, or the story of how he died.

'I'll ask Fiona,' I say. 'She or Mike will know, they've been working on their family tree.' We lapse back into the familiar silence that preceded the conversation, each wandering off in our own thoughts.

Uncle George had married my mum's sister Ann in the early 1950s. They had one daughter, my cousin Fiona, who's now married to Mike. I'd always been fond of Uncle George – a genial, generous chap who cut a handsome figure with a high forehead, steely blue eyes, and a pipe permanently clenched between his teeth, reminding me of Mr Crabtree from the fishing books I pored over as a kid. I knew that he was a journalist and did his training on the local paper in the town where my parents grew up during the war years; I used to listen, fascinated, when he told us stories about how he and his editor on the *Goole Times* would have to operate under Government restrictions called 'D Notices', to prevent them from possibly revealing sensitive information to the enemy in their reporting. He'd impressed me with his seriousness, but there was always a look in his eye that suggested a sense of humour and a strong nonconformist rebellious streak.

However, to a small boy like me, what was really remarkable about Uncle George was that he wore a large built-up shoe, the result, my parents told me, of contracting polio as a child. I'd never seen anything like it and would always have to stop myself from staring. Everything else about his appearance - the pipe, the tweed jacket with leather elbow patches, and the neat plaid tie, gave him the reassuring appearance of those stock characters from 1950s British black-and-white films; doctor, solicitor, teacher, writer, aircraft designer, he could have played any of those parts. But those highly polished, cherry red, mix-matched shoes were endlessly fascinating to me.

By the time I get Mum home we have forgotten all about George's brother. Mum's conversation has taken us down a different road, and at the house there are a few odd jobs for me to do: changing a battery in the kitchen clock, replacing a light bulb, and making Mum a cup of tea. She is tired out from her lunch, so I leave her in front of the television and drive back to my flat in Newark, and it isn't long before I pass RAF Syerston again. When I was younger the Fosse Way used to run directly past the gates of Syerston, and I remember catching fleeting glimpses of hangars from the road and sometimes aircraft parked out on the perimeter. But recently the old Roman road was replaced by a bigger, faster A46 that took a slightly different course through a cutting, and Syerston was suddenly hidden from view.

I'd certainly not had any inkling of the tragedy George had suffered here, losing a brother, and in what were, presumably, such dramatic circumstances. I suppose he'd found it difficult to talk about, and the rest of the family too. Of course, George, like my mum, belonged to that great generation of people who lived through the war and saw personal loss on a regular, almost daily basis. They didn't weep and wail or even expect to talk about their woes – not in public anyway - everybody was suffering and there was a war to be won. They just got on with it, preoccupied with rationing and the Luftwaffe's nightly visits, so I can understand why the death of George's brother might not have been discussed often, or lightly.

Looking back now, I think it's true to say I wouldn't be writing this if it hadn't been for those magical words *RAF bomber station*. If Mum had said that Uncle George's brother had died of some illness, or in a road accident, I can't honestly say that I would have given it a second thought. But a wartime bomber station is something different. Growing up on a diet of black-and-white British war films, they have always held a special interest for me. On the many occasions when I've visited one, I can't help feeling surrounded by the ghosts of the men and women who once inhabited those open spaces beneath wide, lowering skies. History was created around those runways, hangars and dispersal points, and Syerston was no exception.

I don't know it yet, but the thought that a nameless relative who I'd never heard of until now might have had some association with the place, has started something that is going to obsess me for the best part of two years.

Two

I think about my uncle George's brother all the way back home to Newark. It seems odd that Mum shouldn't have mentioned this story before. I can't believe that she has and that I've simply forgotten it; my interest in all things RAF and World War Two would have ensured that I remembered it. My brain is idly stirring, trying to work out what might have happened, and why the story should be shrouded in such apparent mystery, and I have barely been in the flat for half an hour when I open up the laptop, unable to resist the urge to do a little digging. Having next to no information about the dead man, not even a Christian name, I figure where better to start than with RAF Syerston itself.

Syerston was a purpose-built bomber station, one of the last permanent aerodromes to be built at the end of the 1930s, when it had finally become clear that Hitler's Nazi regime was preparing for war; it was also equally clear that Britain, and in particular her air force, was ill-prepared to meet the threat. A large expansion programme, both of aircraft and stations, was rushed through, although it would be some time before the RAF's obsolete bombers would be replaced by anything like what was required, in design as well as numbers. RAF Syerston seems to have been intended to be a major base, as a special decoy airfield was also built two miles to the southwest, near the village of Kneeton. Known as 'Q' sites (which sound like something out of a cheap 1930s spy novel), these decoys were situated near to actual airfields, and dummy runways with lights were laid out in the hope of deceiving German raiders into dropping their bombs on open fields at night. They didn't always work. Just before midnight on 14

March 1941, a German aircraft dropped nine bombs on the real RAF Syerston. All the bombs exploded, causing severe damage but no loss of life. A month later to the day, a lone intruder (possibly a night fighter, hanging around to catch unsuspecting bombers as they landed), sprayed the airfield with machine gun fire during a night flying exercise. Again, there was damage but no fatalities. I don't think the 'Q' Sites lasted long.

Syerston airfield was laid out on an area of land between the River Trent to the west, and the A46 Fosse Way to the east (National Grid Reference SK730480 if you are interested). This ancient Roman road linked Exeter on the southwest coast to Lincoln, some 25 miles to the northeast of Syerston. The flat, open landscape in the east of England is perfect for airfields (and conveniently situated for dropping bombs on mainland Europe) and the area is littered with names such as Scampton, Coningsby and Waddington, bomber stations that would become famous during the war.

Syerston fitted the bill when it came to sites where the Air Ministry wanted to place its new aerodromes: flat, well-drained land, relatively free of trees and buildings, lying above sea level. The Trent ran inconveniently close by however, and there's a famous photograph of a 61 Squadron Lancaster that ended up in the river after a raid on Mannheim, which only goes to show that in wartime you can't always tick all the boxes. The Trent was, I subsequently learned, navigated on many occasions by airmen stationed at Syerston, as they had to make their way across it to get to the nearby Old Elm Tree Inn at Hoveringham, tantalisingly situated on the wrong bank of the river. Sitting with me in the watch office at Syerston one late summer morning, Squadron Leader Mark Williams told me the story of how Guy Gibson, a little the worse for wear, capsized an improvised ferry on the way back from the pub, giving his fellow drinkers a thorough soaking. Just one of many stories about the war hero that may or not be apocryphal.

The cost of building the three intersecting runways and

technical, administrative and personnel buildings that went to make up a bomber station of the time was around half a million pounds in old money. Covering an area of some 2,000 acres, this huge military community lay six miles to the southwest of Newark, a middling-sized Nottinghamshire market town with a colourful English Civil War history, and, coincidentally, the nearest town to the village where I grew up. The same town that I had recently moved to was the place where every Saturday in the mid-seventies I would go shopping with my mum and dad, having saved up my paper round money to buy the latest prog rock album or the next Airfix model. Yes, I was one of those kids.

Aerial view of RAF Syerston at the end of the war. The River Trent is top left and the A46 Fosse Way runs diagonally up the bottom right corner of the photograph. (RAF Cranwell Photograph)

RAF Syerston opened on 1 December 1940, and the next day it became home to two Polish bomber squadrons. That summer the Poles were replaced by a squadron of Canadian flyers, who themselves were transferred that December in anticipation of the arrival of Nos 61 and 106 squadrons, both of which were equipped with the new Avro Lancaster. 106 Squadron was led by Guy Gibson, in the days before he led the 'Dam Busters' and became a VC. Flying from Syerston, the BBC's first war correspondent, Richard Dimbleby, hitched a ride on Gibson's Lancaster to make a special recording of the first large-scale raid on Berlin. Apparently Dimbleby passed out early in the flight, the result of a faulty oxygen pipe which was soon fixed by a member of the crew, and he quickly recovered, recording his experiences for his radio audience. However, his composure only lasted until the raiders reached Berlin, when, according to legend (and almost certainly fact) the determinedly gung-ho Gibson wasn't convinced he had found the correct aiming point and insisted on flying around the heavily defended target three times before finally dropping his bombs. Dimbleby reportedly left his flying meal of bacon and eggs all over the interior of the Lancaster's fuselage, but the next day's broadcast on the BBC was a great success.

More interestingly perhaps, at least in terms of my uncle George's brother, I discover that there had in fact been a serious accident at Syerston, of the kind that I imagined he might have been involved in. On 8 December 1942 a reserve Lancaster, all bombed-up and waiting as the rest of the squadron prepared to take off for a raid on Turin, accidentally dropped a case of incendiaries (probably caused by the vibrations of a passing Lanc). This was seen from the Watch Office by the Station Commander, Group Captain Augustus 'Gus' Walker, a larger-than-life character who, terrified that the burning incendiaries would set off the 4,000lb 'Cookie' in the Lancaster's bomb bay, promptly jumped into his staff car and chased across the airfield to try and help prevent disaster. Although ground crews had managed to alert the Lancaster's crew and got them away from danger, Walker arrived just as the 'Cookie' went off, with an enormous explosion that was felt many miles away. Walker was blown two hundred yards away from the wreckage, losing half of his right arm in the process, and rushed to hospital along with a number of other casualties. As a footnote to the story, it seems that when Walker woke up in hospital, visited by Gibson, his main concern was for the missing brand-new leather glove which was lying somewhere on the airfield, still on his right hand. Again, apocryphal perhaps, but a nice story.

There are no reports of any deaths in connection with the accident, but this is exactly the kind of dramatic incident I imagine Uncle George's brother could have died in. Seized by enthusiasm, I write an email to my cousin:

Hello Fiona,

I hope you don't mind me asking this, but I wonder if you might be able to help me with a bit of family history?
Today I was driving Mum home from Newark, and we passed RAF Syerston. She mentioned that your father's brother had died at Syerston while serving with the RAF, but couldn't remember any of the details, such as his name, the date of his death, his rank and role, or the circumstances of the incident, which she thought had been some sort of accident.
I have done a bit of digging online and found that there had been an explosion in late 1942, but no details about any deaths, so that probably wasn't it, and of course there were bound to be many accidents during wartime. You may not have any of these details either - it is frustrating when we don't ask more questions about these things until it is too late. But if you do, I'd very much appreciate your help. Don't worry if not.
I hope that all is well and look forward to hearing from you.
Very best wishes,
Adrian.

Fiona replies almost immediately:

> Hi Adrian,
> Great to hear from you. We are fine, thank you. Do hope you are too.
> It's very kind of you to take an interest in Uncle Bill. He was William Parkinson, born 30/10/1921 which is easy as he and Dad were twins. It's going to take a bit of searching to find his death certificate (I hope I have it). I was always told that he died in a mid-air collision in poor visibility on his first solo flight. I knew it was in your neck of the woods but didn't know the name of the airfield, so I'm grateful to hear that.
> I'm including a photo of Bill.
> My best,
> Fiona.

I hadn't known that my uncle George had a twin, but I can immediately see the resemblance, in the eyes particularly, and the set of that distinctive mouth and chin. And to me at least, the information helps perhaps to explain why his death was not discussed greatly. I am the father to twin sons myself, young men now, and I know how painful the loss of one would be to the other, not to mention the agony their mother and I would suffer just thinking, never mind talking about it.

But re-reading the emails now I am surprised at my lack of tact. I hadn't begun by giving Fiona my news or asking about her family - I just launched into the subject of her dead relative, asking for details about the tragic circumstances. To simply plough straight in there without any pleasantries seems to demonstrate a mighty absence of sensitivity on my part. The officers who wrote those sometimes blunt, impersonal letters informing parents that their sons had died in the service of king and country at least had the excuse that they were writing letters quickly and regularly, and sensitivity couldn't always be the prime consideration. Direct communication of basic information was probably the priority, as well as security. I could at least have shown a bit more empathy.

Fiona says that Bill died in a mid-air collision (Mum had described it as 'an accident'), which probably rules out my rather fanciful idea that he could have been part of that heroic action in which 'the one-armed bandit' acquired his nickname.

William 'Bill' Parkinson (Fiona Reid)

But I have a name now – William Parkinson, known to family and friends as Bill – and a photograph of a man – no, let's be honest, a boy, because that's really all he is - wrapped up in an RAF greatcoat, ready to play his part in the war. In her email Fiona says that he was born in 1921, so that would have made him around 21 if he had died in 1942, but I can't help feeling he looks younger than that. In photographs and films of the time, men always seem to look older than their actual years, but I'd put him at 18 or 19, just a kid, clearly still wet behind the ears. But joining up would turn him into a man, very quickly, if for only a very short time. I am well aware of the extreme youth of most of the fighting servicemen during World War Two, but the photograph only emphasises that most of the men who fought and died in Bomber Command were really boys.

I immediately find myself wondering what was going through his mind as he posed for the photograph? That he would make his parents proud, in his smart new uniform? That his mother would be able to hold her head up high, producing the photograph when neighbours asked, 'How's Bill and what's he doing now?' Or maybe there was a girl Bill was keen on, and he was thinking that she couldn't help but be impressed by his brave decision to volunteer? Or was his head just full of romantic dreams of aerial adventures, inspired by stories in The Champion, Wizard, and Biggles?

I notice the white flash in his cap and wonder what it signifies. A quick search online tells me it was worn by aircrew under training until they qualified and were promoted to Sergeants or commissioned as Pilot Officers. So, when the photograph was taken he was still learning to fly, and Fiona says that she always understood that he was killed when on his first solo flight. That means this photograph would have been taken perhaps only months or weeks before his death, depending on how long it would take to train a pilot in the middle of the war, which I don't know. Fiona can't remember when he died, but if it was around 1942, with the RAF's bombing campaign increasing in intensity, losses were increasing dramatically, and the need for new aircrew was high.

Would Bill (already I'm thinking of him by that name) have known the risks involved in the life he was preparing for? More importantly, would he have known how many young men died in accidents during training, as he was to do shortly. I hardly think so. Those thoughts couldn't have been further from his mind. Studying this boy's fresh features, I can't help seeing my own twin sons at that age and imagining what might have motivated them to do what Bill did. I also wonder how I would have felt in his parents' position: on the one hand, proud that my son was doing his bit, stepping up to help in the fight against Nazism, and on the other, terrified at the prospect of my precious boy putting himself into such danger.[1]

I hope desperately that his parents were on good speaking terms with their son when he died, that Bill's joining up hadn't been the cause of some terrible family ruction, as it sometimes was. The thought of the physical and emotional distance that exists between me and my sons brings the guilt and shame of my family break-up flooding back. But it's too much to think about, and I distract myself by sending an email straight back to Fiona:

Hi,
That's wonderful - mum wasn't sure if he was aircrew or not. Absolutely no rush for me though!
I hope all's well!
Ade x

---

[1] Overall, 51% of Bomber Command aircrews were killed on operations, totalling more than 55,000 men, and 12% of aircrew were killed or wounded in non-operational accidents. (Imperial War Museum)

Three

'Bill?' says Mum, confused. 'I don't remember a Bill.'

'His name was William, but Fiona referred to him as Bill,' I say. 'I suppose that was the family nickname.'

We are in Mum's front room. I am telling her what Fiona told me about her uncle and it triggers memories. She remembers the house where the Parkinsons lived: '9 Fountayne Street, Goole.' She spells the name out, 'F-O-U-N-T-A-Y-N-E,' as it is unusual, and tells me that Gertrude Parkinson, Bill and George's mother, was a widow. Her husband William, a Minister in the Methodist church[2], had died sometime before the war, so at the time of Bill's death she would have been living with George, and Mum thinks, his elder sister Margaret. Mum says she always felt especially sorry for Gertrude, being first widowed, as well as losing her daughter Margaret to illness, having one son George whose life had been made difficult by polio, and then losing his twin brother William in the war. She pauses for a moment, thinking back to those days, and remembers happier times.

Mum grew up Enid Wilson, in a solidly working-class family in Richard Cooper Street, Goole, a small town on the River Ouse, and the most inland port in Britain (some thirty miles from its bigger neighbour, Hull). The bay-fronted terrace is gone now, recently bulldozed and replaced by ugly modern housing, but she has fond memories of living there with her parents George Arthur, a farm labourer, mother Edith Annie,

---

[2] Bill's grandfather, George Parkinson, was the author of a history of his early life working in the pits and the Wesleyan community in the northeast, *True Stories of Durham Pit-Life*, published 1912.

her two brothers Fred and Roy, and three older sisters Doreen, Edith and Charlotte Annie.

The last of these, Mum remembers, announced one day that she was fed up with people calling her Annie, (or even worse by the nickname Lottie), and wanted to be known henceforth simply as Ann. She had just won a place at Teacher Training College, and Mum could imagine her bringing home a new friend and wincing every time she was referred to as 'our Lottie,' preferring instead the rather more glamorous name of the actress Ann Todd, the star of the 1945 film *The Seventh Veil* and to whom (to me at least) she bore more than a passing resemblance. Surprisingly perhaps, her mother Edith Annie was 'fine about it,' but according to Mum her father George was clearly hurt by his daughter's decision to abandon her grandmother's name, and sulked mightily.

In 1947 Ann married George Parkinson, who was then a reporter on the *Goole Times*. Mum isn't sure how they met, but Fiona tells me that it was in a sweet shop, when Ann was buying sweets and George was stocking up on tobacco. According to Fiona, Ann had already known his brother Bill as they were regulars at the tennis club, Bill being more the sporty type than George. After getting married they lived temporarily with his mother Gertrude in the red-brick house on Fountayne Street, and Mum thinks her sister was annoyed when she saw the house that my Mum (who by this time had met and was engaged to the boy next door, Gerald Bean) had saved up and bought just around the corner in Frederick Street. It looked beautiful, said Mum, because Dad, a painter and decorator by trade, had done it all up, bringing home rolls of wallpaper and tins of paint from work, and once he put his mind to a job, he completed it to perfection. George apparently, was not at all inclined in that way; a wizard with words she said, not so clever with a hammer and paintbrush. Worse still, the house had been advertised in the *Goole Times*, and Ann couldn't understand why George hadn't seen it first. But then George got a new job on the national paper the

Methodist Recorder, and he and Ann moved nearer to London, and then finally to Salisbury, where they remained.

I am keen to bring the conversation back round to Bill and his mother, and ask Mum about Gertrude Parkinson, and she just replies in one word, with emphasis, 'Posh'. She seems to have been a strict and possibly quite imposing character, but Mum is at pains to emphasise that Gertrude was a very kind and generous person. She remembers that when I was Christened, the family gathering took place in the garden at Fountayne Street. By this time my parents had moved to Cardiff with Dad's new job, but Mum wanted me to be baptised at the Methodist church where she had been married, and there seemed nowhere to have the post-Christening party. Gertrude kindly offered to host the gathering in her house, and Mum shows me the photos.

In the mid-1960s, with me and my younger brother Jonathan in tow, Mum and Dad moved from Cardiff to Nottinghamshire, and although this was a long way from George and Ann's house in Salisbury, we often visited each other. I particularly remember one trip to Salisbury in the 1960s when I was about 7 or 8, at a time when kids were still allowed to scramble over the sarsens and bluestones at Stonehenge, and running around the remains of Old Sarum.

As I grew up I saw less and less of the Parkinsons, with little communication for many years other than Christmas cards, and occasional meetings at weddings and funerals. Ann passed away in 1998, looked after in her final years by George until she had to go into a nursing home, where she died shortly afterwards. I can't remember the last time I saw George; Mum was always fond of him, but sadly he was unable to attend her 80th birthday party in 2009, being unwell, and died six months later in Salisbury District Hospital.

I can't help thinking about Bill, and how he would have fitted into these memories had he not died during the war. I would have been so excited to have an uncle who'd been in Bomber Command. The nearest I got to that was my Captain in the Boys' Brigade, who was a navigator on Halifaxes when

My christening party in the garden of 9 Fountayne Street, May 1960. L-R Auntie Ann, Uncle Geoff (with Uncle Philip), Uncle Arthur, Mum, Nan, 'Auntie' Lucy, Uncle John, Auntie Doreen, Auntie Enid, Gertrude Parkinson, Uncle Roy. Fiona is in the white dress (Bean Family)

he was shot down over France.[3] But his untimely death left a Bill-shaped hole in the lives of George and Ann, not to mention his mother Gertrude, and I wonder how he would have impacted on their lives had he lived. What would he have done with his life? Where would he have lived? What adventures would he have had? How would he be remembered, if not as a war hero? Would he have found someone, married, settled down, and had children? Or would he have lived alone? As it is, Bill, as with all the dead, was a ghost, permanently hovering in the background of so many family stories, and yet because he was gone, he, unlike his living relatives and friends, remained as he was all those years ago when he joined the war that changed the course of so many lives.

---

[3] The story of 'Bert' Spiller's escape and return to England is told in his book *Ticket to Freedom*. William Kimber 1988.

Four

Email from Fiona:

Hello Ade,
Do hope you're v well and enjoying the summer so far.
I've finally had a dig around in many dusty boxes and found some more about Bill. Sorry it's taken so long – anyway these are the bones from a pile of letters etc. Haven't yet found his birth cert but know he died 26/06/1940 at 1125am near Beckswood, Newark (I can't find the actual woods but you may know them). Another telegram was from RAF Syerston, as you mentioned, detailing the arrival of the cortège in Goole. He enlisted on 3/9/40 and his rank on discharge was Leading Aircraftman. RAF Trade recorded as Under Training Pilot.
The circumstances were as Dad described, a mid-air collision in poor visibility. His full name was William Wharton Parkinson, Wharton being his maternal grandmother's maiden name (I think).
That's all for now. It's been fun getting a clearer picture so thank you for the prompt.
We're wondering whether we could call on your mother and perhaps take her out for afternoon tea at some point this summer. Does she have any plans to be away that you're aware of? It would be great if we could see you too but it's always so difficult finding a time to suit everybody.
Hope that's of interest/help. Love to your mum.
Fiona X

Well, that has well and truly put the cat among the pigeons. Firstly, Fiona's email seems to confirm that Bill definitely couldn't have died in the Gus Walker incident because that happened in late 1942 and she says he died in 1940. So I can finally put that rather romantic possibility to one side.

But the date Fiona has given for Bill's death (26/06/1940) would actually be *earlier* than the date of his enlistment (3/9/40) so I'm guessing that one or both of the dates is wrong, which only confuses the issue. Is it a typo on Fiona's part, or an official mix-up?

Fiona mentions that Bill died in 'a mid-air collision, in poor visibility,' near Beckswood, Newark. That placename means nothing to me – I'll have to do some searching. But she gives a precise time for the accident, 1125am, so I guess she must have some official document with that information. But a mid-air collision implies another aircraft; would one therefore expect some mention of the other aircraft and/or crew? The mention of a funeral cortege is also interesting; it sounds rather grand and official, not necessarily the kind of thing normally associated with the death of a humble Leading Aircraftman, next to the lowest rank in the RAF in World War Two. And I am surprised that Bill should have been buried in Goole – it is a good fifty or sixty miles away from Syerston and my understanding was that wartime burials would be carried out locally, especially, again, when they concerned a mere u/t pilot.[4]

The information Fiona has provided seems to raise as many questions as it answers. It is mid-evening and I had been going to do nothing more interesting than sit in front of the telly, but I make a mug of tea, fill a plate with chocolate biscuits, and break out a pen and notepad, preparing for a long session on the laptop trying to answer these questions. Having these few details means I should be able to open some doors on the internet. I set a playlist of old prog favourites running and type in Bill's full name and rank. Within a few seconds I get a flush of excitement when I see his name immediately appear in the list of possibilities:

---

[4] Under-Training Pilot.

AIR81 Casualty File Description
Leading Aircraftman WW Parkinson, 19.

I have no idea what an AIR81 Casualty File is, but it looks like I'm on the right track. I click on the link and am taken to the RAF Commands website, a forum where, among other things, researchers share information and cross-reference details about aircraft and aircrew losses in World War Two. I think that Bill died in a mid-air collision, so I'm not surprised to see another name alongside his:

Leading Aircraftman WR Newton, 26.

This was probably the pilot who was flying the other aircraft – as a Leading Aircraftman he could also be an u/t pilot, like Bill. It looks like we have a tragic accident resulting in the loss of two young lives.

But I'm wrong. Further down there are more names...

Flight Lieutenant T Stefanicki, (Polish), Pilot Officer M Wojtowicz, (Polish), Pilot Officer S Kowalcze, (Polish), Pilot Officer A Zirkwitz, (Polish), Sergeant K Mruk, (Polish), Sergeant J Krawczyk, (Polish), killed.

My blood instantly runs cold. Six other men were killed in this incident? I almost can't believe what I'm reading, but have to carry on as the entry goes on to describe:

A mid-air collision near Beckswood between Oxford T1334, 2 Service Flying Training School, and Wellington R1017, 305 Squadron, 12 June 1941.

The enormity of it hits me almost physically – an Oxford trainer, flown, I now presume, by Bill and this other man, collided with a Wellington bomber, carrying a crew of six Polish airmen, *all killed*. This story is no longer that of the death of one young man, which only a few minutes ago I was assuming, but *eight*.

I take a moment to breathe, have a gulp of tea, and think about it. When I saw that list of names, I felt the physical and emotional impact in exactly the same way I would if someone had told me of the death of a friend. And strangely, at the same time, I had the momentary sensation that I was somehow intruding on the private grief of the families of those eight dead men. Reading on, another post gives the same information, but also includes the Christian names of the Wellington crew: Tadeusz, Marian, Stanisław, Aleksander, Kazimierz, Jerzy. Already they have ceased to be a mere list of names and ranks and are assuming characters in my brain. And Bill's fellow crewman on the Oxford begins to emerge from the shadows: his first name is William, the same as Bill's. I have a clear date for Bill's death now: 12 June 1941, so it *was* a typo in Fiona's email after all. And although I already had an idea that Bill was young when he died, I didn't know for sure just how young. But he was 19. He would have had his 20th birthday that autumn, if he'd lived.

I remember reading that there were two Polish bomber squadrons stationed at Syerston when it first opened, and 305 Squadron, it turns out, was one of them, flying Wellingtons. A little more searching also gives me the information that 2 Flying Training School is now based at Syerston, and although the Oxford trainer was from 2 Service Flying Training School, I assume they are one and the same, so maybe Bill was also flying from Syerston at the time of the accident. But it seems odd that an operational bomber squadron and a training squadron would be at the same station, so I put that to one side for further investigation.

And I'm confused about the location of the accident. Mum had said that Bill died at Syerston, which had initially led me down the Gus Walker/Lancaster explosion cul de sac; Fiona had seemed to confirm that in her email, although intriguingly I see now that she refers to Beckswood, Newark. The brief entry on the website I'm looking at now simply refers to a 'mid-air collision near Beckswood.' No mention of Newark.

I don't know of a village called Beckswood in the Newark area, but of course it could be the name of some woods that would probably only be only known locally. It's a habit of mine to always buy an Ordnance Survey map of the area I'm living in, just so I can search out interesting features, or match places I've seen with locations on the map. So I pull my Explorer 271 off the shelf and check the immediate area around Syerston and Newark, but can find nothing with the name Beckswood.

Google, however, comes up with a 'Becks Wood' which is about 20 miles northwest of Newark, and only a mile or so from RAF Metheringham, also a wartime Bomber station, although not operational at the time of the accident. While this Becks Wood does seem to be a long way from RAF Syerston and Newark, at a cruising speed of around 200mph a Wellington bomber flying from there could easily cover that distance in a few minutes, so it is quite possible that both aircraft could have been in that area on the fateful day. A little more searching reveals that a very short distance away from this Becks Wood is Nocton Hall, which once served as an RAF military hospital. Could some injured airmen, including my uncle's brother Bill, have been taken there, only to die later from their wounds, and thus be recorded as having died near Beckswood? And it would tie in with that tantalising detail in Fiona's email - that Bill died at the precise time of 1125. Perhaps the time of death was recorded by a nurse, standing by the hospital bed? This could be the 'Beckswood near Newark' where the mid-air collision occurred after all...

But no matter how much I try to convince myself, it still doesn't seem right. A further check confirms that Nocton Hall wasn't turned into a military hospital until sometime after Bill's death. And the Becks Wood near RAF Metheringham is a 20-odd mile drive along the A17 to Newark. That's not close; you certainly wouldn't describe it as being near Newark, especially when its far closer (and much bigger) neighbour,

Lincoln, is only five minutes' drive by car or speeding wartime ambulance. In that case, it seems to make much more sense to me that any RAF officer, when recording Bill's death, would surely have indicated the death as happening at Becks Wood near *Lincoln*, a place 10 times closer to Syerston than Newark.

Looking again on the RAF Commands website I follow the thread about the AIR81 report and see on another entry further down that the deaths of all eight men are noted as happening 'over Elton' and registered in Bingham. Elton is a tiny village only 5 miles from Bingham, where my mum lives and where I grew up, but in the *opposite* direction from Syerston, and further away from Newark. I immediately assume that the post is incorrect, confusing Elton with *Elston*, which is the village next to Syerston, no more than two miles from the airfield as the crow (or Wellington bomber) flies. It is more than conceivable that the collision happened over Elston, with both aircraft apparently flying from the same station, in the confusion as aircraft take off and land. The mention of Elton is probably a typo, just like the confusion over Bill's enlistment and death dates in Fiona's email. The fog of war, and all that...

Still, I remain confused. But buzzing with the excitement of having unearthed the information about the collision with the Wellington bomber, I push the confusion to the back of my mind, and immediately email Fiona with the news:

Hi Fiona,

The info you've come up with is fascinating – I did a quick dig and found out the following.

Bill was flying with a co-pilot (who was presumably also training as they were the same rank) named William R Newton.

They were flying an Airspeed Oxford trainer and were in collision with a Vickers Wellington bomber from 305 Squadron, flown by an all-Polish crew, who all died, and are buried in the Newark Polish War Cemetery.

It's all fascinating, isn't it?

Anyway, I hope this helps fill in some blanks!
V best wishes,
Ade x

PS. Yes, we'd love to see you over the summer! Mum doesn't have any plans so any date that is convenient for you is good for us.

Five

Okay. Before we go any further, we should get a couple of things straight. Firstly, as the previous chapter will demonstrate to anyone who knows anything about these matters, I am no expert at investigating air crashes that happened 80 years ago. Cards on the table, I know absolutely nothing about the way to go about finding answers.

I know something about aeroplanes, especially those from the Second World War. I can tell the difference between a Vickers Wellington 1c and Mk 11 at a glance and could bore anyone stiff with facts and stories about the Wimpy. But the detective work involved in finding out what happened, where, and how... well, frankly that's all new territory to me.

No shit Sherlock, I hear the experts say. Well, hands up, part of the problem is that the people who *do* know these things, those members of the extremely select community of the initiated, know it all so well that they sometimes don't bother going further than the shorthand and acronyms so beloved of the RAF itself. A novice like me, entering that shadowy, mysterious world for the first time, is wary, cautious, and generally... well, *confused*. 'Check the AIR81,' they say, or 'You'll find that info at Cranwell,' or 'Haven't you tried Hendon? What about Gloucester?' To be honest, armed even with the little starting information I had, anyone who knows anything about this business would have answered all the questions I was asking within a few hours. But my journey was destined to take much longer.

Not that these thoughts were going through my mind when I saw an email from Fiona arrive in my email inbox.

Truly fascinating. Thank you - so much and so quickly. I wish Dad could have known all this, but it might have been painful too. Suppose that's why asking lots of questions when people were directly affected feels insensitive.
Glad to hear Enid is home for the summer.
Will be in touch about a visit soon, hopefully.
Fx

Fiona's reply is surprisingly short, and well... just *short*. She doesn't even open with a 'Hi Ade,' or 'Dear Adrian.' My blood runs cold, realising what I have done by sending her that email late at night. Suddenly I see how it must have felt to her, getting an email about this tragic incident in which not one young man, her father's brother, but eight young men all lost their lives. Which brings me to the second point: my insensitivity. In my haste to share my discovery I'd just dumped this information on her. Unlike me, excited by the actual process of digging and searching and revealing, she just opened an email and the news will have hit her with all the brutal finality of the telegram which was sent to Mrs Parkinson when *her* life was suddenly torn apart. No matter how much Gertrude will have prepared herself for that awful moment, suddenly there was a knock on the door, and then the dreaded telegram in her trembling hand. What I'm now imagining might have happened to Bill's mother in June 1941, in a sense, did actually happen to Fiona this very night, thanks to me.

There's no comparison, obviously, but my mind is taken back to that day when the envelope containing the letter confirming the finalisation of my divorce landed on the mat. I picked it up, knowing exactly what it would contain, but I couldn't open it straight away. I knew that after reading it my life would never be the same again. In a way I wanted life to continue in the same old way, to pretend my family hadn't disintegrated, to drag out my previous, settled existence for just a few more hours, minutes, seconds even. But I knew it couldn't be like that and had to open it. Not that opening it or not would have made any difference anyway – what happened had happened. Of course, I knew that my envelope was only going to contain confirmation of the divorce I'd been waiting for, not the unexpected death of a son. Bill wasn't even on active service, he was still learning to fly, the white flash in his cap showed that. *It can't be true, can it?* his mother must have thought as she sank into a chair, her heart beating wildly. What hell must it have been like for those mothers and fathers, those wives, sisters, brothers?

And what must it have been like for Fiona, to suddenly read, out of the blue, that what had always been 'my uncle died in the war' now became 'my uncle *and seven other men in the two planes that collided in mid-air,* died in the war.'

I have done that to her. I am responsible.

What does that say about me?

Six

I moved into my flat in Newark around six months before Mum and I drove past RAF Syerston on that day in early May. It's not where I ever expected to be living, but how I came to be here is a familiar story: a 30-year marriage disintegrating into loveless recrimination and finally divorce.

We were living in Scotland, in a tiny village, by a loch surrounded by low mountains which were stunningly beautiful in the summer and gloomily oppressive for the rest of the year. In winter the sun barely rose above the jagged black skyline and for days on end the village seemed to be mired in perpetual twilight. But there were eagles in the skies above and stags roared in the hills. Deer wandered into the garden and an osprey fished in the loch. We loved it, telling ourselves we were living in the most beautiful place on earth (which was true). We'd moved up from England a few years before, with dreams of finding an old farm steading and converting it into a place where people could come on artistic holidays, writing, painting and performing while recharging their batteries in the gorgeous surroundings. Maybe it was never going to be anything more than a dream. In truth it was probably just a last-ditch attempt to save our dying marriage.

The new life proved difficult from the start. The artistic holiday plan never got off the ground. I was immediately called away to work down south so my wife was left alone and lonely, a city girl trying to establish relationships in a small, insular and self-obsessed rural community. There were long-standing problems in the marriage of course, which we'd hoped we might be able to work out in the peace and quiet of the Scottish countryside, but somehow they were only magnified by the isolation.

Within a couple of years we separated and when the marriage went into its death throes in the late summer of 2019 I moved out to a small cottage in a neighbouring village about 12 miles down the road. Confused and numb, trying to come to terms with a future I hadn't expected, I began the process of creating another new life. This was easier said than done in a village which comprised one small shop (closing at 3 and never open on Sundays or Bank Holidays), a dismal petrol station straight out of a backpacker slasher movie, and a bar that looked like a good place to have a fight. The cottages and houses were spread along the single street, and that was it. The village's only claim to fame was that it had been burned to the ground by retreating Jacobite forces in the rebellion of 1715, which just about said it all. As with the village I'd just run away from, most of the current residents were either retired, or worked in the city and retreated behind drawn curtains in the evenings. Alone, and an outsider, I couldn't avoid the irony that I was in exactly the same situation my wife had found herself in when we first moved to Scotland. What goes around comes around, as they say.

When I did meet people, I avoided mentioning the separation unless pushed, as it was something I still hadn't fully come to terms with myself. It also wasn't me. For nearly 30 years I had been a family man, and still felt that I was, although I knew it was ending. *Had ended*, I had to keep reminding myself. Like a cheap, ill-fitting suit this new identity as a separated, single man just didn't sit comfortably. I was going to have to look in the mirror, rethink myself, and lose some metaphorical as well as literal weight, if that new suit was ever going to look good on me. As it was, the fact that I spent most of that winter away, working down south and returning only at weekends, meant I made precious few acquaintances, and even fewer friends. My time in the village was divided between long walks in the hills and sitting in front of the log fire, staring into the flames, drinking whisky and generally feeling sorry for myself.

Christmas came and went. Following a difficult and emotional graduation ceremony in November it was clear that I wasn't going to meet up with my sons over the festive period, and faced with the prospect of spending Christmas alone I volunteered to help out at the local homeless shelter, something I'd often thought of doing, and in the event, hugely enjoyable and rewarding. A few weeks later I spent my birthday alone. *Next year*, I told myself, it'll be different next year, when things have settled down. But the television and radio were full of stories of a strange new virus, supposedly originating in bats, which was spreading like wildfire around China and moving into Europe. Next thing, I was preparing a shoot in the studios outside Glasgow, when the producer came into the office and told us all to go home.

'How long for?' we asked.

'No idea', he said. 'Just go home. We'll be in touch.'

The next day I drove into town to deliver my signed application for Divorce to my soon-to-be ex-wife's solicitor. It was mid-afternoon but the office was locked, and the streets were completely deserted. Everywhere was strangely, eerily quiet. A drunk staggered past me, yelling that *I should be at home, didn't I know about the plague?* He carried on weaving down the street, laughing crazily. I felt like I was in some kind of zombie movie. Hurriedly I pushed the envelope through the letterbox, hoping that someone would pick it up before the plague was over, and drove home to enter an involuntary isolation that would last for several months.

I have always been someone who was happy in his own company, and so lockdown began as the extended holiday I'd needed but had denied myself for years. However, the isolation also meant that I was alone with my thoughts, and unable to avoid examining the reasons that had brought me here. That could only be good, surely? But the more I went over who said what and when and why, the more confused and hurt I felt.

Within seconds I would be mentally back in the middle of a vicious, no-holds-barred argument with my wife, and was left feeling sickened, ashamed or furious. One day I felt stupid, blaming myself for my mistakes and failings, for being selfish and not thinking enough about her needs, or guilty for being too stubborn to go the extra mile and try to find a way to mend a salvageable marriage; the next I saw only too clearly that I had done as much if not more than any man could reasonably be expected to do, that there comes a point when, to borrow a cliché, you have to put yourself and your mental health first. Then I was back to self-blame, guilt and regret, going round and round in existential circles, never finding any simple answers. Because there are no simple answers. None of it made sense, although I suppose the one conclusion I was drawing was that what had happened had to be for the best; that if this was painful, at least it wasn't as bad as the awful, drawn-out torture of continual arguments, coldness and recrimination that I had run away from.

And so I would get through the day, then the next day, another week, another month, obsessively watching reruns of *Judge Judy* on the television, and devouring DVDs of old films. As the lovely lockdown spring turned into gorgeous summer I sat in the cottage garden beneath a vast buddleia, watching the flowers emerge below the stone walls, the apple blossom come and go; sometimes I would look up from my book, surprised again that there was nobody walking down the lane, no sound of cars or children playing, no vapour trails high up in the empty blue sky. In the evenings I sat outside by the fire pit, sipping a malt and staring into the flames for long periods, thinking of nothing, feeling nothing except an ashy emptiness, and an aching loneliness; all the time trying to make sense of what had happened, and seeming to get nowhere.

I'd tell myself this wasn't the way it was supposed to be for a man going through a divorce. When I'd first moved out of the family home I'd expected that I'd be able to talk about IT with friends over a pint or a meal, at work, or at the football, but just when I needed to talk, lockdown had made that practically impossible. My grown-up sons, living with their mother in the family home only a few miles down the road, could have been a thousand miles away for all the difference it made. Boris's insistence on socially distanced households even within families meant we were unable to see each other in person. In phone calls to friends or my mother I avoided the subject; it didn't seem right or fair to ring friends in order to pour out my misery, particularly when other people were really suffering because of the pandemic – losing friends and family to the virus – so I chatted about the banalities of lockdown, giving the impression that I was dealing with it all just fine, and the reality of my situation was filed away for possible later discussion. Three hundred miles away, down in England, my mother was also going through the pandemic alone, having lost Dad some ten years earlier, and although on the surface she never admitted to feeling lonely, lockdown had obviously increased her isolation. When we talked on the phone, Mum found it especially hard to understand that I'd not seen or spoken to my sons for weeks, even months on end. As did I, although that was more from a refusal to dwell on the situation than anything else. It was just too painful to face what was happening, alone. And of course, Mum and I avoided discussion of this difficult emotional subject.

But despite my inability or refusal to discuss them, the dark thoughts were still going round and round in my head and becoming darker with every turn. In a rare moment of clarity I saw that my fascination with *Judge Judy* probably came from some unhealthy subconscious desire to see a wrong righted, a guilty party identified, and a just punishment meted out. Crazy, I know. The solution was easy - no more *Judge Judy*. One day I realised with a shock that I hadn't actually touched another human being for several months, and couldn't remember the last time I had laughed, except when watching something on the telly, or reading PG Wodehouse. But I wasn't sharing that laughter with another person. Not so easy.

There was a nice bottle of Champagne sitting in the fridge which I'd kept since an awards ceremony in pre-Covid days (how long ago that seemed) and I nursed a dark fantasy that perhaps I'd open it on The Big Day when the divorce was finalised. Bizarrely, it seemed a suitably ironic way to celebrate what would be a significant milestone in my life. But with no end to lockdown in sight would I have anyone to celebrate with, or would I be drinking alone? That would indeed be ironic. Then, in another massive emotional swing, I hated myself for harbouring self-pitying thoughts. If anything, I started to think, far from feeling angry and bitter I should actually be happy now – I had escaped the conflict and pain of a failed marriage, I was set up, in my own place, able to do what I wanted, when I wanted. Maybe that was what other people would think, anyway. And the next day I would be down again.

Then, one morning towards the end of that long beautiful, strangely unique lockdown summer, a letter arrived from the office of the Clerk of the Sheriff Court. I made a cup of tea, trying to ignore the bottle of Bolly in the fridge, went out into the sunny garden and sat on the bench in the shade of the buddleia. The garden is beautiful, I thought, as I sat there listening to the bees buzzing, and watching the red admirals, tortoiseshells and peacock butterflies flitting all around me. It felt too unreal. I needed to focus on the reality of what was happening to me. I breathed deeply, and looked at the envelope for some time before finally opening it and read the expected news that my divorce was, in fact, now final.

So that was it. In the end I didn't feel anything – neither elation, relief, misery or regret. I didn't tell anyone. I couldn't go out and celebrate or commiserate. The Bollinger remained unopened. The letter from the court confirmed that my past life was now irrevocably over, which should be a relief, but my future remained uncertain; if anything, it seemed even darker and more confusing than what I'd already been through. Like Bill's mother, receiving that awful telegram in June 1941, I knew that my life would never be the same. And I had to get on with it.

Lockdown eased and I was able to return to work, grateful to be amongst people again, albeit still at a socially distanced level; the summer passed into autumn and with the cold of winter lockdown was resumed. The pandemic seemed to be never-ending, and despite the return of the sun in the spring, and being able to walk in the hills again, I remained unhappy still living so close to the scene of the crime. Although I still loved Scotland, and it had never occurred to me to return to England when we separated, I was clearly in the wrong place now. Everywhere around me there were reminders of my previous life, either places we'd once been happy and looking forward to the future, or the sites of torrid arguments and bitter silences. Although I could now go to church again, instead of watching the priest conduct a lonely Mass online, it felt strange to be there on my own, without the family. On top of everything else my unease and guilt at not being able to see my mother and be there to help her through lockdown was only growing.

So it was perhaps not surprising when one Sunday morning in the early summer of 2021, sitting on a socially distanced pew and singing a hymn through a face mask, I realised the situation was actually ridiculous and was only going to change if I did something about it. Suddenly it all seemed very clear. I should up-sticks and move back down to England. It was as simple as that. Not exactly a divine revelation, more a case of the blindingly bleeding obvious.

Not pausing to think about it or change my mind, I rang Mum with the surprise news that I was moving south, gave notice on my rented cottage, and began planning to move house for the second time in less than two years. I felt instantly re-energised, focused, and positive about the future. A couple of months later, I was in my new flat.

Seven

I wander into the kitchen and flick open the blinds, letting the morning sunshine flood in through the window, and make a pot of coffee. I've been in the flat for a good nine months now, and I like it, still taking pleasure in seeing the squirrels chase each other around the churchyard outside my window. In some ways Newark feels as if it is caught uneasily between different ages; full of impressive buildings with important historical associations (the castle, where wicked King John died, the beautiful half-timbered 15th century Governor's House where Prince Rupert slept after arguing bitterly with his uncle Charles before the King's eventual surrender to Cromwell's forces). These sit uneasily among the more modern buildings. There was a ceremony in the market square on the day I first came to look at flats, with the Town Mayor and assorted officials parading in full regalia: tricorns, chains, tights and buckles, which seemed a bit odd, and made me wonder if this really was the place I wanted to settle in. But when I heard the familiar growl of a Merlin engine and looked up to see a Spitfire make repeated low sweeps over the town, I felt as if I had come home. This was definitely the place for me.

This morning, however, I'm feeling a bit off-centre, thinking about the discovery I made last night, and disturbed about the effect it may have had on Fiona. I'm still feeling guilty for the way I dropped the news on her. I'm not sure that there is an easy way to tell someone that the accident their uncle died in also killed seven other men, but I'm sure that wasn't it. And as usual, when I identify that I have done something wrong, or hurt someone, I don't tend to do the obvious, normal thing, like face up, accept and apologise. I deflect. One of the posts I read last night mentioned that the Polish airmen had all been buried in Newark, and so, after finishing my coffee, I decide to take a walk to the cemetery. As well as being the resting place of the great and the good of Newark since the mid-19th century, the cemetery is also home to a special plot containing the graves of some 80 Commonwealth and 400 Polish servicemen. I am also going there with a desire to find out more about Bill's story, to get closer to the incident and to the mystery surrounding it.

It only takes me a few minutes to walk across Newark and along the London Road to the cemetery. It's not a place I've visited before (why would I?) but now it seems to be exerting a magnetic pull, drawing me ever more strongly towards it. I have no idea of exactly where I will find the plot, but I know roughly what I am looking for once I am inside: those rows of white headstones so reminiscent and evocative of Verdun, Ypres, Normandy and Arnhem. In my back pocket I have a piece of paper, containing a list of the names of the seven other men, six Polish aircrew and one British u/t pilot, who had died together with Bill and were all buried in the cemetery. Perhaps I will find some clarity, some certainty here.

I enter through the dark red- and gold-painted iron gates and begin to make my way through the grounds, wandering between dozens of Victorian tombs, columns and statues, reflecting on how proud these people must have been of themselves. What exactly did they think they had done in life that was so special as to justify such a theatrical memorial of their brief time on this earth? I know they will be in stark contrast to the rows of identical, simple headstones that I am looking for.

Along the tarmac pathways, young mums are pushing prams, mindful of their toddlers running between the gravestones. Others are walking their dogs, talking on their mobile phones, or just stretching their legs, enjoying the warm spring sunshine. Eventually I see a tall white stone cross partially hidden among the trees, and then, around it, the rows of white headstones I have been looking for. Not much higher than the low, neat hedge surrounding the plot, the headstones are laid out in straight rows either side of the large central cross. I walk around the outside of the plot, wanting to get a full impression of the look and feel of the place before getting closer to the graves. I have to stop myself from glancing at the headstones for fear of seeing a name I recognise before I'm ready. Standing in front of the cross, I see from the inscription that this is the spot where General Sikorski, the wartime commander of the Polish Forces and first Prime Minister of the Polish Government In Exile, was once buried. He was killed in July 1943 when the B-24 Liberator aircraft he was on board crashed into the sea shortly after taking off from Gibraltar; all on board were killed, with the exception of the pilot, and questions about what happened remain to this day. Sikorski was buried at Newark with full military honours, including a eulogy delivered by Winston Churchill and a flypast by Polish bombers, and I remember reading somewhere that his body was removed from this spot and flown back to Poland shortly after the fall of the Berlin Wall.

A council van is parked nearby, and a workman is noisily operating a leaf blower, clearing rubbish from around the headstones, and I can see that the graves are very well looked after, some with older or newer bunches of flowers by them, all immaculately clean. Finally, excitement and anticipation rising in me, I wander up and down the lines, looking for the words 12 June 1941. There are lots of dates, and nearly all have an impressive Polish Eagle carved into the stone, but they don't seem to be in any specific order, and although I see many dated 1941, I find none for June 12th.

L MALYSZ, Z STAERZ, R WALCZAK... Seeing so many Polish names is quite moving. All these men who came from a country in flames, learning to speak English and to fly, (not necessarily in that order) so they could get back into the fight against Hitler. And they all died, in various circumstances, and now they're here. According to the cemetery's website, most of the deaths were the result of accidents, or from aircraft crashing on their return from action over Europe. Many injured airmen were taken to the military hospital at RAF Nocton Hall near Lincoln, and those who failed to recover were buried here.

Polish War Graves, Newark Cemetery (Author)

The workman turns off his leaf-blower and in the sudden quiet I hear someone speaking Polish, and turn to see a middle-aged mother and her teenage daughter walking through the cemetery together, and I think of the men who didn't die, who survived the war and settled here, marrying local girls or bringing their families over from Poland to settle down in the town which they made their new home, the place where they fought and flew and drank warm beer in English pubs.

Then I see it - the first grave.

The date draws my eye first – 12th JUNE 1941, and above it the already familiar name of KPL K MRUK, 305 SQDN. I stop and stare at the headstone. Next to it is the grave of KPT TJ STEFANICKI, and behind them are POR MJ WOJTOWICZ and POR AA ZIRKWITZ. Finally, behind these two, and next to each other again, ST SZER J KRAWCZYK and POR S KOWALCZE, the last two crew members of Wellington R1017.

It seems fitting that all six members of the Wellington crew are buried together, and all within a few feet of the spot where General Sikorski would later lie. They would have liked that – I am sure their fierce Polish hearts would have burned with pride to know they would rest so close to their commander. I stand back and look at the graves, six identical white headstones amongst more than 400 others, and try to picture what happened on that last tragic flight in June 1941. One second they were flying through the air; a training flight perhaps, or a night flying test, maybe having a laugh and looking forward to landing back at Syerston and getting warmed up over a mug of hot tea in the mess. Or maybe they were relieved to be returning from an op, after God knows what they'd experienced over Germany, or the North Sea, laying mines or leaflet dropping. And the next second there's the awful crash as they collide with another aircraft, followed by the noise of grinding, rending, shattering metal, screaming engines, the terrible knowledge of flames, burning, the ground rushing up at speed, and seconds later…

I imagine that with the exception of the rear gunner they would probably all have been within a few feet of each other when they died, so it's appropriate that they are buried close together here. But what about Leading Aircraftman William Newton, who was flying with Bill on the Oxford? According to my notes he is buried here too. Less than a minute later I find him. Curiously, he lies just the other side of the central monument, only a few feet away from the Poles but amongst some non-Polish graves.

Maybe it was felt that it was somehow inappropriate or insensitive to bury him alongside the Polish crew? Again, I take a few minutes to stand and look at the grave, and I think of him and William Parkinson, sitting together in the Oxford on their first solo flights, nervous because they are flying in such dreadful conditions, (I'm imagining the poor visibility

Fiona mentioned) and at the same time exhilarated because they are that bit closer to finally getting their wings.

Job done, the workman slams the back doors of his van and starts it up noisily, shattering the peace and quiet of the cemetery. The radio comes on in his cab as he turns the ignition, and an Ibiza-type dance tune blares out, fading as the van drives away. I take some photographs of the gravestones, step back for a final moment of reflection and wonder about whether any of the families have visited them, and when, and how they felt. There are certainly no flowers, fresh or otherwise, on these particular graves, and yet several others do show evidence of recent visits. The mother and daughter I saw earlier were clearly visiting a grave that meant something to them. I realise that I could put something below the headstones, and wonder if that would be appropriate, then decide that as I don't have anything to give anyway, the question is redundant. I'm here, I'm paying my respects to them, and I hope that is enough.

I say a short prayer, and leave the cemetery, feeling rather better than when I'd arrived; curiously not saddened by what I have found, but uplifted. Somehow I feel more certain, of what I'm not sure, but in a way, just seeing the graves, just being nearer to these men, has brought me closer to the truth of a tragedy, a tragedy I know hardly anything about.

Eight

Back at the flat, I quickly write an email to Fiona:

Hi Fiona,
You're right about the sensitivity of the subject. After I'd sent the email I started to worry - suddenly knowing more details can be quite upsetting. All those lives lost in one incident. It was only one of hundreds of similar stories (many so much worse) but still I hope it wasn't upsetting for you.
I took a walk down to Newark Cemetery this morning and found the graves. Bill's co-pilot lies a few yards from the six Polish airmen in a very special spot.
It would be interesting to know if there was a detailed investigation into the incident. Given the number of such incidents at the time it's unlikely, but I might do some digging...
There's some confusion over whether the accident happened at Becks Wood or Elton, which is odd, as they are a long distance (two counties) apart. I'm sure I'll find out.
All the best,
Ade x

It didn't take me long to get back into battlefield detective mode, did it? After a few cursory words trying to evoke the atmosphere of the place and not quite apologising for my previous insensitivity, I'm off again, talking about doing some more digging into the incident. How unthinking am I? It occurs to me that if that's how I was with my family, it's no wonder they couldn't bear to live with me anymore.

Visiting the graves had disturbed me, despite what I'd hinted at in my email to Fiona. I was thinking about war, about death, and heroes. It was all feeling very close, uncomfortably so. The news on TV and radio was full of Putin's bombing of Ukraine, of bloody bodies being dragged from wrecked buildings, of tearful bereaved mothers, and of young men with thousand-yard stares, wearing body armour and yellow/blue armbands hastily improvised from electrical tape. Like the Poles lying in Newark Cemetery, they are desperately fighting for their homeland. In the last few months, as my paranoia about the conflict increased, I'd bought in emergency supplies of water, painkillers and energy bars in case the shooting war spread, or in case Putin decided to wage cyber war on us for supporting his enemies. It's not just thinking about Bill that makes war seem to be very close.

I look out of the window, past the churchyard, and see the young mums picking up their children from the nursery over the road; another ordinary summer afternoon, just like the one William Parkinson's mother was probably having in Goole before she got the news she feared. The same thing will have happened to the mother of William Newton, wherever she was. I think it's unlikely that the mothers of those Polish airmen, back in Poland presumably, and under Nazi occupation, would have received anything so formal as a telegram informing them of their son's/husband's deaths. If they heard anything at all from their loved ones during the war, it might have come through some underground network, via the Polish Resistance I suppose, but it is possible they might never have known about these deaths until after the war, and even then it couldn't be guaranteed, as Poland quickly moved from Nazi to Soviet occupation in 1945. But they might have felt something had happened. Some sixth sense, transmitted across hundreds of miles, may have made itself felt, alerting them to the fact that something terrible had occurred. I'm fictionalising now, but the stark vision of those graves has underlined the fact that I am now looking at a story involving the deaths of eight young men who are no longer just names, but people, with families, and history.

I find myself wondering why William Parkinson isn't buried here in Newark, alongside the seven others who died on that day. Fiona mentioned that he was buried in Goole, close to the family home. I had read an account somewhere of a similar incident where the mother of a dead airman had requested that his body be brought home for burial, so I know that despite all the wartime restrictions on travel and so on, it did happen, and I assume that it would have been Mrs Parkinson's choice. Having already lost her husband and daughter, it is more than understandable that she would want her son buried close to home. It is also possible that her decision could have been motivated by some feeling of anger, related to her sense of loss, that saw her rage in her heart against the war, the RAF, and these men in particular, who had taken her son from her so cruelly. Perhaps Bill's mother had been against him joining up, to the extent that there had been arguments, and now, proved right in her fear that she might lose her son to the war, she was determined that he wouldn't be laid to rest in a military cemetery, but back at home, with the family, where he belonged.

These thoughts beg the question why the family of William Newton didn't ask for *their* son to be buried closer to home. Were the Newtons not as close-knit a family as the Parkinsons? Or maybe they didn't have a matriarch with such a strong personality as Gertrude. Of course, William Newton could have been one of those Commonwealth volunteers who had come from South Africa, Australia or Canada to join the RAF, and it would have been impossible to send his body home. Or he may even have been a local man, and his family were happy for him to be buried in Newark. They might have found the idea of their son lying in a military cemetery was befitting of the sacrifice he made for king and country. And he may not even have had a family as such; he could have been an orphan, an only child. I am speculating about what happened, but I know absolutely nothing about this man except his name, rank, number and the fact that he died alongside my uncle's brother. Just as I know nothing about the six Polish airmen buried here as well. Yet…

How did all of these men die? At the moment all I have is a simple, if blunt, reference to a National Archives Air Ministry Casualty File (AIR81) describing a 'mid-air collision near Beckswood between Oxford T1334, 2 Service Flying Training School and Wellington R1017, 305 Squadron, 12 June 1941. 8 men killed.' And the names.

Was it simply a freak accident, two aircraft flying practically blind in poor weather, and colliding with each other? Fiona mentioned that the family had understood the collision occurred in 'poor visibility', but how did they know that? There's no mention of weather conditions in the brief reference I found online. But if the family believed that the accident was the result of poor visibility, that information could only have come from the RAF. Would the RAF tell them that? And why? I quickly remind myself that although I know Bill's death occurred in an incident which saw the loss of seven other men's lives as well, that won't necessarily have been known by his family at the time. Apart from anything, the RAF would not want that kind of information released. How would it look if it got out that accidents like this, with such an awful and tragic loss of life, were happening regularly, not at night over Germany, but in the British countryside, and in broad daylight? The grim total of lives lost would certainly be kept secret, as far as possible, not even revealed to the immediate families. As far as Bill's family and friends were concerned, his death was a sad, tragic, and possibly heroic death. I am reminded that Fiona said they believed he was on his first solo flight – they didn't even know that William Newton was on the Oxford with him.

The nagging thought returns: why did I know nothing about this story until now? Is it just chance, the simple fact that I wasn't in the room whenever Bill was mentioned, and grew up completely ignorant of his story? Or is there some other reason? There are questions I need answers to: who were these men who died that day? What brought them together, literally and metaphorically, to die together? Where exactly did the crash happen? And why?

I remember the mother and daughter wandering through the graves earlier today. I assumed they were Polish, which would be very likely considering the large number of Poles living in Newark, and probably visiting a family grave. There are other families who are part of this story, some of whom may be living in the UK, possibly even be my neighbours. I need to find out, and if possible, make contact.

I am aware that I am on the brink of moving into unknown, emotionally difficult, possibly dangerous territory. I don't know if I should though. What began as a simple desire to be able to provide a few facts, a date and place, has already taken on more significance. And having established those facts, the deaths and the aircraft involved, shouldn't that be enough for me? It would be very simple to close the laptop now, step back and walk away, satisfied that I have added some previously unknown details to an old family story. I only started out on this because of something my mother happened to mention, at random. Am I right to ask these questions, to research and bring this story into the light? Mightn't it be better to leave it in the shadows where it has lain for so many decades? And if I carry on, do I have any idea of what I will unearth, what secrets I may reveal, and what it will mean? Do I dare disturb these ghosts?

All I know is that I have to know. I don't know why yet, but I just do. I need to find some answers. At night I lie in bed, my brain shuffling and reshuffling images, trying to make sense of them. Individually they don't mean much, but the more I think about them the more they seem to grow and spread ganglion-like, making connections and taking on a life of their own. It feels as if there might be a story in there, one which I don't fully know yet, but which I might be able to pull together. I need to find out more about the characters in this story, the u/t pilots William Parkinson and William Newton, and the Poles from 305 Squadron, whose paths crossed tragically on a summer's day in 1941. I need to know where they came from, what kind of men they were, get an idea of how they thought and felt and saw the world, if I am to understand anything of that fateful day.

I want to know what life was like on the station, in those squadrons, flying those aircraft. I need to soak myself in the period, re-reading all my old books and watching my collection of war films on DVD: *The Way To The Stars, The Dam Busters, One of Our Aircraft is Missing* and *Appointment in London* for starters. I need to know about the aircraft themselves, the Oxford trainer and the Wellington bomber. I already know something about these aircraft, but I need to really *understand* them: how were they designed and built and what were they like to fly? I want to find out everything I can not only about the types, but about these actual aircraft, *Oxford T1334* and *Wellington R1017;* what their stories were, where they were built, and their operational or training histories.

And I'm going to start with the Wellington.

Nine

In Michael Anderson's 1955 film *The Dam Busters*, one of my favourite moments comes at around 17 minutes in. Barnes Wallis, inventor of the bouncing bomb that would be used to attack the Ruhr dams, is seated opposite a pinstriped civil servant from the Ministry of Aircraft Production, who is clearly reluctant to sanction the loan of the Wellington bomber that Wallis needs in order to test his fantastic idea.

'They're worth their weight in gold,' the pinstriped one protests. 'Do you really think the authorities would lend you one? What possible argument could I put forward to get you a Wellington?'

Wallis, played in the film by Michael Redgrave, stares owlishly through his round specs and replies simply, 'Well, if you told them that I designed it? Do you think that might help?'

We cut to a shot of the first aircraft to be seen in the film: a Vickers Wellington taking off, the bomber speeding directly towards the camera before lifting into the air with only feet to spare. It's a brilliant and memorable moment, but one that was probably never played out in so many words; the dialogue between Wallis and the jobsworth pen-pusher presumably no more than a dramatic fiction created by the screenwriter RC Sherriff, (implying incorrectly that Wallis designed the aircraft when he only designed the airframe) but it highlights the importance the Wellington still played to RAF Bomber Command in 1943, several years after its introduction. A Lancaster does not appear in the film until 10 minutes later, and we are reminded that it is the humble Wimpy, not the more famous Lanc, that is the mainstay of the bombing campaign against Germany.

The story of the Wellington begins with a document, RAF Specification B.9/32, in which the Air Ministry invited tenders from companies to build a monoplane bomber that could carry a bombload of at least 1,000lbs, capable of defending itself against fighter attack, with a minimum range of 720 miles flying at 'a reasonably high speed.' As well as being rather vague, these specifications seem frighteningly unambitious now, given that we know Britain would be at war with Germany before the end of the decade. But in 1932, when B.9/32 was issued, the RAF's main bomber strength consisted of aircraft such as the Vickers Virginia, a biplane with a top speed of only 98 mph. This was not regarded with particular alarm by the RAF or the British Government at the time, because in 1932 Hitler was not perceived as the threat he was to later become, and for planning purposes the main enemy was still regarded as France. Vickers jumped at the chance to tender a design, and Wallis and the company's Chief Designer Reginald 'Rex' Pierson pulled together their ideas for what they called the Type 271. The name of Barnes Wallis is inextricably linked with the Wellington principally because of his design of the aircraft's geodetic superstructure. His work on airships such as the R100 had convinced him that a light metal alloy framework covered by a fabric skin would give his design an advantage in weight, strength and durability, increasing the Wellington's ability to take punishment from flak and fighters, and to increase its potential bombload and range. Building on its previous bomber design, the Wellesley, Vickers met the Air Ministry specifications for a new twin-engine medium day bomber capable of bettering any current design.

With Hitler's eventual rise to power the political and military situation in Europe changed rapidly, and so did the Air Ministry's requirements for their new bomber. The design went through many alterations and improvements, but by 1936 an early prototype was able to fly (with Wallis on board!)

and the aircraft, known at this time as the Crecy, was accepted for production. Coincidentally, this was the same year as Bomber Command was formed, to meet the growing threat from Hitler's Luftwaffe.

Vickers Wellington Mk 1 (Shawshots/Alamy)

The Mk 1 variant, now known as the Wellington, first flew in December 1937. It was highly advanced for its time, boasting an increase in crew size from four to six, several machine guns in revolving turrets in nose, tail and ventral positions, and a bomb-carrying capacity of 4,500lb, more than one-fifth of the aircraft's total flying weight. Powerful twin Bristol Pegasus radial engines gave the aircraft a maximum speed of 235mph at 15,000 feet, with a maximum ceiling of 18,000 feet and a rate of climb of 1,120 feet per minute. In appearance the Wellington was unusual and distinctive – a swollen fuselage designed to accommodate the large bomb load meant that the open bomb bay doors almost touched the ground, and the aeroplane was soon given the nickname 'Wimpy', after the portly hamburger-munching J Wellington Wimpy from the Popeye cartoons. Add to that an enormous tail fin and the aircraft had the appearance of a Wellington boot, making it easily identifiable.

As the likelihood of war with Germany increased, so did orders for the Wellington, and Vickers were forced to rethink their production process to meet demand. The geodetic airframe, initially regarded with suspicion by the Air Ministry as being too complicated to manufacturer easily, proved to be surprisingly simple. The sections were built at various factories, coming together for assembly at the main Vickers works at Weybridge, Surrey. Wooden battens screwed to the metal geodetic frame and covered in Irish linen, doped to provide a tight skin, could be assembled quickly and easily. In the early days it took around 60 hours to build each aircraft, but with the outbreak of war in 1939 production was streamlined and intensified so that a completed Wellington was rolled out every day at Weybridge. Shadow assembly factories at Blackpool and Broughton in North Wales were established to take the pressure off the Weybridge plant and move production further away from German bombers. The works at Broughton was soon rolling out Wellingtons at the rate of 50 a month, and in October 1943 a morale-raising propaganda film was made at the factory showing the attempt to build a Wellington in record time. The factory workers gave up their weekend off to build Wellington LN514 in only 23 hours and 50 minutes, and the bomber took to the air 58 minutes later.[5]

A total of 11,461 Wellingtons were produced, at an average cost of something over £14,000 per machine (more than £750,000 in today's money), a number greater than that of any other bomber in the RAF ever. By comparison, only 7,377 of the more well-known Avro Lancaster were built. The Wellington was produced throughout the war and had the distinction of being the mainstay of Bomber Command's frontline force. By the spring of 1942 Wellingtons made up 40% of the RAF's total bomber strength, and in the first '1,000 Bomber Raid' on Cologne in May of that year, 599 of the 1,046 bombers were Wimpys.[6] Overall, during World War

---

[5] *Workers' Week-End, A Tribute to the Workers of the British Aircraft Industry.* Crown Film Unit/Ministry of Information 1943.

[6] 101 of those Wellingtons were flown by Polish aircrews.

Two, Wellingtons flew 47,409 operations, and dropped 41,823 tons of bombs, at the cost of 1,332 aircraft destroyed.

Eventually the Wellington would be produced in 16 variants, each with modifications in armaments, navigational aids and performance, and it would serve in every theatre of war in a multiplicity of roles, including day and night bombing, anti-submarine warfare, mine sweeping, transport, and training. Tests were carried out to see if it was suitable for glider-towing, but the Wellington's unconventional airframe was apparently stretched by some 18 inches after towing a Horsa glider and the idea was abandoned.

As a flying machine the Wimpy was popular with crews, who found it reliable and simple to fly, even 'docile' or 'ponderous.' Take off and landing were generally easy, with good all-round visibility for the pilot, although apparently the brakes often left something to be desired. Early variants were cold and draughty, leading to cases of frostbite, and the smell of the interior of a Wellington will never be forgotten by those who flew 6- or 7-hour operations in one. A heady mixture of hydraulic oil, high-octane fuel, the pungent pear drops aroma of fabric dope, spilt coffee and the stink of the Elsan chemical toilet made for a unique brew which seemed to never leave the aircraft (and all too often was accompanied by the stench of fear and the coppery smell of blood).

Wallis' geodetic design caused the aircraft to shift and settle in flight, the wings to sway up and down, and even the tail section to 'wag', which could prove disconcerting to its crews. But the flexing movement was an inbuilt design feature, which also enabled the Wimpy to withstand enormous punishment. Night fighter shells and shards of red-hot flak shrapnel inflicted less damage on the fabric covering than on stressed metal skins, and there are many examples of Wellingtons returning home after suffering damage that would have seen other bombers fall out of the sky.

In the very early days of the war, day bombing was the strategy favoured by Bomber Command. The British government, led by Sir Neville Chamberlain, refused to allow the RAF to bomb German territory for fear of killing civilians and encouraging reprisal raids on British cities. Bombing was restricted to military targets, and consisted mostly of attacks against German shipping, well away from centres of population. These attacks were carried out by Wellingtons flying in tight formation in 'vics' of three,[7] the theory being that they could protect each other against fighters, and close formation flying, often at low level, was practised intensively.

But these tactics were soon proven to be ineffective, even disastrous. On 18 December 1939, the 'Battle of the Heligoland Bight' saw 12 out of 22 Wellingtons from Nos 9, 37 and 149 Squadrons shot down by German fighters in an unsuccessful attempt to bomb the German fleet. Initial reactions from the RAF command was that the bombers must have failed to maintain close formation, although the reports of Luftwaffe pilots gave the impression that attacking bombers flying close together actually increased their chances of getting a hit. Daylight raids continued, but by the fall of France in May 1940, night bombing was becoming more popular, especially as with the replacement of Chamberlain by Churchill the restrictions of bombing civilian areas had now been abandoned.

Flying night-time operations was a hugely dangerous and terrifying job, and it took unimaginable courage simply to get into a bomber night after night, knowing that your chances of returning were not good. But there are also numerous stories of remarkable heroism associated with Wellington aircrew, not least among them the case of Sgt James Allen Ward, a New Zealander flying as second pilot with 75 Squadron. Ward's Wellington took part in a raid on Munster in July 1941, and was attacked by an Me110 night fighter as it crossed the Dutch coast on the way home. The rear gunner, Sgt Allan Box, managed to shoot down the Messerschmitt, but not before it had strafed the Wellington, leaving it badly damaged.

---

[7] A formation where three or more aircraft fly close together in a V-shaped formation with the leader at the apex and the rest of the flight following to the left and the right.

A punctured fuel tank in the wing was leaking fuel which was burning at the rear of the starboard engine and threatened to explode or burn the fabric skin off entirely. Faced with the option of baling out or ditching in the North Sea, the crew agreed to press on, with the pilot telling Ward to do something about the fire. Trying to aim a hand-held fire extinguisher through a hole in the fuselage fabric proved useless because of the violent slipstream, so Ward's solution was to grab a rolled-up canvas engine cover and climb out onto the wing to try and smother the flames. Ward attached himself to a rope, and with the aircraft's speed slowed to 100mph edged out onto the wing, punching and kicking hand and foot holds in the canvas skin as he went. Risking falling off in the slipstream and trying to avoid being burnt by the sheet of flame coming from the fuel tank, Ward finally reached the fire and attempted to bung the hole with the canvas. This proved much harder than he had expected, but eventually he managed to stuff the canvas into the breach, and the flames subsided.

With Ward safely back inside the aircraft the pilot successfully flew the Wellington back to England, landing with all the crew safely accounted for, although the aircraft itself was written off. Ward was awarded the Victoria Cross shortly afterwards, and his heroism meant he was featured in newspapers across Britain. Sadly, he died two months later when the Wellington he was piloting was shot down over Hamburg.

The last flight of a Wimpy took place in January 1955. Ironically it was Wellington MF628, which had featured in *The Dam Busters*. During production of the film it was used as an aerial camera platform for the dramatic flying sequences and appeared in that memorable first shot of a bomber taking off. Its final flight was from St Athan to Wisley, and it was later transported to the RAF Museum at Cosford, where it underwent a programme of intensive restoration, and can be seen today in all its wartime glory.

Ten

On any relatively clear day when I am passing RAF Syerston on the way to visit my mother, I will see a glider or two soaring high above the airfield and the surrounding countryside. I often think that with their long fuselages and wide wingspan they must compare in size to what Wellington R1017 would have looked like, flying in those same skies 80 years ago.

But I'm wrong.

With a length of 26 feet and a wingspan of nearly 60 feet, the Grob G103 Twin glider that the RAF Gliding School use to teach Cadets how to fly looks enormous, but next to a Wellington it is tiny. The Wellington is nearly three times as long at over 64 feet, and with a wingspan of 86 feet the bomber must have seemed huge, just as it would have done next to the aircraft used to train pilots like William Parkinson – the Airspeed Oxford.

In the mid-1930s his predecessors would have done their initial flying training on a De Havilland Tiger Moth biplane, progressing to an Avro Anson if they were intending to pilot medium bombers such as the Whitley, Wellesley or Blenheim. Piloting an Anson he would learn the challenges presented by twin engines, flaps and retractable undercarriages. But by 1936 the Air Ministry realised that with bigger and more advanced bombers in the pipeline, such as the Hampden and Wellington, a new twin-engine trainer was required.

Airspeed Ltd, of Portsmouth, appeared to have what the Air Ministry was looking for. The company was founded by Neville Shute, who had worked with Barnes Wallis as a designer on the R100 airship and would eventually be more

Pre-war magazine advertisement for the new Airspeed Oxford
(courtesy *The Aeroplane*/Key Publications)

famous as a novelist. No giant among British aircraft manufacturers, Airspeed had the advantage of already producing more aircraft equipped with retractable undercarriages than any other British manufacturer. Since 1934 the company had been building a small airliner, the Envoy, featuring an all-wood construction and, crucially, a hydraulically-operated retractable undercarriage. A simple upgrade to meet the Air Ministry's specifications was all that was required, and Airspeed was invited to tender for the project. In the event Airspeed's AS10 went through an entire re-design, and in 1937 the first prototype, now renamed the Oxford, took to the air. Pleased with the Oxford's performance and capabilities, the Air Ministry placed an initial order of 136 aircraft, although by the time the Oxford ceased production in 1945 more than 8,750 had been built. Production was spread around a number of factories, and in the early days it took an average of 3-4 weeks to build an Oxford from start to finish.

The aircraft that was to become the workhorse of RAF Training Command was a simple affair. With a length of 34 feet and wingspan of 53 feet, it was powered by twin Cheetah X radial engines, giving the trainer a maximum speed of 188mph at 8,300 feet (without its gun turret) and a range of 925 miles, enough to allow long cross-country navigational exercises. Its angular, boxy appearance was due in part to its construction – wooden beams, spars and ribs covered with stressed-skin plywood, with all the joints held together by glue. The aeroplane was affectionately nicknamed the 'Ox-box' for obvious reasons. Although seemingly basic and old-fashioned, this method of construction was to give the Oxford a remarkably long life of at least 10 to 15 years active service. A hand-operated gun turret situated half-way down the fuselage on the Mk 1 variant allowed for in-flight gunnery training, fitted with a single 0.303 Vickers 'K' machine gun. A Perspex window in the nose was used to train bomb aimers, and as there was provision for up to three crew, it was fitted for wireless, navigation and camera training as well. The cockpit was spacious, with good all-round visibility and a sensibly laid-out instrument panel and had alternative single or dual controls.

Initially, the training of bomber pilots was carried out in Britain, but with the outbreak of war the skies became more congested and dangerous, and many flying schools, along with their Oxfords, were transferred to the safer skies of the Commonwealth, to Canada, South Africa and Rhodesia, and to Australia and New Zealand. In its predominantly yellow colour scheme (yellow being the brightest colour visible to the human eye and the traditional colour indicating caution) the Oxford appeared large and daunting to pilots who had learned to fly on Tiger Moths – deliberately so, as the intention was to teach those would-be bomber pilots how to handle the bigger two- or four-engine aircraft they would graduate to. Take off was often difficult, the aircraft showing a pronounced wing drop, and it had a dangerous tendency to fly off in any direction on landing. Pilots would usually amass around 150 hours of flying on an Oxford before they were deemed proficient enough to take the controls of a Wellington or Lancaster.

Oxford T1334, the Mk 11 variant which Bill Parkinson and William Newton were flying on June 12 1941, was built at the Airspeed factory in Portsmouth, part of an order of 16 which was delivered to 2 Service Flying Training School at RAF Brize Norton on March 25, 1941, only three months before its last flight. Throughout its service the Oxford required little modification or upgrading, being used in only two variants, and although production ceased with the end of hostilities in 1945, it continued to be operated by the RAF until 1954. It was also widely used by air forces and airlines across the globe, and although there are no flying examples left today, several can be seen on static display in museums. I visited the example on display at the RAF Museum in Hendon and was struck by its small size. Even though I knew that I was going to be looking at a small aeroplane, particularly when compared to the collection's B-24 Liberator and the enormous Lancaster, 'diminutive' seems to be the perfect adjective to describe the aircraft that William Parkinson would learn to fly bombers in.

Eleven

There is a plaque on the side of the NatWest Bank in Newark's marketplace, erected by the Bomber Airfield Society and dedicated to:

> the thousands of men and women of many nations who served on the nearby airfields and walked and enjoyed these ancient streets of Newark during the war years 1939-1945.

Strangely, the plaque is placed about twelve feet high, well above the eyeline, and I'm sure that most people don't even know it is there, but those who do stop and crane their necks to read it are reminded that:

> in the morn they came and passed a few quiet hours. In the evening twilight their aircraft in countless numbers circled above the town and surrounding countryside, climbing higher and higher. In the blackness of the night they fought and died. Remember them as you pass by, these brave young men who fell from the sky. 55,573 airmen died in the night skies over Europe, many have graves known only to God.

When I first returned to the area after nearly 40 years away, Newark struck me as more than a little quaint, with its timber framed pubs, splendid Georgian town hall and townhouses - a kind of Trumpton marooned in the 21st century. But I soon got used to the narrow, cobbled streets and low roofs, unchanged for centuries, and grew fond of its character and undoubted charm. The aircrews memorialised on that plaque must have appreciated Newark too, and it is not hard to imagine happy gangs of them roaming the ancient streets by day and night, enjoying what they knew might possibly be their last few hours on earth.

The average age for bomber aircrew in the middle of the war was 22. They had to grow up fast, learning about themselves and life whilst doing an unbelievably dangerous job. And so, with such little time and with the stakes being so high, these young men did what others have done for generations in similar circumstances. Facing the very real possibility of death and not knowing if they were 'up to it', whether they could trust themselves or their friends in a tight spot – they would go out and get drunk. If they were going to get slaughtered together in the night skies over the Ruhr, they might as well get slaughtered together in the pub as well, could have been their thinking.

It is quite likely that some of the Polish crews of 305 Squadron downed a pint or four in the Fox and Crown, the Saracen's Head or The Ram. RAF Syerston lies only a short bus or cycle ride up the Fosse Way, so it seems a pretty safe bet they would have been familiar with some of the watering holes I now find myself frequenting. With their alien accents, elaborate Polish Air Force cap badges and distinctive 'POLAND' flashes on their shoulders, an over-exaggerated politeness and very un-English sense of self-confidence, these strangers would have seemed quite exotic in sleepy old Newark. The Poles certainly enjoyed themselves while they could, and by all accounts played as hard as they fought. No doubt there would have been riotous nights, too much beer drunk leading to arguments and fights with local men, resentful at the Poles' legendary success with the women. Before the Yanks were viewed as being 'over-paid, over-sexed and over here,' in cities, market towns and villages across eastern England the Poles were regarded with a mixture of admiration and suspicion (depending on your perspective) and I'm sure the situation in Newark was no different.

Curiously (or perhaps not, given what I am quickly learning about the Polish attitude towards their war heroes) it is easier to find out information about the Polish aircrew than the two

Williams, and there are many sources of information online and in books. This could be because they constituted only a relatively small proportion of RAF Bomber Command personnel, and as operational crews they have a more visible online presence, but maybe it is also a result of the Polish determination to never forget the contribution their forbears made to the war effort. Wandering around the internet I soon find that there are many websites dedicated to the Polish fighter and bomber squadrons that served with the RAF in the Second World War, and begin to gather some interesting details about what life must have been like for the crew of R1017, far from home, strangers (and not always welcome) in a foreign country, united by their fierce determination to avenge what the Germans had done, and were still doing, to their country.

When trawling through the online archive of the Polish Institute and Sikorski Museum in London, I come across an impressive album, chronicling the story of 305 Squadron's history from its arrival in England to the end of the war, compiled at the time. It is full of newspaper cuttings and photographs, evocative drawings and paintings of the stations they were based at, including Syerston, and humorous cartoons of the crews, notably a wonderful caricature of Aleksander Zirkwitz, rear gunner on R1017.

There is also the Squadron's *War Diary*, beautifully handwritten in Polish, including a short entry for 12 June 1941, listing the crew of that aircraft. There are also a few brief lines which seem to be a reference to the accident, but as they are written in Polish, they mean nothing to me. I will need a translator if I am going to be able to make full use of this resource, and figure that it won't be difficult to find one given the number of Poles living and working in Newark. I write a few postcards appealing for help (in English) and put them up in the windows of local Polish shops, and wait.

There are, however, many other useful websites in English translation that are full of valuable nuggets, some dedicated to recreating 305 squadron's time in the UK at airshows, others acting as simple memorials to their airmen. They each contain galleries of photographs from the war, all very atmospheric, helping to create a vivid picture of what life must have been like at Syerston in early 1941 – cold, wet and muddy. And yet the faces of those young men in the photos are cheery, smiling. They were obviously putting some of it on for the camera, hoping perhaps that they would be seen and recognised back home. And of course, they may genuinely have been enjoying their chance to get back at Hitler or looking forward to a good night at The Ram... Disappointingly there are no photographs of Wellington R1017, but I put this down to the fact that the aircraft was lost quite early on in the squadron's history. There is, however, something of interest in the photo gallery of the website *polishairforce.pl*, which is, as its name implies, a treasure trove of all things to do with the Polish Air Force, run by Wojciech Zmyślony. The website's gallery includes a rather indistinct photo of Sgt Kazimierz Mruk, second pilot on R1017, standing in front of a Wellington along with his ground crew. The Wellington bears the codes SM-B so cannot be R1017 (which bore the codes SM-K) and the caption acknowledges that this is not the aircraft he was lost on. I also find a biography of Sgt Mruk, supplied (and presumably written) by a Krzysztof Mruk, who I assume must be a family member. Reading the piece, I learn that Mruk was born in Turostówko, a village in western Poland, was a baker by trade but trained as a pilot with the 3rd Air Regiment in Poznan, flying RWD-8 and PWS-26 aeroplanes. At the time of the German invasion he was considered to be too inexperienced to fly combat missions and was evacuated to Romania after the Soviet attack on Poland, eventually making his way to Britain via France. The biography gives a brief account of his death in the collision with the Oxford, and then, surprisingly, mentions that an extra man was also on board the Wellington when it crashed. This name, which I have never seen before, was of a Sgt Armourer B Brottell.

This is very odd. The name Brottell doesn't appear on any of the documents I've read that report the deaths. I know that there are many cases of ground crew, often WAAFS, hitching a ride on a bomber, strictly against the rules, but surely a passenger who was killed whilst doing so would be named in the official documents. I do some Googling of Sgt Brottell's name but can find nothing anywhere. I try variants of the name, and still no luck. It's the same in the Newark Cemetery lists. I put it down to a rumour, a mistake or a family story that has no actual basis in fact. But if it's there on the website where so many more experienced researchers than I will have seen it, why has nothing been made of it before? Was there really another man on the doomed Wellington? And why? I will have to do some more digging and ask some more questions.

Wojciech's website also opens up another interesting question: who was piloting Wellington R1017 on the day of the crash? The biography of Sgt Mruk suggests, or rather states, that Mruk was piloting the aircraft on the fatal flight, rather than Flight Lieutenant Stefanicki, who is listed as pilot in all the other sources. Could this simply be an assumption on the part of a family member, that because his relative was a pilot, then he must automatically have been piloting the aircraft, or does he have more concrete information? Doubting the latter and favouring the former, I make a note to get in touch with Krzysztof Mruk and try to find out, just in case.

The website also contains a link to another site, with the rather formal title *Personnel of the Polish Air Force in Great Britain 1940-1947*, popularly known as 'Krzystek's List'. This astonishing resource began life at a 1998 meeting of the Historical Commission of the Polish Air Force Association in Great Britain, when it was decided to prepare a complete list of the personnel of the Polish Air Force serving here during the Second World War, and Anna Krzystek was chosen as the person responsible for compiling and classifying them. Taking almost four years to complete, Krzystek's List includes the names, ranks, service numbers, trades and biographical details (including, in some cases, photographs) of the 17,000 Polish men and women stationed here and proves invaluable when trying to connect the dots. The current website is edited by Piotr Hodyra, who has the job of updating all the entries.

I begin by entering the names of the Polish crewmen on board Wellington R1017, starting with the highest-ranking officer and the man I assume was the pilot, Flight Lieutenant Stefanicki, age 36. Nothing comes up other than his name, service number and date of birth, which I already know. Next, I try Sergeant Mruk and this time I find a head and shoulders photo of a young man, in uniform, with his cap at an angle, looking rather like the actor Tim Roth. More photos come up, including one of Pilot Officer Stanisław Kowalcze, in full uniform and strikingly handsome, a smiling Pilot Officer Aleksander Zirkwitz, and a studio shot of Sergeant Jerzy Krawczyk, beaming in his uniform. This final image was supplied by a Shaun Noble. I do a quick internet check and discover that Shaun has an association with Polish groups in Newark, which looks promising. Unfortunately, there are no photographs of Flt Lt Stefanicki, or PO Marian Wojtowicz, although I do later find them elsewhere. Notably, Krzystek's List records that all six members of crew were recipients of the Krzyż Walecznych (Cross of Valour), awarded to a person who 'has demonstrated deeds of valour and courage on the battlefield,' (PO Wojtowicz being awarded the medal twice), and each was also posthumously awarded the Medal Lotniczy (Air Medal) at the end of the war.

But I'm tired now. I send off emails to the websites and to Krzysztof Mruk and Shaun Noble, explaining what I'm researching into and appealing for help, before falling into bed, exhausted, but feeling strangely satisfied with what I've achieved.

Twelve

Email from Fiona:

Hi Ade,
So sorry for the delay in replying to your last email. No excuses really. The days just fly by and the to-do list grows ever longer!
Thank you for your kind words re the details of Bill's accident. It was strangely poignant, even though I never knew him, but I'm so grateful none-the-less to know more about it.
The discrepancy over the site of the accident is odd. In a letter from the RAF Record Office, Beckswood is stated. I'll take a pic of the letter and attach. I imagine there was much confusion over facts at the time - as we all know there often is now, even with all our rapid communications.
Anyway, as I should have said at the beginning, I do hope you're well and everybody else. I haven't yet thrashed out a date to visit but it's on that list!
Fiona xx

I click on the attached jpeg and see the letter, photographed on Fiona's mobile phone. It is from the RAF Record Office, Gloucester, dated 14th June 1941:

Dear Madam,
It is my painful duty to confirm the death of your son, 1067083 Leading Aircraftman William Wharton PARKINSON of No 2 Service Flying Training School, Royal Air Force, who was killed in a flying accident near Beckswood, Newark, Nottinghamshire, at 11.25 am on the 12th June 1941.

The Air Council desire me, in conveying this information to you, to express their sympathy and deep regret at your son's death in his country's service.
Your Obedient Servant (etc)

Well, there's no doubt about it: an official letter, posted two days after his death, stating that Bill was killed at Beckswood, Newark. This confirms the information contained in the note about the AIR 81 file that I found at the beginning of my search. But I still can't find a Beckswood anywhere near Newark on the map or by Googling the name. Although there is a note in another post mentioning Elton, the village not far from my mother's house, I have always assumed this is a typographical error, and that the location is actually *Elston*, another village just outside the boundary of RAF Syerston.

Elston is small and sleepy, and still feels very much as it would have done in 1941, the kind of quiet English hamlet featured in *Went The Day Well?*, *The Way To The Stars*, and later, William Wyler's documentary *The Memphis Belle*. Simple red-brick cottages, a church and a pub, and that is pretty much the story. I've been using the Ordnance Survey Landranger 271 map, which covers Newark, Syerston and Elston, and concentrating my search for evidence of a Beckswood in the area. Interestingly, there is a Brecks Lane heading south-east out of Elston – I wonder if this could be a clue, possibly a confusion with Beckswood, but driving up and down the road reveals nothing, and nobody in the village seems to know anything about a crash. They're mostly incomers now anyway; anyone who knew anything about an incident that happened 80 years ago would have died or left the village long ago. But I *want* the collision to have happened here, it feels so tantalisingly close; for days on end I have wandered the lanes around the village, staring up into the vast sky, imagining a small yellow Oxford trainer lifting into the clouds from the direction of Syerston and into the flightpath of a huge, black Wellington, coming in to land. It seems so logical that the collision should have occurred here at Elston, rather than this Elton...

Then, at home one evening, I am researching another strand of the story online and have to examine another OS Map, Explorer 260, and laying it out on the desk I see the name of Elton-On-The-Hill and, less than a quarter of a mile south of the village, a small area of woodland, marked The Becks Plantation. Not the exact same name as Beckswood, or Becks Wood, but close enough. Idiot! All this time I have been barking up the wrong tree. Obviously the crash must have happened here. How could I have wasted all that time and energy focussing on the area around Elston? I feel so stupid.

Becks Plantation has a rather archaic ring to it which might well have fallen out of common usage. I can imagine that when the recovery operation was taking place at the crash site a villager might have identified the location to the RAF officer as 'Beck's Wood', and what was said became written down as Beckswood, and the rest, as they say, is history… I realise that what Fiona said in her letter (that she can 'imagine there was much confusion over facts at the time') is bang on the money – but embarrassingly, when she says 'as we all know there often is now, even with all our rapid communications,' she has predicted exactly the mistake I made. I wanted Elston, the village next to the airfield where Mum had said Bill died, to be the place, because it suited me to believe that and was blind to the obvious, when the truth had been staring me in the face all the time.

Elton-On-The-Hill (it was called plain old Elton when I was a kid – Mum says they only recently added *On-The-Hill* to make it sound posh and push property prices up) is a tiny village comprising a church, a manor, a few houses and some farms, lying at a crossroads on the south side of the A52 Nottingham to Grantham road. I used to cycle through it on my way to go fishing at the nearby Orston ponds during the school summer holidays.

I get in the car and drive down the A46, past Syerston, and Bingham where I guess Mum will be dozing in front of the telly, and along the A52, following the route I used to ride as a kid, with my fishing rod and tackle strapped onto the bike and sandwiches and squash in an army surplus haversack over my shoulder. In the '70s you never had to worry about speeding cars and lorries thundering past you. You hardly saw any. Life then, it seemed, like the roads, was safe, quiet, unhurried.

Still thinking about those glorious days spent staring at a motionless float tip, I approach the small hill that gives modern day Elton its name, but instead of turning left where the old Manor Arms pub used to be (now converted into smart apartments) I turn right to drive through the village, looking for any possible clues, like a name plate on a house, cottage or farmgate that might give something away: *Becks Cottage*, *Beckswood Farm*, or *Beckswood Drive*...

Nothing.

It takes less than half a minute, even driving at a crawl, to pass from one end of the village to the other. I glance through breaks in the thick hawthorn hedges for a sight of the woods that according to the map should be somewhere on my left. Through one gap I catch a brief glimpse of some substantial-looking woods in the distance, lying a few hundred yards from the road, beyond a locked farm gate. I stop, reverse and park, checking it against the map. It could be the Becks Plantation...

I carry on round, turning left and taking the Redmile road, with the familiar sight of Belvoir Castle sitting high on the ridge a few miles away. I keep glancing from my rear-view mirror to the map and back to the hedgerow, but the hawthorns are thicker and taller here. I come across another locked farm gate, but I can't see the woods from here, and carry on, turning left again back onto the main road until I have come full circle. I get a few more tantalising glimpses of what I am certain must be the Becks Plantation and note what looks like the main farm entrance (also locked). There's no sign of life, but that's going to be my way in. I head home, knowing from previous experience how awkward and frustrating it can be just to turn up and knock on a farmer's door asking nosey questions about their land. Instead, I'm going to write a letter explaining everything I know about the crash and hope that they'll get back to me. They're sure to know if I've found the right place. Letter written, I drive back to Elton and pop the envelope into the post box attached to the wall by the farm gate.

My first view of the Becks Plantation - the woods at the end of the track (Author)

The quiet of the evening is broken by the faint drone of an aeroplane engine and I look up to see a small aircraft, descending slowly out of the clear blue, cloudless sky. It's obviously on its landing approach to Langar airfield, another ex-wartime bomber station, now used for skydiving and charity parachute drops, a few miles to the south-east.

Shielding my eyes from the glare of the setting sun, doing the same thing I had done at Elston, but now, I feel sure, in the right place, I imagine that the pilot's view must be similar to what Bill's would have been, if he had indeed flown over these fields the morning of 12 June 1941. A few seconds later the aircraft disappears beyond the trees, the drone of the engine fades, and all I can hear is a lone blackbird singing in the woods.

Thirteen

'I wonder if you can help me? I'm doing some research into an incident that happened during the war and thought there might be someone here who could point me in the direction?'

I am standing in the shop of the Newark Air Museum, a collection of aircraft and exhibits at what used to be RAF Winthorpe, on the northern outskirts of the town. Surrounded by stacks of model kit boxes, books and aircraft memorabilia, the young man at the till looks up wearily.

'Maybe,' he says. 'Do you have any details?' Clearly they get a lot of this. Behind him, on the phone at a desk, a grey-haired woman peers over her glasses, looking me up and down. I jump straight in.

'Yes, it involves a mid-air collision between an Oxford trainer and a Wellington from 305 (Polish) Squadron flying out of Syerston...' But before I have even finished my sentence, I am aware of another head emerging from behind some shelves at the back of the shop.

'If it involves the Poles then he's your man,' says the grey-haired woman. 'Knows everything there is to know about them, don't you Ian?'

'I'll give it a try,' the man says, moving forward, with what looks like a box containing a 1/48 scale Hawker Hurricane in his hand. 'Ian Shaw's the name.'

Several days have passed since I dropped the letter into the box at the farm gate and I've heard nothing. Keen to keep some forward momentum I drive one Saturday morning to the Newark Air Museum, hoping to find some answers. It's a place I used to go to as a lad, accompanying my next-door neighbour Ralph, a workmate of my dad's and fellow model aeroplane nut who spent his Sundays as a restoration volunteer at the new museum. Too young to get my hands dirty on the actual aircraft I was free to watch or wander around the other exhibits, gazing in wonder at the sleek Hawker Hunter, the enormous Avro Shackleton and bits of other aircraft filling the hangars.

Talking to Ian, I quickly realise that he is an expert on the Polish Squadrons, with a particular affection for the Wellington bomber. This is unusual, as most aeroplane nuts, like me, go for the more obvious Lancaster. Ex-RAF, Ian's dad's best friend Stan was a Polish pilot with one of the squadrons stationed nearby during the war. After the war ended, like so many other Polish fighters, Stan couldn't go home - or rather, had no home to go to, the old country now being part of the Soviet empire. So he settled down as a painter and decorator in Spondon, Derby, near where Ian's dad was working as an engineer at Rolls Royce. Ian used to listen to Stan and his dad talking about the war and learned that in the Battle of Britain the Polish airmen's record for fighter kills was proportionately higher than that of the British pilots, due to their penchant for getting as close as possible to their targets, often having recalibrated their machine guns for the job. Ian says he wished he'd listened to more of their conversations when he was a kid, particularly because Stan would often 'go AWOL' for periods on end. Apparently, Stan's experience as a combat pilot had been useful to the Americans, and he flew secret missions in and out of East Germany during the Cold War. Being a Pole gave him added 'plausible deniability,' as they say. At least that's what Ian thinks.

But I digress. After Ian has told me about the Hurricane he's going to paint up in Polish markings and shown me all the photos of the Wellingtons he's already made up, each with individual squadron markings, we get down to details. I explain that I am trying to pinpoint the location of the collision between the Wellington and Oxford, which I now think probably happened over Elton, and hopefully find the crash site, aware that the lady with the grey hair is listening intently. She mentions that she knows of a roadside memorial in one of the villages near Elton, which she thinks involved an Oxford. She can't remember which village but she can see the memorial now, at the corner of a field, near where the farmer has erected some large haybale sculptures. This doesn't ring a bell with Ian, nor me. I'm confused, and the fact that there is a memorial somewhere in the vicinity both excites me (it may lead me to the location of the crash) and depresses me (if it does, someone has beaten me to it). But more than anything it reminds me that this kind of accident happened regularly around here during wartime; hardly surprising, considering the close proximity of one aerodrome to another, and the pressures of flying in wartime, with tired, possibly inexperienced crews flying war-weary aircraft. The woman nods in agreement and wanders off. It looks as if this is as far as I am going to get with my enquiries.

But Ian is still thinking about the crash. He is surprised, because, as he says, he is knowledgeable about pretty much everything that happened in these parts concerning the 'guys from Poland.' Although he doesn't recall this specific incident, he takes down the Wimpy's serial number and promises to get back when he's had a chance to look up what happened to the airframe. (Reader, there are books full of this arcane information, telling you, should you care to learn, where and when each specific aircraft was built, to which squadron it was delivered, and what ultimately happened to it.) And Ian is surprised by what I say about the Oxford flying from 2SFTS out of Syerston. 'Well, that's where they are based,' I point out. 'Now they are, yes,' says Ian, 'But not during the war – it was an operational bomber station – there would have been Oxfords and Ansons around, used for flying aircrew to and fro, admin etc, but the last thing they wanted was hordes of unqualified pilots whizzing round in the skies.' I mumble something about thinking the same thing myself, and make a mental note to find out more, feeling rather embarrassed. I'm starting to feel that I've rather shot my bolt here, clearly an amateur in the presence of these professionals, and am about to make my excuses when the grey-haired lady reappears.

'I was looking to see if we had a copy of the 305 Squadron history,' she says, 'You know the Chris Ward/Grzegorz Korcz Bomber Command Profile, but it's still on order. Sorry.'

But Ian has got a copy at home, as well as a shelf full of other similar titles, and he'll try and check them tonight, see if he can find some clues. I'm grateful but make a note of the title and authors so I can order my own copy.

'Of course, the AIR27's what you really want,' the grey-haired lady says to Ian. He nods, sagely. It's like they're incanting strange spells, using magical words to conjure up the spirits of the past. I feel like a complete novice, an outsider, in the presence of the initiated, someone not yet permitted entrance into this secret world of aviation history, lacking the special knowledge that will allow me through its portal. 'Good luck anyway,' she says. 'Let us know if you find anything,' before returning to her desk.

I mention to Ian that something has been bugging me: the suggestion that a seventh man, Sgt Armourer Brottell, may have been on board the Wellington when it crashed, even though he doesn't appear to have been buried along with the rest of the crew. 'Well, things like that did happen,' Ian says, thinking. 'He was an armourer – he could have been testing the guns or something. And maybe he was buried elsewhere, like your uncle. Anyway, it's an interesting story. Give me your email and I'll do some checking and get back. Now I better pay for this before someone gets cross.' We swap numbers, he pays for his Hurricane, and I head out into the bright sunshine, taking a deep breath of summer air.

That night, after a long evening spent scouring the internet for more leads, and finding, to my shame, that 2SFTS was not based at Syerston in 1941, as Ian had said, but at RAF Brize Norton, a hundred miles away in Oxfordshire, I am about to shut the laptop and go to bed when an email pings into my inbox. It's Ian. He says he has gone through his reference books and found what he was looking for. He's attached a copy and hopes it will be of interest to me and finishes by saying that he'll keep looking and let me know if anything else turns up.

Attached to the email is a jpeg of an extract from an AIR27, (AIR27/1672 to be exact). It's a scan of a page from a wartime squadron operational record book, a type-written account of how the accident was reported by an administrative officer at RAF Syerston on the day of the accident. AIR27/1672 is gold dust. On a page which lists the routine mundanities of day-to-day operational life on a wartime bomber station (weather conditions, movements, promotions and so on) the day's entry for 12 June 1941 is dramatic precisely because of the understated, matter-of-fact manner in which it is recorded:

> A warm day commenced with local patches of thick haze. Light NW wind increasing to 10 mph towards dusk, little cloud at 3000 to 4000 feet. At about 1140 Hrs [sic] a XXXXXXX regrettable flying accident occurred to Wellington No 1017 'K' which was engaged in a formation flight with Wellington No 1696 'P', visibility being poor owing to local patches of haze. When over ELTON near BINGHAM a mid-air collision occurred with an Oxford aircraft of No 2 SFTS which was flying at the same height and on an opposite course to that of 1017 'K'. The accident was seen by the rear gunner of 1696 'P' which was leading the other Wellington in formation. The two pilots concerned took what avoiding action was possible but owing to the haze had not observed each other's aircraft in time to prevent a collision, the Oxford striking the Wellington at the astrodome carrying away its tail unit. Both aircraft crashed from about 900 ft and fell about 700 yds apart, bursting into flames, both crews losing their lives. The crew of Wellington 1017 'K' were F/LT STEFANICKI T, SGT MRUK K, P/O KOWALCZE S, SGT KRAWCZYK J, P/O WOJTOWICZ M, and P/O ZIRKWITZ A.[8]

Talk about the stiff upper lip. It is so matter of fact and restrained in its description. I can practically see the officer, pipe tightly clenched, pacing up and down in a fug of tobacco

---

[8] AIR27/1672 National Archives.

smoke, dictating quietly as a clerk types up the report. There's a telling moment just as the account begins where a word has been crossed out and changed: '*At about 1140 Hrs a XXXXXX regrettable flying accident occurred...*' I can't help wondering if the officer had said 'crash' at first, or instinctively used some emotive adjective, and then, with an eye to history, and remembering that this log would be read in the future, thought better of it.

I start to imagine the feeling as word got round the squadron about the regrettable accident, and the terrible loss of life. The mood on the station on that warm summer afternoon must have been sombre, to say the least. The amazing revelation to me is that the log makes it clear there had been a witness to the incident, the rear gunner on the leading Wellington, R1696, SM-P. The unnamed gunner clearly describes the Oxford trainer coming out of the haze, on a course directly opposite that which the Wellingtons were flying, and at the same height, and one can imagine the split-second during which the pilots must have seen each other and tried to take evasive action. Presumably the pilot of the Wellington might have dipped his aircraft's nose to try and fly under the Oxford, as the trainer hit the bomber on the astrodome, which is on the top of, and nearly half-way down, the Wellington's fuselage. The two aircraft were probably flying at a combined closing speed of well over 300mph, and the impact of the collision must have cut the Wellington in two, so that it carried away the bomber's tail section.

How must that Polish air gunner have felt, seeing the collision happen before his very eyes, unable to do anything about it, watching transfixed and horrified as the two aircraft ripped each other apart and fell hundreds of feet to explode in flames in the fields below? Remember, he was not just watching two aircraft crash and burn, horrific as that would be; he knew the crewmen on the Wellington, had possibly known them since they served in Poland together. He may have stood them pints the night before, in the Saracen's Head, or stepped excitedly into a Nottingham dancehall with them, eyeing up the local talent together. Sudden violent death is the kind of thing these crews would have prepared themselves for on operations, at night over Germany, but flying above the peaceful Nottinghamshire countryside, in daylight, on the way home for lunch in the mess? One minute you're on a routine training flight, the next, the cold bony finger of Death taps you on the shoulder, reminding you that He is always there, and you could be next...

The log is also revealing in what it says about the weather conditions. My cousin Fiona had always said that the collision happened in 'poor visibility', and I am sure that she, along with the rest of her family, and certainly me, imagined that could only mean one thing: murky, possibly cloudy and rainy skies. It's the way 'poor visibility' has been depicted from Howard Hawks' *Only Angels Have Wings* to any number of modern air-disaster movies. But the log says that *haze* was the problem, which is a new one on me. It was 'a warm day... with local patches of thick haze...' There was 'little cloud' and 'the two pilots concerned took what avoiding action was possible, but owing to the haze had not observed each other's aircraft in time to prevent a collision...' I would have to be more realistic and restrained in my fantasies if I was to get an accurate picture of what really happened. I remember that my friend Megan has recently started flying as a commercial pilot, and make a note to talk to her to get an understanding of haze from the horse's mouth.

In all this talk of death there is a positive though: the question of the crash site, or as I am now thinking, *sites*. I hadn't really imagined the details of the collision yet, assuming I suppose that the aircraft had become entangled in each other's airframes and plummeted down together, but the report makes it clear – they fell *separately*, with the Oxford dragged down by the weight of the Wellington's tail section leaving the Wimpy spinning wildly out of control, ending up 700 yards apart. It occurs to me that the rear gunner in the stricken Wellington might have gone down in his turret, entangled with the Oxford. I hope that he and the others knew nothing about it, but sadly, I am probably wrong. I reassure myself that both aircraft would have taken only seconds to hit the ground and explode, and that the final impact would probably have killed anyone outright.

However, one question seems to remain unanswered. My understanding had been that with so many airfields lying in close proximity to each other during the war, each would keep its own aircraft flying within strict height limits, precisely to avoid this kind of accident. The report states that the Oxford was flying at the same height and on an opposite course to that of the Wellington. It doesn't say that either was flying at the correct or incorrect height. I wonder whether that is something which I will ever be able to get to the bottom of, or indeed, whether I will even want to.

I make a note of the details of the AIR27 and remind myself to order a copy of the full log along with that of 2SFTS from the National Archives at Kew. Hopefully the information in them will answer more questions I have about the squadrons, their aircraft and crews.

One mystery however, looks like being solved now. Remembering the suggestion that an extra man had been aboard the Wimpy, and looking carefully at the jpeg of the report I notice that the name of Sgt Armourer Brottell appears immediately after the name of PO Zirkwitz A, typed so closely that it could appear to be an additional name in the list of casualties. But on the line below, the report goes on to note that Sgt Brottell was 'promoted T/F/SGT w.e.f 1/6/41,' actually confirming that Sgt Brottell has been promoted with effect from June 1st. That extra line could easily have been cut off on any photograph or scan of the page. The mistake made by that member of Sgt Mruk's family is an easy one to make, but one which could have had me barking up another wrong tree for a long time.

With a faint glow of pride (not to mention relief) at having solved a mystery, I email Ian, thanking him for the document and apologising for putting him to so much trouble. Before I can close my laptop he replies, grateful that I'm grateful. Ian tells me we obviously share an obsessive character trait: several years ago he was caught up in a battle to find the war grave of his Great Uncle Charlie who was mortally wounded on the first day of The Somme. He eventually found the grave, organised a new Commonwealth War Graves headstone, and included on it the name of the sergeant who had saved Charlie's life by pulling him back into the safety of a trench. Searching the family ancestry websites he was also able to locate the sergeant's family and many Shaw relatives, and the story now lives on.

I can empathise with Ian – that's me, already, obsessively working to try and bring an obscure, unknown family story to wider attention. Ian and I met quite by chance only a few hours ago, but already we have a kind of understanding, and his inspirational story encourages me.

Fourteen

'And these are what Tony found with his metal detector. He had them framed for us, which I thought was a nice touch.'

I'm peering closely at five small coins, mounted in a simple square wooden frame, hanging on the wall of the farm office, while Gillian Roberts tells me her story. The coins are in various states of preservation, the newest being a George V1 sixpence from the 1930s, and the oldest a tiny medieval coin dating back to the reign of Edward 11. It still looks as bright and new as the day it slipped from someone's fingers or fell out of a leather purse back in the early 1300s.

'Tony found these as well,' says Gillian, indicating two more small frames. The first contains a small medieval dagger fitting, but in the second there's something much more interesting, to my eyes at least: a bracelet, with a chain made of small silver bars, and in near-perfect condition. Curiously, on a small oval plaque it bears the simple inscription: *Toby Dec 1939*.

'It looks like it belonged to a child,' Gillian says, breaking my thoughts. 'Maybe it was a baptism present?'

I'm not so sure. I've seen photographs of the identity bracelets worn by servicemen in World War two, not official, but often given by a loved one, sometimes as a lucky charm. It looks much too big to be a child's baptism present. But it's the date, Dec 1939, less than two years before the crash happened, that makes me think this might be significant. And the name Toby is unusual, possibly short for Tobias. Could it be Polish?

I had received a reply to the letter I'd posted about Beckswood. It was a phone call from Gillian Roberts, telling me that she and her husband Barrie owned the land I was interested in, and that I was welcome to chat about the story. We arranged to meet the following morning, but bizarrely I had slept through my alarm and now found myself hurrying nervously to Elton.

How (or rather why) had I slept through my alarm, today of all days, when I knew I had an appointment to meet Gillian? Like anyone who did a paper round as a kid, I never sleep through an alarm, unless, of course, there is a good reason for it. Is my brain telling me not to go to this meeting? This is a meeting I should be really looking forward to, an opportunity to discover something important, possibly stumble on a clue, or even locate the crash sites. But deep down, subconsciously, do I really know that this whole thing is nothing but a wild goose chase and a monumental waste of time? Do I really want to avoid the disappointment? Or is it something even more fundamental?

The traffic is bad, a combination of roadworks around Victoria Street and the morning rush hour, but miraculously the country roads are clear and I get to the farmhouse just a few minutes past the appointed time. I ring the doorbell and wait. It's hot. No answer. I try again, gazing around at the farm and wiping the sweat from my brow while I wait for someone to come to the door, which they don't. Damn. I've missed her and I have nobody to blame but myself.

But of course, I haven't missed her. Gillian operates on Farmer's Time, and arrives ten minutes later, greeting me pleasantly, but with a brusqueness that suggests she doesn't expect our business to take up much of her morning.

Gillian obviously doesn't believe that the crash happened on her land and is convinced that I won't find anything to support my theory at all. She says she has spoken to the only people who might know (most of them are dead now) but has drawn a complete blank. Am I sure I've got the right Elton? I explain that I had been looking at Elston and she agrees that with it being so much closer to Syerston, Elston does sound like a safer bet. But she kindly takes me into the farm office, where I look at the metal detectorist's finds, and shows me the boundary map of the farm, dated 1877, where the Becks Plantation is clearly marked, not *Beckswood*. Repeating for the umpteenth time that she doesn't hold out much hope for me, she finally says she will drive me to the plantation where I can have a mooch around on my own so long as I am careful (whatever that means).

The farm is around 500 acres, mostly arable, and on this boiling hot day the few sheep she owns are grateful for the precious shade of the oak trees. Gillian and Barrie have lived here since about 2004, when they amalgamated what used to be two smaller farms. As we drive to the plantation I tell her about the eye witness report from the rear gunner on Wellington R1696, describing the collision over Elton and the two crash sites some 700 yards apart. I try to sound convincing when I tell her that I am sure that at least one of the aircraft crashed near the plantation, but she remains firmly sceptical. In all the time they've been living on the farm no-one has ever mentioned this story, the metal detectorist who has worked the area has found no evidence of a plane wreck, and more importantly, the area around the Becks Plantation shows no signs of a crash. It was 80 years ago, I say, but even I can detect the lack of conviction in my voice.

Gillian's car pulls away over the hardcore track and disappears around the bend, quickly hidden by the trees. Suddenly it is quiet and still. I turn and look at the woods in front of me, a tightly packed tangle of mixed deciduous and evergreen trees and bushes. Before leaving, Gillian had warned me that the surrounding fields were all seeded so I mustn't walk on them, and that there are thousands of pheasants in the woods, being reared in blissful ignorance of the shoot. She was keen not to see them disturbed, but I had permission to wander into the woods and see what I could find.

I'm not actually expecting to find anything at all. Not because Gillian's pessimism has affected me (although it has) but because I'm pretty sure that after more than 80 years any evidence of even the biggest crash will have been hidden by now. Any trees that were blown apart by the impact of an aircraft and subsequent explosion and fire will have recovered, and more trees, bushes and brambles will have reclaimed any gaps. And if an aircraft came down in the surrounding fields, decades of ploughing will probably have levelled out any disturbance of the soil.

But I'm here, and as I walk into the woods (there's no actual path of any description, I just enter and wander between the trees) it is with a kind of reverence for what I want to believe happened here all that time ago. Maybe reverence is the wrong word. Respect is better. If any of those men did die here, it is only right that I should treat the place with respect. And as I duck below the branches, moving in and out of the shafts of sunlight, aware of absolutely nothing but the sound of my own footsteps and breathing, there is something almost sacred about it. This is not like the bleak, muddy battlefields of the Somme, or the grim, concrete and steel brutality of Stalingrad or Berlin. It's a beautiful, peaceful place.

About 20 or 30 yards into the woods I stop, noticing that the ground seems to be much more uneven here. There is a sense of timelessness, as there always is in the woods, but also a sense of history. I can feel it. It's as if all those hours of thinking about the two pilots in their Oxford and the Poles in their Wellington are focussing in on this spot. Is it wrong of me to imagine a stricken, mangled aircraft, falling down directly onto this ground? Is that macabre? Ghoulish? I don't think so; I am just imagining what happened, recreating in my mind what that rear gunner on R1696 saw. And that's what this whole journey is about, isn't it? I look up into the canopy, shading my eyes as I watch the clouds move slowly beyond the tracery of branches and leaves. No more than a dot, a buzzard soars in gentle circles high above.

A little further into the woods I discover a pond, almost hidden amongst the trees. I say a pond, but it looks more like a hole in the ground, filled with stagnant, stinking water. It doesn't appear to be fed by a stream or anything; it's just there, almost scarring the beauty of the woods. Around the water I note a curious kind of blue-grey shale, layers of semi-rock, and the pond has a strange shape. Not that ponds are supposed to follow a regulation shape, I know, but this hole in the ground is, well... angular if anything. I can imagine it being created when a large aeroplane fell from the sky and exploded.

I check my OS 260 map and see that it is marked – a smallish blue shape in the middle of the woods. And a few inches roughly south of this spot, just south of the Redmile road, is another blue dot, even smaller. I recall driving past the spot that first time and noticing a few trees growing out of it. It's several hundred yards away from this feature - another crash site perhaps?

Emerging from the woods I gaze across the surrounding fields in the direction of Elton. They are flat and completely featureless with no obvious signs of a crater or anything else that might indicate a crash site. Finding where Oxford T1334 crashed is not going to be easy.

Back in the farm office I ask Gillian about the curious bomber-shaped hole in the woods. 'You mean the fishpond?' she says, showing me the old map again, and there it is, just inside the woods: marked Fishpond. So, no wartime crash site there, after all. I mention the other possible site, in the field on the other side of the road, but she doesn't know who owns that land.

After promising to keep in touch and let her know if anything interesting comes up, I take my leave and drive away from the farm, suddenly feeling a deep despondency and emptiness. Despite my upbeat and positive attitude as I say goodbye, the hopes that I might find some sort of clue here have come to nothing. There is going to be a lot more to this journey than I had expected.

Fifteen

This story is taking over my life.

Every spare moment, it seems, I'm either thinking about, reading about, or imagining what happened on that morning of 12 June 1941. The name Toby and the date December 1939 keeps returning to me and won't go away. Tobiasz turns out to be a relatively common Polish name, and in late 1939 any of the crew could have been making their way from Poland to England. Could the bracelet have belonged to one of the crew of R1017, a gift from a friend?[9] I can't drive down the Fosse Way in the direction of RAF Syerston without remembering the Poles who were stationed there for six months in 1941, thinking about the nightmarish operations they flew and the grand times they spent in Newark on their down nights; visible from the road, the officers' quarters which most of the crew lived in are now derelict, huge gaping holes in their roofs and graffiti painted all over the walls, a far cry from the quaint watercolours painted by some unknown artist in the 305 Squadron *Chronicle*.

On sweltering hot summer days I go north and drive around the airfields spread around Lincoln, exploring the nearby villages with names like Boothby Graffoe, Wellingore and Navenby. In Navenby I stop for lunch at the Lion and Royal pub, sipping my pint in the sunshine of the beer garden. Well before his Dam Busting days, Guy Gibson was stationed not far away at RAF Digby, flying Beaufighters with 29 (Nightfighter) Squadron, and he and his new wife Eve lived in

---

[9] Tobiasz is the Polish variation of the Hebrew name meaning 'God is good,' with the diminutive Toby

rooms in this pub, before their marriage began its slow and painful decline. I visit Metheringham Airfield Visitors Centre, one-time home to Gibson's 106 Squadron, and see the fragments of wheel hydraulics from the Mosquito he was flying when he crashed and died in Holland in 1944. They have a wonderful exhibition in one of the huts at Metheringham, where a recorded voice reads out the names of the aircraft and crews who were lost from the station, and looking up you can see dozens of models of Lancasters hanging from the ceiling, each painted up in the markings of those aircraft, a simple yet powerful reminder of the cost of war.

Not far from RAF Scampton, home to the Dam Busters, there's a small collection of huts on the outskirts of what used to be RAF Ingham, where a new heritage centre is being built by volunteers, dedicated to the work and memory of the Polish Squadrons who flew from Ingham, Syerston and many other airfields in the area, most of which have since disappeared under the plough or concrete. Nobody there seems to know anything about the crash I'm investigating, but they are busy with rewiring and plastering, so I leave them to it, making a note to return when the centre is open and (hopefully) I have answered more questions myself. It's the same story at The International Bomber Command Centre at Lincoln, where archivist Dan Ellin tells me he doesn't know about the crash but will keep an eye out for me.

I go to the Lincolnshire Aviation Heritage Centre at East Kirkby, where they've got a Lancaster (NX611 'Just Jane') that doesn't fly but taxis along the field from where 57 and 630 Squadrons used to launch their raids on Germany. Among the bookstalls on an open day, I bump into Tim Chamberlain, a local historian and bookseller who I had earlier contacted about Bill's crash, hoping he might have some information. He didn't, not having heard of the incident, but he was very useful in putting me onto people who knew about organising memorials to such things. I also come across the people from the Lincolnshire Aircraft Recovery Group, (LARG), who specialise in tracing crash sites. Again, no immediate help, but a contact for the future...

And of course I visit RAF Syerston, in the company of Squadron Leader Mark Williams, Commandant of the Gliding School, who kindly shows me around the surviving station buildings and tells me stories (inevitably) about Guy Gibson. We drink tea in the room where Gibson worked, and stand on the balcony of the Watch Office, from where the WAAFs and admin staff watched the aircraft set out on raids and waited for their return. He shows me the only remaining 'H' Block, where the lower ranks were accommodated, and indicates the area near the bomb dump where that 4,000lb 'Cookie' went off, nearly killing 'Gus' Walker...

Every time I'm out walking in the country or through the town and hear a propellor engine in the sky above, I look up and imagine the Wellington and Oxford, their courses converging. I don't know how to gauge 900 feet in the open sky but discover that it is a little less than the height of the Shard, or twice the height of the London Eye, (or for those fortunate enough not to live in London, that's roughly twice the height of the tallest onshore wind turbine). Not living in London myself, it is hard to imagine, but when Squadron Leader Williams and I are watching the gliders being launched from the runway at Syerston he waits till the glider levels out and says, 'That's about 1,200 feet.' The glider is lower than I had expected and for the first time I realize that the Oxford and Wellington would have been flying lower than I had imagined when they collided.

On my phone one day I see a number of recently-posted videos of a mid-air collision between a B-17 Flying Fortress and a P-63 Kingcobra at the 'Wings Over Dallas' air show in 2022. Flying in good visibility at a height of about 200 feet over the spectators they hit each other and break up before crashing to the ground a few seconds later in a ball of orange flame. It's horrifying to see, but I have to watch it over and over again, trying to work out how on earth the pilot of the fighter hadn't seen the huge bomber right in front of him.

The investigators still don't know the full story, although it seems to be a combination of factors. That then starts me off down a more macabre path: just how long would it have taken for an aircraft flying at around 200mph to hit the ground from 900 feet? About *7½ seconds*, I am reliably informed by someone with a bigger brain than mine. Only a few seconds, but it must have felt like an eternity to the men in those aeroplanes...

My head is full of dark thoughts like these, and it doesn't help that the only books I read now are about Bomber Command, the history of the Polish Air Force within it and the stories of their aircraft and crews; I endlessly watch DVDs featuring wartime documentary films on the same subjects, and re-watch old movies: *The Way To The Stars*, T*arget For Tonight*, and *Millions Like U*s. The inbox of my email pings incessantly with notifications about new books and DVDs to be delivered, website links to investigate, or old contacts to be followed up; I wake each morning thinking about Oxford trainers and fall asleep thinking about Wellington bombers. After only a couple of months since starting down this road, I am obsessed, not only with Bill's story, but with the whole world of excitement, danger and death that he and those other men lived in 80 years ago.

One day I strike gold, when a book I've ordered online arrives. *Bomber Aircraft of 305 Squadron* by Lechosław Musiałkowski is a glossy hardback which catalogues all of the various types of aircraft the squadron flew during the Second World War. The book is reliant for most of its value on the fantastic photographic collection of Flight Sergeant Gabriel Milosz, who served as a photographer, and then head of the photographic section of the squadron until 1945 and took thousands of shots of the crews and aircraft, determined to preserve their contribution to the war. Although Wellington R1017 SM-K was lost relatively early in the squadron's history, during the six months they were stationed at Syerston, there is a photograph of the aircraft (quite possibly the only photograph of R1017 in existence), and I find myself staring at it, literally open mouthed. The Wellington is pictured on the eastern runway (judging by the trees in the background, still visible today), possibly running up its engines before take-off, and a cloud of dust blows up around the tail and the rear turret, where the gunner sits. It's a very ordinary moment captured in time, nothing dramatic or exciting, quite unremarkable in fact, but to me it is like a long-forgotten family photograph found in an old shoe box in the attic. I feel connected to it. It looks like a warm, sunny, cloudless, possibly hazy day. Who knows, it could have been taken as R1017 took off for its last flight.

The only known photograph of Wellington R1017 (SM-K) on the runway at Syerston (Reproduced by permission)

My preoccupation with the summer of 1941 also gives me something else to talk to Mum about – her wartime memories, and more specifically, what she remembers of George and Ann. Of course, if I hadn't moved back south to be nearer Mum I wouldn't have had that first chance conversation with her as we passed Syerston, and none of this would ever have occurred, and I often consider where I would be and what I would be doing if that conversation had never happened (certainly not working out how long it takes for an aircraft to hit the ground flying at a certain speed and from a certain height). My younger brother Tim has recently moved with his family back to the area, also keen to be nearer Mum, which is a great help. Our decisions to move back home have certainly worked out well for Mum; aside from the convenience of having someone on hand to do the odd jobs around the house – things which since Dad died have become increasingly difficult for her - she appreciates having members of the family living nearby who can drop by for a cup of tea, sit with her and have a chat. Making dates for Sunday lunches, afternoon teas and shopping trips sharpens her mind; Mum visibly brightens, and I see the vague fog of depression and loneliness lift and disappear as she gets out of the house, and I feel it in myself too.

Sometimes after lunch at a pub we go for long meandering drives through the countryside. Like me, she says, my dad used to drive just where the fancy took him, taking surprise turns and going down unknown lanes as he came to them, and everywhere we go she chatters away like a bird, commenting on the villages we drive through, the people she knew, mostly gone now, and remembers stories from the past. However, most of these stories I've heard before, and I notice that more and more now she is repeating not only the same stories, but also thoughts, even sentences verbatim. Each time we drive through a new development of houses, or pass the numerous cars parked in the village, she expresses genuine surprise, as if noticing these changes for the first time, just as I know she will again on our next drive. It's as if she has started wearing mental blinkers, which focus only on the here and now, right in front of her, and forgets what happened yesterday, or last week. But this is not a big thing; I put it down to old age and the natural fading of memory and try not to pick her up on it in case she finds it confusing.

Just as Mum's mental health and outlook seem to be benefitting, so I am enjoying the simple pleasure of being able to talk to a human being on a regular basis. The end of my marriage has left me hollowed out, mentally exhausted and shot to pieces, emotionally. I still don't really know who I am, what I have become since the family break-up, or how I really feel about it. So although we rarely, if ever, discuss my divorce, both of us carrying on the family tradition of not talking about 'personal matters', I feel better for being with someone who I know is instinctively on my side.

One fine morning I pick Mum up in the car, surprising her with the news that I'm taking her for a drive to the seaside. She loves a trip to the Lincolnshire coast, and often remembers the drives she and Dad used to take out there. I could also do with a day off, not staring at the laptop or reading yet another airman's autobiography. When I was young, we often went on caravan holidays in the villages along that coast – Chapel St Leonards, Ingoldmells and Sutton on Sea, and would take day trips to the bigger, noisier and more colourful Mablethorpe and Skegness. She's excited, and quickly packs a bag with sunhat and suncream, grabs a windcheater in case it turns chilly, and talks about the fish and chips we are going to eat on the seafront. We did something similar the summer before lockdown, and she has reminded me of it ever since.

We head east, passing through Grantham, which to Mum is the birthplace of Margaret Thatcher and to me is the Headquarters of Bomber Command's 5 Group during the war. Guy Gibson drove these very streets to and from Scampton, as he prepared for the dams raid, putting thoughts of Eve and his failed marriage to the back of his mind...

'We used to see Richard Todd in Morrisons,' Mum says, in response to my mention of Guy Gibson. 'He'd often be in there on a Saturday. Your dad would lean over and whisper to me, "Look – over by the fruit and veg - it's Richard Todd, Guy Gibson from *The Dam Busters*." And it was. He always looked very well turned out but he's much smaller than you think.'

We leave Grantham's industrial estates and fading villas, winding through the gentle hills of Kesteven, rich with cattle and fields of still-green wheat. Before we know it, the irregular shapes of meadows and trees give way to the immense wide, flat Lincolnshire fenland, laid out in geometric rigidity, the long straight roads lined on each side by deep ditches, and vast endless lines of cabbages, brassicas and potatoes. Beyond, row upon row of plastic polytunnels stretch into the distance, reminiscent of the aircraft hangars and Nissen huts that used to give this place the name of Bomber County.

It's not long before we are in sight of the sea, and Mum's excitement is rising. But we've picked the wrong day for our trip to the seaside: it's a Bank Holiday and Skegness is *heaving*. So we drive up the coast towards Chapel St Leonards, where I buy fish and chips which we eat in a quiet spot just north of the village, at Chapel Point, surrounded by sand dunes. It was over dunes like this up and down the coastline that many aerial scenes from *The Dam Busters* were shot by Erwin Hillier and his camera crew in Wellington MF628.

In his fascinating book *Filming The Dam Busters*, Jonathan Falconer explains that among the pilots who were loaned to the production by the RAF to fly the Lancasters (which by this time had to be taken out of storage for the film), two of them were Polish: Flt Sgt Joe Kmiecik of 83 Squadron and Flt Sgt Ted Szuwalski of 97 Squadron. Both had made remarkable escapes from the Soviet Gulags where they had been held since the Russian attack on eastern Poland in 1939, eventually arriving in England where they, like the crews of 305 squadron, joined the RAF and the war against fascism.

The job of flying the modified Lancasters in tight formation and at very low level over water was extremely difficult and dangerous. This kind of close formation flying was no longer practised in the age of the atomic bomb, and the film makers constantly pushed the pilots closer and lower, requiring specific shots for their action sequences. The result though, speaks for itself. In the age of computer-generated flying sequences, the live-action scenes in *The Dam Busters* make it still one of the finest flying films ever made. Sitting on a picnic bench among the dunes it is not hard to believe that those very aircraft may have flown at zero feet over this spot.

On my phone I have the photograph of Bill that Fiona sent me, in his RAF greatcoat and with the white cadet's flash in his forage cap, and I show it to Mum. Shading her eyes from the sun she peers at this image of a man she never knew, and remarks on the strong resemblance to his twin, George, and it triggers more memories. 'They had a dog, with a funny name, was it Rack? I think so, something like that.[10] He was a scruffy little thing who used to trot about the streets of Goole, which dogs could do in those days,' she says, 'So long as you had a dog licence, but people don't bother with those now do they? Anyway, he was a very friendly dog was Raque, but a bit of a rascal. He used to sneak into the butcher's shop and steal strings of sausages off the counter!' She remembers George laughing about the angry, red-faced butcher in his striped apron, chasing Raque through the Goole backstreets. According to Mum, when anyone told George what Raque had been up to, he just laughed, saying, 'Good old Raque!' I laugh with her at the vivid pictures she paints of incidents, places and people she sees with clarity as the memories come flooding back, triggered by Bill's photograph.

Mum is pleased that Fiona and I have been working together on the project. 'It must be nice for her to discover all this information about Bill,' she says. 'I don't think George ever really talked about it very much. People didn't in those days, and I expect it must have been upsetting for him to lose a twin brother like that.' Hearing the word twin, I am again reminded of my own twin sons, and the distance I have got to go to try and mend our damaged relationship since I moved out. It's something I could talk about, but don't, and we sit in silence, picking at the fish and chips in the stiffening sea breeze.

Having eaten as much as she can, Mum says she is starting to feel cold, and we drive back home in the early evening sunshine. I take a detour, going along the road to RAF Coningsby, the home of the Battle of Britain Memorial Flight

---

[10] Talking to Fiona later I learned that George's dog was called *Raque*, and that's the name I'll use here.

and where Lancaster PA474, one of the only two Lancasters in the world that are still flying, now lives. I was lucky enough to hitch a ride on board her many years ago, in another life, flying from Coningsby to the south coast, but that's another story. I always get a thrill when I see her, and it would be nice to make her acquaintance again. I park up near the perimeter fence, alongside a few other Lanc fans, me with one eye scanning the vast Lincolnshire skies, hoping to see this special Lanc returning from an air show. You never know - we could strike lucky.

Anxious to fill the silence, I talk about how I'm settling into my new life in Newark, desperate to give the impression that I'm making new friends and am not lonely, both of which are untrue. The reality is that first winter in Newark was dismal and cold; not like the bright, bitterly cold, snowy winters I had become used to in the Scottish hills, but penetrating, damp and depressing. The new flat felt sterile, and I missed the warmth of a log fire, so useful for staring into for hours on end. I told myself I shouldn't be feeling lonely when my new home had so much to offer. Apart from when I was doing my research I spent as little time as possible indoors, making the most of the new experience of living in close proximity to people, shops, pubs, restaurants, and – luxury of luxuries – a theatre and cinema. Newark is a small town but coming from a tiny village in the Highlands I felt like I was living in the middle of Manhattan. Eventually the first tentative signs of spring arrived, the weak sunshine became warmer by the day, and before I knew it cherry blossom covered the trees in the churchyard outside my window. Squirrels scampered through the grass, digging up the nuts they'd buried the previous autumn. The days were getting longer and it was even possible to sit out and drink coffee in the market square again. Slowly, day by day, I felt like I was returning to life.

But my moods were still swinging violently, from exhilaration and hope one day to depression and despair the next. The more you are around people, the more you realise how isolated you are from them. No sooner had I started to believe that I was in a place where I could make a new start than I feared things would never change, because I could never change. My isolation and depression became worse. Of course the remedy was simple – I needed to get out and meet people.

Glossing over that, I tell Mum about the pub quizzes I've started going to, some of which even serve chip butties at half time, which Mum thinks sounds as good a reason as any for going. What I don't tell her is that I haven't made any friends yet and that I think the main reason is that the kind of people who frequent these quiz nights fall into three main categories:

1. Lonely and competitive
2. Nerdy and very competitive.
3. Obsessively hyper-competitive, and therefore extremely nerdy and lonely.

Clearly, these are not necessarily the best or easiest people to make friends with.

I also scoured the local newspaper and websites for details about organisations that I might join – archery, swimming, meditation (*really?* Yes...), local history, even crown green bowling. But in the long shadow of lockdown a lot of societies and clubs still weren't fully up and running again. By chance I saw that a new book club was starting at a café in town, and I went along. At that first meeting I was one of six people, including the café owner, and we all eyed each other up and down suspiciously as we drank coffee and muttered about who we were, why we had come along etc. Nobody, of course, admitted the truth, which was that we were lonely and only here to meet people, the books being a convenient excuse. Needless to say, of the five women and one other man in the group, I was the only one who had Antony Beevor and Max Hastings at the top of my reading list, and I probably extolled their literary virtues a bit too strongly. It was never going to end well...

My last hope was a writer's group. Again, like the book club it wasn't something I'd ever been a part of before, and I was by now pretty pessimistic about how it would work out. Ironically, my main worry was that I am, technically at least, a writer, or more accurately, I sometimes get paid real money to write for TV and radio - so I wasn't sure if I was the kind of person who would fit easily into what I imagined would be an essentially amateur group. I had visions of a bunch of sad old cases reading their work to a similar audience, who would immediately regard me with suspicion and resentment. I couldn't have been more wrong.

The Fosseway Writers (named after that same Roman road that RAF Syerston sits on) were meeting in the LetsXcape Together coffee house, which turned out to be a weird and glorious den situated on the marketplace, where you could find coffee, cakes, and more boardgames than you can shake a Harry Potter wizard stick at. Entering the café, I was directed to an area at the back where half a dozen people sat around a big table, surrounded by books, shelves of wargames and weird steampunk ephemera (Newark is very big on steampunk). Most of the group had glasses of wine in front of them. Feeling a bit like I was joining an addiction recovery programme I resisted the temptation to say 'Hi, I'm Ade and I'm a writer,' and was instead warmly welcomed by Nick, the leader of the group and the man I'd contacted online about joining. Trying to look like I knew what I was talking about, I told them I was writing a novel. Since the separation and divorce I had, truth be told, begun what I called a 'crime novel', which had petered out through a combination of my total ignorance of a) what was actually required to write a crime novel, such as a decent plot and interesting characters, and b) anything like a basic understanding of the world of crime itself. Afraid of looking like an idiot, I avoided admitting this, preferring to blame the usual suspects of self-prevarication and distraction for my lack of progress, expecting sympathy and nods of support. However, the sceptical looks on their faces revealed that this kind of pat excuse for not getting on and doing it wasn't going to wash – yes, they knew about those problems, but they'd all, to a greater or lesser extent, surmounted them. It quickly became clear to me that some members of the group weren't just aspiring writers – they had finished, sold and published their novels and stories, they had book deals, and an audience, and had learned the discipline of sitting down and writing. They were writers, and they knew what they were doing. This was more like it.

Searching for something that might sound authentic, I said I was thinking of abandoning the novel altogether, and that I wanted to write something more personal. 'What does that mean?' asked Nick, perplexed. I muttered something about wanting to find a way to write less commercially, not really knowing myself what I actually meant by that. I explained that in the past I had been lucky enough to be commissioned to write some scripts for television and radio, and these tended to be mostly for continuing series, in which case I was simply picking up characters, situations and plots that already existed, or writing one-off scripts based on historical events or dramatisations of novels. They were enjoyable to write, and did quite well, but I was always conscious that there was very little of me in them. If my writing did reveal anything about me, it was that I didn't reveal much about myself in my writing. And although I had continued to write speculative scripts with television in mind, rarely did anything ever come of them. That was why I had started to think about writing prose, and the abortive attempt at a crime novel.

The problem, it seemed to me, despite all the emotional turmoil I was experiencing in my life, or maybe because of it, was that I couldn't find anything personal to write about. Or rather, I didn't know how to write to about it.

But I enjoyed the meeting and was disappointed when it came to an end. It was great to spend an evening talking to like-minded people, so when a few of us gathered outside on the steps in the rain, I plucked up the courage to ask if anyone was up for the pub? Surprisingly, all three said yes, and we sloped off to the Flying Circus, where we spent the rest of the night hunched over our drinks, swapping stories about stories.

I found myself taken back to my early days in theatre, when having a laugh or a cry over a drink or two after work was the expected norm, and the best way to make friends.

There were four of us – Nick, a bloke in a pork pie hat called Martin (the bloke, not the hat), a woman named Linda, and me. After they finally threw us out of the pub, we said our goodbyes on Castle Gate where the rain had now turned into a fine, steady drizzle. Martin, the bloke in the hat, hung back a little and we chatted in that ironic, self-deprecating way that men who don't know each other yet tend to do, laying out our life stories in broad chunks, each sizing up the other to see where we came from and what we were made of, and testing the ground before giving too much of ourselves away. It turned out that he, like me, was a relative newcomer to the town, having moved here after his own relationship broke up and finding a flat down by the castle. Aside from writing we shared an interest in football, music and pubs; so far, so blokey. More importantly, Martin asked if I'd enjoyed the meeting and whether I was going to come again. I said I had and would, and he said he was glad, as no-one had ever suggested going on to the pub until I did tonight. We laughed, agreed that it would be great to go along and watch the local non-league Newark Town FC on a Saturday afternoon, shook hands, said goodnight and headed our separate ways.

Even though I was still walking back to an empty flat in the drizzle, I felt warmer and happier than I had in a long time. This was what I'd been missing, what I'd looked forward to, and I loved every minute of it. I felt a little more of me returning.

Of course, I don't tell Mum any of that. All I tell her is that I've joined a writer's group, that it went well, they were nice, friendly people and that I was hoping it would encourage me to do some more writing. And I don't tell her that when I did get back to the flat after that first meeting, I lay in bed, staring at the ceiling, trying to work out what to do about it, the arguments and possibilities running around and around in my head like bombers circling a target. But I knew then, as I know now, that when I was talking about pub quizzes, book clubs and writer's groups, I should really have been talking about my failed marriage and how guilty I felt about it. As always, I pushed those feelings to a safe place at the back of my mind, where I buried them.

At Coningsby it's getting late. The sun is low in the evening sky and there's no sign of the Lancaster, no more activity on the airfield. Maybe she was tucked up in her hangar all the time. One of the nearby cars starts up and drives off, the occupants having given up waiting. Mum asks what time it is; she is bored of waiting and wants to go, so I pull away and head home.

Sixteen

It is easy for me to forget, with all this concentration on the technical details of the aircraft, and the war, that this is a human story, and I need to find out more about the players in the tragedy. As the story begins with Bill Parkinson, and my mother's random but vague memory of his death, it is obvious that he should be my starting point. His niece Fiona has already sent me a photograph of him as a 19-year old u/t pilot, taken only a few months or even weeks before his death, looking rather young and fresh-faced, clearly eager to get into the skies and do his bit for the war effort.

Initially I had assumed that he was flying from Syerston, as his unit, No 2 Service Flying Training School is now stationed there, but I was wrong: I now know he was flying from RAF Brize Norton in Oxfordshire, where 2SFTS was stationed in 1941.[11] As he was flying a twin-engine Airspeed Oxford, I imagine he was training to fly multi-engine aircraft and may have been hoping to join Bomber Command after completing his training, although a posting to Coastal or Transport command would not have been out of the question. However, bomber crews were in high demand in 1941, so I stick with my first assumption... Aside from these details, all I know is that he was the twin brother of my uncle George, now passed away, and the son of a widower, Gertrude Parkinson, of Goole, Yorkshire. I want to get a more complete picture of the man, finding out as much as I can about the kind of person he was, about his early years and his time in the RAF leading up to his death. Searching online for his service record

---

[11] No 2 Service Flying Training School was re-named No 2 Flying Training School after the war.

produces nothing, but I send more emails off to the National Archives at Kew, and to the RAF at Hendon and Cranwell asking for any information on Bill and 2SFTS, or where to find it. Trusting that Fiona will also be happy to tell me what she knows about him, and perhaps allow me access to any documents or photographs she may have that could throw light on him – photos, letters, anything at all – I write to her explaining what I am looking for, and turn to the other man who was killed on the Oxford that day - William Newton.

Other than that he shared Bill's Christian name and was sitting beside him when they died, I know precious little about William Newton. The only biographical details I have about him are carved on the headstone in Newark Cemetery: Leading Aircraftman WR Newton (1018127) was an u/t pilot with the RAF when he died on 12 June 1941, aged 26. I also know from the online post referring to the AIR81 report that like William Parkinson he was with 2 Service Flying Training Squadron at the time of his death. That is all.

Having researched my own family tree some years before I still have active subscriptions to ancestry websites and am pretty familiar with the procedure for finding an individual, which usually begins with typing a name and date into a search engine and seeing what comes up. Typing in the information on his headstone I am led to a website called *Find A Grave*, which tells me that he was born on 3 November 1914, in County Durham. That's something – I already have a rough geographical location and can now imagine the accent he probably spoke with. I'm thinking of the beautiful Northumberland coast, the bleak hills I used to drive through on my way to Scotland, and James Bolam in *The Likely Lads*. The website also includes two photographs. One is of William's grave in Newark, which I visited earlier in the year. The second immediately sends my pulse racing.

The black-and-white photograph is titled '*William Robson Newton with his aunt and cousins. The Dingle, Chester, about 1930*'. It is a very nice group shot of a middle-aged woman, two young girls and a teenage boy, sitting on a park bench against a gentle backdrop of trees. The boy, William Robson (so that's what the R stood for) looks like any English middle-class kid of his time: he's wearing a blazer, with an array of badges on the lapel, and a white open-necked shirt with the collar outside his jacket. Flannel trousers with turn-ups, woollen socks round his ankles and firm leather shoes.

Robson Newton, cousins and aunt (Chris Kemp)

I feel sure there must have been a professional photographer involved, or at least someone who knew what they were doing with a camera, as it is nicely composed, the children perched naughtily on the back of the bench, and told to look away from the camera, as if noticing something of particular interest away to the left. The girls are both dutifully focused on the same spot as directed, but the woman, William's aunt, is staring directly at the lens, almost as if to tell the photographer to hurry up, and William seems to have let his gaze drift. His shoulders are ever so slightly slumped and his hands are held loosely between his knees, in an attitude that seems somehow familiar but which I can't quite pin down for the moment.

If the photograph was taken around 1930 that would make William about 16 years old. He is a good-looking kid, with dark, wavy hair, rather intense dark eyes, and a mouth that is either trying to conceal a grin or a look of irritation. Maybe he felt silly posing for the camera or didn't get on with his rather severe-looking aunt, or his cousins, both of whom are wearing cloche-style hats, and pretty summer dresses. I guess it must have been a warm day because the girls are holding their knitted woollen cardigans on their knees. William's aunt, sitting primly at the far end of the bench, feet crossed, in coat and hat with her handbag on her knee, looks serious, preoccupied even. It's a perfect depiction of the uneasy peace that characterised Britain in the inter-war years.

I notice the name of the person who posted the photograph on the website, a Chris Kemp, and hopeful that he might be a Newton family member, I fire off an email, explaining that I am researching the incident in which William died, and wondering if he might have any more information.

It's a good start. A photograph of William, who it turns out was a Durham lad, with some family members (although not close family), and I may be able to trace some descendants or relatives. Inspired, I continue searching, and the Census return for 1921 throws up more details. The Newton family lived at 24 Devon Gardens, Deckham, Gateshead. All I know about Gateshead is that it is a town on the south side of the Tyne, close to Newcastle, and that Brendan Foster came from there and ran with Gateshead Harriers.[12] I've never been there myself. William Robson Newton was 6 years and seven months old at the time of the 1921 Census, and his father, also named William and born in Gateshead in 1886, was a Post Office clerk. His wife Beatrice Mary, also from Gateshead, was a year younger than her husband, with no occupation registered. She was 24 when they married in 1911. There are no other children recorded.

---

[12] The runner was in fact born in Hebburn, a short distance up the road from Gateshead.

From tracking down the few family trees that include references to William or his parents I am able to find that he took his middle name Robson from his mother's maiden name, and that her parents were Thomas Robson (1851-1892) and Elizabeth Jane Gillender (1852-1937). The Census of 1911 records William's grandmother as Elizabeth Jane Robson, then 58, a widow and a woman of 'private means', living with her daughter Beatrice and a son Thomas Gillender Robson, both single. Thomas, then 21, was a mechanical draughtsman, but there are no more details.

William Newton's mother seems to have had three brothers: Thomas, born in 1890 and who died in childhood; James, born a year later, and a second Thomas, born in 1899, who married Florence Ada Rutter, a girl from nearby Chester-le-Street. Their older sister Elizabeth Jane, born in 1881, married a Matthew Wilson Hindhaugh (a civil engineer) and produced three daughters, but neither of these, as with their uncles, have left any traceable descendants that I can find. There is, however, a photograph of Elizabeth Hindhaugh's headstone in Gateshead East Cemetery, an impressive affair that attests to her obvious wealth and status in the community.

There appears to be some confusion over the actual date of William Newton's birth. All the reliable sources I can find relating to William show him being born on 3 November 1914, but there is also a record in the Births Index of *another* William R Newton, who was also born in Gateshead to a mother with the maiden name of Robson, but two years earlier, in 1912. I wonder whether our William Robson had an older brother who died in infancy, and his mother named him in memory of his deceased sibling, as happened with her own brothers?

The 1939 England and Wales Register also shows a William R Newton living at 2 Maple Grove, Felling, Durham, also born on 3 November 1914. He is living in the same house as Sarah Morris (83) and Jane Morris (51) with a James P Browell (46) also there, so I'm guessing maybe he was lodging now? He is recorded as an insurance agent, age 19, single. It seems to be the same person, so why was he registered as living with his parents in Deckham at the time of his death? Perhaps because he had moved back there before enlisting? Or had returned home when the house in Maple Grove was bombed? I don't have any proof yet that that's what happened, but the house on Maple Grove seems not to exist on the maps, so that could be the explanation.

On this first trawl I don't really find very much else relating to William, except that he left £766 17s 10d to his father in his will. That's worth around £48,000 in today's money, a huge sum for a 26-year old to have in his bank account at that time. But we have to remember that flying was not a poor man's pastime, and that the RAF had a rather traditional attitude about the social backgrounds that it drew its pilots from. Maybe William had benefitted from his grandmother's 'private means'? His mother Beatrice died in 1952, also leaving a decent sum to her husband, who died 3 years later. After that the Newton trail seems to go cold and finally disappears. I email the people whose family trees I have searched, asking for more information, but aware that very often these ancestry accounts remain dormant and unused for years at a time, I am not particularly hopeful of a reply. I am also aware that this process of tracking down the family history of an individual can be a) massively time-consuming, b) expensive and c) fraught with confusion, contradictions and dead ends, so I don't want to get too bogged down by it. I would rather move on to the other characters in the mystery.

I do though, find something interesting in the Newcastle *Evening Chronicle* published on Monday 16 June 1941, four days after his death. Tucked away on page 7, in the Roll of Honour column, there's an entry for:

NEWTON, 24 Devon Gardens, Gateshead. Leading Aircraftman Robson Newton, RAF, aged 26, dearly beloved son of Mr and Mrs W Newton. Interment at Newark.

It is interesting because it suggests that William was actually known to his family and friends by his middle name of

Robson. There's a curious coincidence, because both pilots of the Oxford, in addition to being named William, had middle names in memory of their mother's side – Wharton, Bill's Grandmother's maiden name, and Robson, after his mother. It is a help for me though, because it allows me to distinguish between Robson and Bill, and I will refer to him by that name from now on.

As with my enquiries about William Parkinson, I can't get immediate access to his service record, and write to the RAF asking for more help. But there is one more thing to do before leaving Robson; I want to see if the Newton family home is still standing. Google Earth comes up trumps, taking mere seconds to fly me around the globe, zoom down from space towards the UK, homing in on the north-east of England, and finally Gateshead, before hovering drone-like above 24 Devon Gardens. The house where Robson lived sits in the middle of a street of late-Victorian or Edwardian houses. Devon Gardens seems to be on a hill, with views from the back down over parkland and a lake, and using the Street View tool I try to get a closer look. The street itself appears to have been pedestrianised at some time, with access to cars permitted only at the *back* of the houses, so I'm not able to get a clear view of the front of number 24. But at least the house is still standing.

An email pings into my inbox. It's from Chris, who posted the photograph of Robson on the park bench in Chester. Chris explains that he isn't actually a friend or relation of Robson's, but a taphophile. I didn't know there was a name for a person with an interest in cemeteries, gravestones and funeral rites, but there is – I have to look it up - the word comes from the ancient Greek *táphos*. In answer to my questions Chris is able to tell me that an elderly neighbour of his, knowing of his interest in things funerary, asked him if he could trace her cousins grave in Newark. That old lady was Beatrice Parry (nee Robson), Robson's cousin, one of the little girls in the photo. Either side of Beatrice sits her sister Lillian and their mother Florence Robson. It didn't take Chris long to trace Robson's grave, and he scanned and blew up the small contact photo of them all in The Dingle, which thrilled Beatrice.

I now know the names of the girls in the photograph, and have an image of Robson, albeit one aged 16. Chris is able to give me an address in Hoole, Chester, where Florence's family lived, but not much more. I think that Florence died in the Birmingham area in the early 1980s, and Chris says that Beatrice has also passed away, dying in Hoole at the grand old age of 97. Thankful that I've been able to get this far so quickly, I get back to Chris, thanking him for his help and promising to keep him up to date if I discover anything. I immediately do some online searches relating to the names he has provided, but nothing of interest comes up.

After writing a letter to the present occupant of the house in Hoole I go to bed that night with an idea that maybe I should contact the local papers or media outlets in the Gateshead and Chester areas to see if they can discover anyone who knows or knew about the Newton or Robson families, and even make a visit to Gateshead itself, but will leave that until later. Meanwhile I can't get that photo, and the image of young Robson Newton out of my mind. It's not the look on his face, although there is something quite powerful and intense about his expression - it's something else, something to do with the way he is sitting. And then I realise what it is: with his head held forward, shoulders dropped and hands between his knees, he is sitting in exactly the same posture as the small plastic pilot figures I used to paint and glue into place in my 1/72 scale model aircraft. The boy Robson looks for all the world as if he is a pilot, holding the tiny model aeroplane's control column.

Seventeen

I had passed the shop a few times but never dared to go in, scared of what might happen once I'd stepped over the threshold. Not that I was afraid of breaking the law or anything like that – what they were selling was entirely legal after all – it was more what going into the place would *say* about me. After the divorce I'd chucked out boxes of the stuff, pulling it out from cupboards and under the bed where it had been hidden for years, and now – well, I think I've convinced myself I'm not that person anymore. I have moved on. But just seeing me standing outside and peering in as another customer makes a hurried exit gives any passer-by a pretty clear impression about what I probably get up to of an evening, so I walk past the shop deliberately looking the other way. Interested in that sort of stuff? *Me?*

Recently however, I've found myself thinking about the shop more and more, particularly late at night as thoughts go round and round in my head looking for answers, and I feel the need to relax. But I have fought the temptation to go in, reminding myself from bitter experience that what is sold behind that door can become all-consuming if not actually addictive, and turning over in bed I've tried to put it out of my mind.

Deep down though, I know I am weak, and easily fall victim to my darker impulses. I know that eventually I will give in, and sure enough one day, after walking past the shop a couple of times to check that no-one is watching, I push open the door and step inside. The man behind the counter looks up briefly, muttering a simple 'Morning,' before returning to whatever he is looking at on his computer. I gaze at the shelves, piled high with stock. There's enough stuff here to keep any man of a certain age occupied for the rest of his life. There's a familiar smell to the place too, a mixture of cigarette smoke and something else, something sweet... It's something I've not really experienced for years now, and it feels kind of good.

From around a corner, I can hear snatches of a low conversation: two men are discussing how much more difficult it has become to get the latest imports from eastern Europe now that there's a war on in Ukraine. They turn and look at me and I pretend I'm not listening, so they return to their conversation, extolling the virtues of the latest Russian models. Thinking that maybe it was a mistake to come in after all, I decide to hurry up, choose something and get out, and start peering at the piles of stock, piled up from floor to ceiling on every shelf.

'Looking for anything in particular?' The shop owner has emerged from behind the counter and is hovering uncomfortably close. 'If it's not in stock I can usually order it online.' He waits for me to answer. The two men pause their conversation and look around at me again, identifying a possible fellow addict.

My heart is thumping and my mouth is as dry as sandpaper; I try to get the words out without sounding like someone who has anything to hide. 'Well, actually I'm looking for a 1/72 scale Airspeed Oxford and a Wellington. I think Frog make an Oxford, don't they?'

The two men return to their conversation, clearly uninterested in my choice of kit, and the shop owner breathes in, sharply. 'I know I haven't got the Oxford – haven't had one in for a long time, and someone told me Frog threw away the moulds. Shame, cos it wasn't a bad little kit, the Oxford.'

I nod, in what I hope looks like a knowing way. 'Ok... and the Wellington..?' I ask, hopefully.

He wanders over to a shelf. 'You're spoilt for choice with the Welly. Airfix, Trumpeter, Revell, MPM all do one. The Revell kit is the old Matchbox tooling, not great but okay, depends how much you want to pay.'

Airfix and Revell are familiar names – back in the seventies I probably kept those companies going single-handed. Trumpeter and MPM I've never heard of. 'I'm after the Ic,' I say.

'The Ic... that narrows it down a bit. I don't remember seeing the Airfix Ic for some time now, and I'm sure Revell only do a Mk X/XIV option... but Trumpeter and MPM both do the Ic.'

'Oh right. Have you got either of them in stock?'

He looks up and down the pile of boxes. 'No, sorry. Plenty of Mk 11s... Does it have to be the Ic?'

'Yes, I'm afraid so.'

'I can order one in for you. Might be some time though.'

I don't really have time. I'd made the Airfix Wellington B.111 when I was a kid and really liked the box art, a dramatic study of a Welly, one engine out action, scudding low over the sea as shells from a pursuing Me109 thrash the surface. Roy Cross at his best. I hoped the Ic would be as good. 'Have you got the Airfix version?' I say.

'That's the best build, and the most expensive,' he says, running a finger up the pile of boxes, 'But we're out of stock. Sorry, mate. Best try eBay, you might strike lucky.' The phone has started ringing and he's already on his way back to the counter. I follow him like an apprentice in the presence of a sorcerer. 'And the Oxford?'

'Same there. You could pick one up for a tenner. Yeah, nice little kit, the Oxford. Might have a go at one myself... Hello, Access Models, can I help you?'

I don't know when I made my first kit, but I have a vivid memory of coming downstairs in my pyjamas early one Saturday morning and finding my dad making an Airfix 1/72 scale English Electric Lightning jet fighter on the living room coffee table. I can't have been more than 7 or 8 at the time. I could smell the polystyrene glue as I came down the stairs, the same odour that had hit me when I walked into Access Models. As he worked, Dad told me about my uncle Malcolm who was in the RAF, a fitter on Lightnings at romantic-sounding locations like Binbrook and Lossiemouth. Seeing that small, silver, arrow-shaped machine take shape on Mum's tea tray, with the bright transfers (we never called them decals) sliding from a saucer of warm water onto the fuselage and wings via Dad's paint-smudged fingers, there was a magical connection, and I was transported to another world. There was a small, helmeted pilot under that transparent canopy, and when the transfers were dry and Dad said it was mine, I held the finished model in my hand and gazed in at that tiny figure, before flying the Lightning around the room. As it roared over the settee and swooped between the coffee table legs, I imagined I was that pilot, screaming over RAF Binbrook at the speed of sound, chasing MiGs and launching my Firestreak missiles to deadly effect.

Why my dad was actually down there, sitting in his vest and pyjama bottoms so early on a Saturday morning, I had no idea – it never occurred to me and I didn't ask, being only 8 years old and much more interested in the model he was making. Looking back now it seems obvious to ask. Perhaps he'd had a row with my mum, or he was simply eager to make the most of his weekend off and get the model done before concentrating on the dreary family stuff like shopping and mowing the lawn. Either way, I just sat there, watching him, enjoying the strange, mystical incense of polystyrene glue and enamel paint and thinners, and listening to him reminisce about the balsa and tissue-paper gliders his dad had shown *him* how to make when he was a kid.

My bedroom was soon a museum to Airfix, Revell and Frog; small plastic aeroplanes in various states of assembly littered my worktop, sitting on shelves, or attached vertically with fishing line to a special pegboard my dad screwed to the wall. Some models I displayed in small dioramas (I had no idea what the word diorama meant, or even how to pronounce it properly, but that's what they called these miniature scenes in my *Airfix* and *Scale Modeller* magazines) mounted on offcuts of wood which Dad would bring home from work: Spitfires being re-fuelled at dispersal, with OO/HO scale RAF personnel in attendance, or crashed in a Polyfilla field, with propellor blades bent back by holding them near a lighted match, and cannon shell holes in the wings made by puncturing the plastic with a needle, stuck in an old paintbrush and heated in a candle flame.

Most exciting though, were the models which hung from the ceiling on lengths of cotton. Although they were prone to instant destruction when my mother tried to clear them of gathering dust, up there they allowed me to recreate the aerial dogfights that I watched on the telly in *633 Squadron*, *The Battle of Britain* and *The Flying Tigers*. At night I could turn off the bedroom light and use a torch to simulate German searchlights as my Lancaster, Stirling, Wellington and Halifax bombers hung in the skies over pretend Berlin, Essen and Hamburg. I could imagine what it was like for those crews, thousands of feet up in the freezing night sky, prey to the unending streams of tracer, flak and the deadly Ju88 night fighter that was creeping up behind them. I'd provide my own running commentary to the aerial drama as the bomb aimer guided the pilot over the target:

> *Steady... Steady... Skipper! There's a fighter on our tail! Calm down rear gunner and give him a burst! (dagga dagga dagga!) Steady... Steady... (dagga dagga dagga!) Got him! Bye Fritz! Bombs gone skipper! Right, job done boys, let's go home! The pints are on me in The Bull tonight!*

When I watched that Spitfire swooping low over Newark there was something of the same imaginative boyhood thrill, and I can't believe the lucky pilot at the controls of that aircraft wasn't getting a similar kick as well. Over the years of course, those models were lost, thrown away or destroyed – some meeting a dreadful end as my brother Johnny and I shot them down with elastic bands or attached pieces of rolled-up tissue paper to their wings, set fire to them and threw them out of the bedroom window, watching them crash and burn in the back garden.

And then, as much more interesting things like prog music and girls took over, I kind of forgot about making models. When I went to university a lot were cleared out, and despite my best efforts the ones I'd tried to hold onto lost their delicate propellors, aerials and undercarriages, and were themselves eventually consigned to the dustbin. Years later, I bought the odd one, usually at times when I was feeling down, or lost, and thought I needed to remind myself of who I was and what had once made me happy. Just looking at those boxes, piled high in a model shop, was like going back to my childhood, and I couldn't resist buying them. And so I steadily amassed boxes full of unmade or half-finished kits. I had always kept a Tupperware box full of the all-important and totally irreplaceable spare parts which I had collected as a kid – wheels, pilots, bombs etc - priceless treasure – but bought new paints, brushes, and scalpels. But making these kits was never quite the same as it had been back in the day. I didn't have the time to take the same care over building them, skirted over fine details that would have absorbed me for hours in years past, and was wasteful with the glues, paints and brushes that I would once have looked after so lovingly. Each time we moved house they all came with me, much, I see now, to the horror of my ex-wife, to whom they were probably just a useless waste of space and money. I, on the other hand, was sure that one day I would have the time and the space to devote to them that they deserved. Maybe next year, or the year after that, when my life was sorted out...

When the marriage collapsed and I moved out it wasn't difficult to decide which models I would keep and which would go. *They all went*. In a Puritanical fit of remodelling myself after the breakup, and particularly when facing moving into a tiny Scottish cottage, I threw them all out. Completed, half-made and unopened - the lot - paints, modelling magazines, even the priceless Tupperware treasure chest of spares. I felt I could breathe when I had done it. I really was getting rid of emotional baggage which had been weighing me down for years. It was much too late of course, but it felt good.

So why was I creeping shamefully into a little model shop on Castle Gate, and drooling over the stock like some old pervert? Obviously, thinking so much about this wartime accident, and especially about the Oxford and Wellington's central roles in the story, I need to make them, to see them in three dimensions, even on a small scale. I need to understand their relative sizes, design and features, characters and distinctive behaviour. Actually building the kits, trimming the excess flashing off the parts, cutting them neatly from the sprues, trying a dry-run assembly to make sure the propellors and wheels and turrets are going to move, and making sure I pay due attention to the painting both inside and outside the airframe will, I am sure, help bring me closer to those aircraft that flew through the air so magnificently before ending their days in an awful tangle of metal, flames and death. Like that little boy, peering in at the bone-domed Lightning pilot under his transparent canopy, I will be able to imagine, perhaps even see what happened.

More than that. *I will be there.*

Back home, in front of the laptop, I open up eBay. Yes! There's a Frog Airspeed Oxford. I remember seeing that box on the shelf of the newsagents back in the 1970s, but for some reason I never bought one. Perhaps as it wasn't a fighting aeroplane I wasn't interested. I also remember how much I used to be able to buy these kits for when I was a kid, handing my hot handful of coins over the counter at the Newark Woolworths (now gone), and I can't believe how much the guy wants for this one. *Twenty quid..?* I have a moment of cold, rational, self-doubt. Should I really be doing this?

Sod it. With a click of the mousepad I am suddenly the proud owner of a 1/72 Frog Airspeed Oxford, exactly the same variant as the aircraft my uncle's brother and his friend were piloting in June 1941. A little more searching and I find its companion – a newly-tooled Airfix Wellington Mk 1c. This one is up for auction, and I am soon the highest bidder, with only three more days to wait until I own it.

Shame the artwork isn't by Roy Cross. The box art on this kit really is inferior to the Great Master's work – I could do better myself. I think for a moment, then, worried that I'll be pipped at the post, I remember what this kit is really worth to me now...

I double my bid.

Eighteen

'I suppose I'm a bit ashamed of it really. It's not something I can admit to most people, but it's true.'

Martin places his glass carefully on the beermat, looks me in the eye and finishes his confession: 'I'm a bit of an aeroplane nut too.'

We have been meeting for a pint or a Sunday lunch for several weeks now, since meeting at the Fosseway Writers, and feel relaxed and confident enough in each other's company to talk honestly, and to go a little deeper than football. Every other Wednesday evening we go to the Organ Grinder for the Quiz Night, and we're not bad, considering the 'Mid-Table Hopefuls' are only a two-man team, not the determined five- or six-man efforts that usually win. I look forward to these sessions, we can talk relatively freely, for men, and I value Martin's company. He's younger than me, but has been through similar problems following divorce, and it's good to share and compare, or just offload over a beer. And now he's confessing to sharing my fascination with aeroplanes...

Since moving to Newark I have been through some pretty extreme mood swings: veering wildly from the highs of a creative and positive meeting of the writer's group, or moments of connection in the research for Bill's story, to the dark depths of loneliness and lack of purpose. It's almost as if the more I fill my life with things to do, to lift and energise me, the emptier and more directionless I ultimately feel when I've nothing to do. Like Newton's Cradle, the higher my hopes rise, the more extreme my depression is when it returns.

Part of it is that I still don't know what to write. I start something, like that ridiculous crime novel idea, only to abandon it half-way through, aware that it is fake. It might do all the right things, press all the right buttons, as it were, but it doesn't *fire*. I'm not excited, because I'm not writing truthfully, from my own experience, or from the heart. I'm writing formula.

This lunchtime Martin and I are at a table in the faded grandeur of the Victorian Butter Market, and after the usual preliminaries involving the fortunes of Charlton Athletic and Portsmouth Town, work, health, films and books, the conversation comes around, as it always does, to What We Are Writing. Martin is much more diligent than I am about doing the exercises and prompts which the group set to keep us writing; he's already had work published in their recent collections, and regularly posts what he has written on the group's forum for discussion and comment. I am nowhere near as productive as he is, partly because I need more than a prompt to kick me up the backside, but also because I lack the confidence to show the others anything I do write. He's working on a novel which sounds so brilliant I know I could never write anything like it and hesitate over whether or not to describe the idea I'm nurturing, but he asks, and I think *oh what the hell.*

With my head full of the research into the crash I tell him I'm thinking of writing a book, something I have never done before. Not a novel, but a *book*, starting possibly with the chance conversation I had with my mum about Bill and Syerston, and telling two parallel stories, one about the unravelling of the mystery surrounding Bill's death, and another, about me.

I realise that sounds completely egotistical and self-centred, so I rewind and try to come at it from another angle: it's going to be a book about trying to find the answers to a story that may not actually have any answers, but that doesn't matter because in so doing I might discover something about what makes me the person I am, seeing the world the way I do, trying to make sense of it... through aeroplanes.

There's a pause. Martin takes a sip of his beer, inscrutable. *Go on...*

I warm to my theme, talking about one wonderful afternoon during the summer when I waited for the Battle of Britain Memorial Flight Lancaster to make a series of sweeps over Newark. I'd seen an article in the *Advertiser* giving the precise time it was due to appear and duly found a bench in the churchyard to wait for the Lanc to arrive. Having previously flown on the Lanc –

'You flew on the Lancaster?'

'Yes.'

'Bastard. Sorry – go on.'

...Having previously flown on the Lanc I know that precise timings are important because of fuel etc and so if she was due at 3.15 that was when she would appear. But she didn't, and I began to wonder where she was and if she was going to turn up at all. While I sat waiting on the bench it occurred to me that the situation was a little like a man waiting to meet a lover. Eventually, a few minutes late, like any self-respecting beauty, she did arrive, appearing low over the rooftops, with that comforting Merlin roar and the love affair, for a while at least, was re-ignited. Seeing her, I felt somehow renewed, validated, alive.

I then tell Martin about the plaque in the marketplace, memorialising the bomber crews and the sense of connection I feel with the ghosts of those men who drank in the same pubs we now drink in. I talk about *The Dam Busters*, and about sitting with my mum in the dunes near where the Lancs flew when they made the film. I talk about the Polish guys who flew the Lancs in the film, and the crew who died on the Wellington, and about the deep Polish connection with Newark. And I talk about the strange, vague but growing feeling I have that there must be something more than coincidence about all these things happening just when I come back home, here, to Tom Tiddler's Ground, trying to recover and heal after a divorce. Maybe there *is* a book to be written about the kid who spent all his time up in his bedroom making model aeroplanes when he should have been focussing on girls, who is now a grown man, obsessing in the same way about Wellington bombers, Airspeed Oxfords and the death of an uncle he never knew when he should be coming to terms with the disaster of his marriage and doing more to rebuild his relationship with his sons. Why am I thinking all the time about the death of a man I never knew? Is there anything to discover about his death, and the death of the seven men who died with him, that will have any meaning, and what, if anything, will it ultimately reveal about *me*? I can't be sure, maybe it is all nonsense, but it feels like there is something there.

I come to a stop, unsure whether Martin will have any idea about what I'm getting at. Having finally said it out loud I don't even know myself whether there is anything here more than a crazy beery lunchtime pipedream, the deranged ramblings of a lonely man of a certain age who is fascinated by stories of Bomber Command.

Martin lifts his glass again, a faint smile beneath the thin white moustache of foam on his lip. He obviously thinks this is the worst idea he has ever heard. But a moment later he smiles broadly, then laughs, and makes his solemn admission of guilt: that he is an aeroplane nut too. He was never a modeller but confesses that like me he used to go to air shows as a kid, wandering wide-eyed along rows of parked-up Tiger Moths and Spitfires, and stood in awe as an English Electric Lightning streaked low across the sky, its polished metal surfaces glinting in the sun. And we share a memory of how, when the mighty Avro Vulcan filled the sky, everything would suddenly go dark and strangely chill, like during a solar eclipse, and remembered the unbelievable howl of its engines as it climbed almost vertically into the clouds, setting off car alarms and making dogs bark for miles around.

I'm relieved, pleased that he recognises at least something of what I'm talking about. I think he understands the magic that I'm alluding to, the mystery of why warplanes appeal to something deep and unknown in men like us. He doesn't go so far as to say it, but maybe he even shares the feeling that they allow us to access the child in us, that they help us make sense of the world, and of ourselves. Most importantly, he agrees that yes, maybe my searching for an answer to the mystery of Bill's death is something that could be the basis of a book.

'But will anyone want to read it,' he asks, 'Apart from men of a certain age who love aeroplanes?'

'That's just it,' I say, cynically. 'There's loads of us out there. All I have to do is put the word Lancaster into the title and it'll sell like hotcakes...'

I head home, ideas flying around in my head. This idea really could be the basis of a book, the thing I've been looking to write.

But soon the effect of the alcohol wears off, and I start to see the flaws in the idea, probably the same weaknesses that Martin was seeing when I rambled on so enthusiastically over lunch. It's a great idea, yes, but all my current research is actually into Wellingtons, not Lancasters; the Lanc really doesn't fit into my story at all, it certainly isn't the star. I'd be shoehorning it in and how disappointed would any model-making reader be when he discovered the Lancaster of the title (whatever that was) didn't actually relate in any way to the book's contents.[13]

Perhaps, after all, the book idea was just another distraction, or at best a way of trying to avoid the fact that what I was really supposed to be doing was finding out more about what happened to Bill Parkinson, and I really wasn't getting very far.

---

[13] This idea for a title was eventually used in *L For Lanc*, a collection of short stories by the author. Published 2023 by Another Small Press.

Nineteen

The winter of 1940/41 was bitter, with heavy snow restricting training. Unable to fly, the crews of 305 Polish Bomber Squadron were stuck in their freezing hangars and huts, listening to lecture after lecture on navigation, meteorology, wireless operation and the naming of aircraft parts. It was cold and boring, and far from the life of action they had anticipated when they escaped from Poland. They wanted desperately to get into the air and fight. Spirits were lifted in late January, when RAF Syerston was visited by King George VI and Queen Elizabeth, accompanied by the Commander-in-Chief of Bomber Command, Air Marshal Sir Richard Peirse. The crews of 304 and 305 Squadrons were presented to the King and Queen in the No 1 Hangar, specially decorated with the colours and flags of both nations flanking a Polish Eagle. The King took the salute at a march past, the Polish Guard of Honour was inspected and the King and Queen spoke admiringly of the loyalty and determination of the Polish airmen.

On that day, an additional unofficial member of the squadron strength followed close on the heels of the squadron's commanding officer. The 305 Squadron mascot, a terrier named Ciapek, had been adopted as a stray by Corporal Tadeusz Karkowski, but quickly became popular with the entire squadron for his character and uncanny ability to perform tricks. Although an English dog, Ciapek (pronounced *Chapek*) only obeyed orders in Polish, and ignored, or even snarled at anyone who spoke English to him. It is not recorded how he behaved in the presence of their Majesties.

Ciapek had a kennel, built to look like a traditional Polish cottage, which sat outside the main hangar, and he was given the unofficial rank of Corporal. He appeared regularly in Sgt Gabriel Milosz's squadron photographs, standing on top of a gun turret, or astride a 500lb bomb, and often featured in Polish-language newspapers and magazines, wearing a tin helmet, clearly enjoying playing to the camera. Strictly against King's Regulations, he even flew with some Wellington crews on a number of operations, including a raid on Berlin, where he was listed in the flight log as 'passenger.' He wore a leather jacket embellished with the badge of the Polish Hussars, and a special harness was made for him, incorporating an oxygen mask for flying at altitude, and a lifejacket and parachute for emergencies. Sadly, in 1943 the Wellington Ciapek was flying in on his eighth operation failed to return. The aircraft was presumed lost at sea, and the word 'Missing' was chalked up on the operations board, with the name Ciapek included in the crew list. Ciapek's story is, however, one of those where fact easily becomes confused with legend, as there are several different versions of what followed.

One story has the squadron receiving a telephone call from the Police in Cromer on the north Norfolk coast, saying that a stray dog had been found wandering the town, identified only by the collar he was wearing, which included the RAF Syerston telephone number and, more unusually, a number of small wooden bombs hanging from it (the 305 crews made a point of awarding Ciapek one of these bombs for each operation he flew). Fearing that the dog would be destroyed if not claimed, a squad of airmen was despatched to the seaside town to pick their mascot up and return him to the squadron, where he was received with full honours and lived happily until the end of the war...

Another version has him found by a search party, lying apparently lifeless on the seashore, only to die shortly afterwards from his wounds. The third, and less romantic though possibly most likely story is that Ciapek, like the other members of the crew of the Wellington, was simply never seen again.

305 Polish Bomber Squadron, known as '*Ziemia Wielkopolskiej*' (Greater Poland) after the western part of Poland, was the last of the four Polish squadrons to join RAF Bomber Command, and was made up of air- and ground crews who had escaped from Poland following the German invasion in September 1939. These men (and women, as a large number of Polish women joined the WAAF)[14] had mostly seen action with the Polish 2nd Air Regiment at Krakow, and the 6th Air Regiment at Lvov. Operating in hopelessly obsolete and outnumbered aircraft, the Polish aircrews flew extensive bombing missions during the September campaign, against vastly superior German armour and troop concentrations. But despite their brave resistance, losses steadily increased, and the outcome was never really in question. Following an agreement between the British and Polish authorities, thousands of Polish air- and ground crews managed to escape via Romania to France, where they were part of the first Polish squadron to be formed in the French Army Air Force, but were forced to evacuate to Britain following France's surrender in June 1940. The remainder managed to get to Britain via North Africa, landing at Liverpool before heading for Blackpool where they gathered to begin the process of enlisting, square bashing and ultimately fighting, with the RAF.

The 305 Squadron *War Diary* (finally intelligible to me after finding a wonderful translator in Magda Brown) records the feelings of the Poles in those early days:

> The bitterness and resentment resulting from the two huge defeats we witnessed were partially lessened by the news that Polish fighter and bomber squadrons were being formed. Everyone wanted to join them, to finally have the chance to fight the hated enemy. The fear that England would be bombed altered Churchill's plans,

---

[14] WAAFs constituted over 13 percent of the Polish ground personnel in the RAF

prioritising the formation of fighter squadrons, with bomber squadrons coming second. In August [1940] a message came from Blackpool saying that bomber squadrons were now organising... How it was decided who could join is unclear. Some had been flying for a long time, others were assigned to flying duties only a month before the war in Poland. Some were helped through recommendation, others placed requests in the hands of influential people, others were chosen as they were well-trained, and some people were removed from Blackpool as they were seen as individuals likely to endanger morale.[15]

After completing elementary training covering the basics of King's Regulations and the English language, the successful crews assigned to 305 Squadron were transferred from Blackpool to RAF Bramcote, near Nuneaton in Warwickshire. The squadron was officially formed on 29 August 1940, and given the squadron codes SM, which would appear on the side of each aircraft, along with its individual letter or call sign. Wellington R1017, which Tadeusz Stefanicki was to captain on the day it was lost, would bear the squadron letters SM-K. The aircraft itself arrived at Bramcote from RAF Yeadon in Yorkshire (now Leeds/Bradford airport), probably flown by a female pilot of the Air Transport Auxiliary. Members of the ground crew would quickly paint its squadron codes on the fuselage sides in large grey letters, along with the distinctive red and white square chequerboard Polish badge beneath the cockpit, and the process of fitting it out and training the crews continued.

The Wellington was affectionately known to its Polish air and ground crews as 'Grandpa Wellington' or the 'Sooty Giant', referring to its predominantly (and powdery) matt black colour scheme, and each pilot was given five hours of dual control instruction on one before flying solo. This was a remarkably low figure considering the skill required to fly a fast two-engine bomber, although flying training continued around the clock. In late 1940 the squadron was informed it

---

[15] Polish Institute and Sikorski Museum, Archive Ref No: LOT.A.V.37/8A

would be transferring to RAF Syerston, which was nearing completion and was more suitable for the Wimpys, and in early December the aircraft, equipment and personnel of 305 Squadron left Bramcote for their new home in Nottinghamshire.

The squadron was led by Wing Commander Jan Jankowski, with Flight Lieutenants Czesław Korbut and Szczepan Ścibior commanding 'A' Flight (*City of Lida*) and 'B' Flight (*City of Poznań*) respectively. Additionally, a small number of British personnel were also posted to oversee the Poles, to act as liaison and ensuring that RAF protocols were observed. By this time the squadron strength stood at forty-eight Polish and four British officers, and 190 Polish and 46 British other ranks.

Unsurprisingly, the process of training non-English speaking airmen in the intricacies of flying a strange aircraft presented many problems, but this was more than made up for by the Poles' enthusiasm and determination to strike back at Hitler. Perhaps more surprisingly, there was not an official system for putting together bomber crews in the RAF. From the outbreak of war to the end six years later, new crews had an informal way of forming up, based very often on little more than luck and guesswork. Thrown together in a hangar on arrival at an OTU[16] station, navigators, wireless operators, bomb aimers and air gunners would be selected by pilots rather like players picked for a playground football team. A pilot might ask a gunner what his gunnery scores were, or a navigator which school he went to, but more often selections were made on the basis of simple hunches: someone 'looked right', or just seemed to be made of 'the right stuff'. It seemed to work though. It obviously made sense to try and form a crew from men who would like and trust each other, rather than on any objective criteria; after all, each man's life would depend on the skill and the others in the crew. They had to

---

[16] Operational Training Unit.

stick together, supporting each other in the air, and also on the ground. Nobody wanted to fly with an unhappy crewmate.

Of course, it helped if a pilot knew a potential crew member, or one could be recommended by a friend, and it is quite likely that many of the Poles in 305 Squadron knew each other from the old days. In fact, it is interesting to note that some of the men who would go on to form the crew of Wellington R1017 had RAF service numbers which were close together, possibly because they had been standing near each other in the queue when they enlisted at Blackpool; Stefanicki is P0057, followed by rear gunner Aleksander Zirkwitz (P0074), then Marian Wojtowicz (P0076), and finally 28 year-old Stanisław Kowalcze (P0080) – only 22 places separating them.

These men had quite possibly known each other in Poland, facing the German invasion and seeing the devastation wrought on their homeland by the Wehrmacht and Luftwaffe; they had shared gruelling marches, packed train carriages and stinking boat cabins during the ignominious retreat through Romania to Britain via North Africa and France, and stuck together wide-eyed and bewildered when they arrived in the bizarre surroundings of wartime Blackpool. They would have trained together, partied together, and found it easy to talk about the old country and their loved ones, instinctively understanding their shared reasons for wanting to get back at the Nazis. Equally, when someone didn't want to talk, his mates would understand, and leave him alone with his thoughts. The short stories in the collections *G For Genevieve* and *L For Lucy*, written by 'Flt Lt Herbert' (the *nom de plume* of Janusz Meissner, a writer and pilot in the Polish Air Force) appear to be based, in part at least, on the men who flew with 304 and 305 Squadrons, and illustrate the tight-knit sense of kinship and camaraderie that existed between many of the Polish bomber crews.

Training continued as the winter of 1940/41 gave way to spring, with the squadron concentrating on bombing exercises at Wainfleet Sands and air-to-ground firing practice at

Cardigan Bay. Crews also took part in long-distance cross-country navigation exercises, and night flying training, both severely limited because of continuing poor weather. The war never felt far away however, as the Luftwaffe was raiding Britain on a daily basis, and Newark found itself on the receiving end of it one Friday lunchtime in March when a Heinkel 111 bomber flew from the south along the LNER railway line to attack the Ransome and Marles factory, in the Beacon Hill area of the town. Ransome's was responsible for producing large amounts of armaments, which German intelligence was well aware of, and the aircraft dropped bombs and strafed the factory with machine gun fire before departing. A second Heinkel attacked about an hour later, catching the Home Guard and emergency services as they were recovering the dead and injured. Altogether, 41 people were killed and 165 injured in the attack, the worst that Newark suffered during the war. Many of the victims of the raid are buried in Newark cemetery, a matter of feet away from the men who died on Wellington R1017.

Pressure was building to see the squadron become fully operational, and the crews were naturally desperate to be let off the leash. With morale beginning to suffer, Wing Commander Jankowski was replaced by Squadron Leader (later Wing Commander) Bohdan Kleczyński, and the mood improved immediately. More men and machines joined the squadron and finally, on 22 April 1941, Kleczyński was able to report that a total of four crews had attained combat readiness. 305 Squadron was finally ready to take the war back to Hitler.

Twenty

A vivid flash of colour catches my eye, standing out brightly against the monotonous greens and browns of the hawthorn hedges lining the narrow winding road. Without slowing, I glance at the red ribbon tied around the telegraph pole, holding in place a dismal bunch of flowers, once bright, alive and strong, now pale, brown, broken and dead. Someone died here, a driver in a car crash possibly, or a cyclist, knocked over by a speeding vehicle. It could have been someone out for their morning walk or evening stroll, lost in the sights and sounds of the countryside, or headphones on, oblivious to the sound of the lorry until it was too late. Maybe it was a child, running out to meet her friend, or to retrieve a ball, forgetting momentarily that this is a busy road, and Death stalks these places.

Over recent decades we've become accustomed to these roadside markers, indicating a loved one's last moments. As I drive through the Nottinghamshire countryside on a bright, sunny, Sunday morning, I reflect on how the crash site, the actual spot where death has occurred, has now become popularly memorialised by people placing flowers and photographs at the spot. Not just the sites of road accidents, but stabbings, shootings, fires, terror attacks, even suicides; where death occurred, particularly if it involved some sort of trauma, unexpected violence, or great emotion, people are drawn to the spot to leave photographs, candles, flowers, anything that possesses some connection to the dead person, something that says *I loved you, I remember you and everyone who passes this spot will be aware that you died here.*

Sometimes, if the dead person is a child, we leave a favourite toy, a teddy perhaps, desperate to believe that wherever they are now they'll still be able to play happily as they once did. If they're older, it might be a football scarf or team shirt, the one they always wore to the game, just as an ancient warrior was buried with his sword and shield, and sometimes his favourite dog, horse or slave, to accompany him on his way to the other world.

Despite our highly technological and rationalistic lives, there still seems to be a recognition of the fundamental, mysterious, maybe even magical sense that the place where a person died, where life was one moment and was not the next, is a special place. *This is where they died.* Think on that, you driver, as you speed past this spot, texting on your mobile phone. This could be you, it seems to say – happily oblivious one second and the next – just unhappy oblivion. *Memento Mori.*

My mind also goes over all those examples through history where death, especially death in battle, has been memorialised. All those standing stones; stark, lonely, but resistant to the decay of memory and the elements, proudly reminding the world that sometimes death, even when brutal and violent, can be glorious and heroic. Is there a sense that something of the spirit of the dead person lives on here, in these fields, this air?

I'm driving to Orston, the little village just north of Elton[17], where I'm meeting Brian Gunn. A few days ago I received an email from Gillian Roberts, the farmer who owns the land including the Becks Plantation, and who I had visited recently. Her conviction that neither of the aircraft had crashed on her land had left me feeling pretty negative, but Gillian did give me the names and telephone numbers of three local people who she thought might possibly have some information. I left a message with the first, the phone rang out on the second, but my third was a hit – the phone was picked

---

[17] Despite its recent name change, and in order to avoid confusion, I am going to continue to refer to the village as Elton, as it was known in 1941.

up by John Johnson, who told me he didn't know anything about the incident himself but knew someone who might – he said he would talk to them and get back to me if anything came up.

A few mornings later I was lying in bed, half asleep, but already feeling slightly down, when the phone rang. In that crazy, contradictory way that depression works, instead of leaping out of bed to answer it, pleased that someone was contacting me, I turned away, unable to face whoever or whatever it was. The fog of depression meant that the ringing phone represented only problems and disappointments, not opportunities, requiring a superhuman effort to answer. I pulled the duvet over my head and hoped it would just go away and leave me to fester in my pit. Eventually the answerphone kicked in and after the beep I heard an elderly man's voice, speaking in that familiar Nottinghamshire accent: 'Hello my name's Brian Gunn, it's about this plane crash during the war...' I threw myself across the bed and picked up the phone, suddenly alert, desperate to get there before he could hang up.

We talked and he told me that he was 91, lived in Orston and remembered a crash between two aircraft on training flights during the war, when he was a 13-year old boy. I interrupted him before he could go any further – the crash I was investigating involved a trainer and a Wellington bomber, with a Polish crew. 'Ah yes, well one of the crew were Polish,' he said. 'They told me his name when I spoke to the folk at the Newark Air Museum about it.'

I let Brian continue, reminding myself that time can play tricks with the memory, with details being forgotten or changed as they are passed down the years, but any clue he could give me might just put me on the right path and help me to discover Bill's story. He went on, describing how he saw a blinding flash in the sky, a flaming object falling to earth, and ran to see where a plane had landed, 'Near the Girl Guides' hut, just up from the old plaster pits.'

In a flash I was transported back in time to Orston ponds, the old plaster pits where I used to fish for Tench on long hot summer days in the 1970s. I must have walked past that Guides' hut a hundred times – how strange that something like this should be leading me back there after all these years.

Suddenly focussed on this new lead I asked Brian if he could show me exactly where the plane crashed and suggested that I could meet him today if he wasn't busy. Brian agreed, saying he'd meet me at his cottage, 'Down the lane, after the Ox,' meaning the Durham Ox pub, but in that curious way country people have of expecting you to know exactly where they mean he refused to go into any more detail other than, 'You can't miss it.' And of course, not wanting to look like some idiot townie, I said I knew exactly where he meant, hoping I'd be able to find it without too much trouble.

And that's how I come to find myself driving to Orston, seeing a limp red ribbon flap pathetically against a telegraph pole, and contemplating the mysteries of death and memory. All the way my excitement is growing in anticipation of what I am going to find. Brian has promised to show me the exact spot where the plane had crashed - maybe I'll be able to walk the site, possibly even find something in the ground, a bit of twisted aluminium airframe turned up by recent ploughing, some actual proof that this was where Bill's story ended? I imagine telling Fiona about what I've found, and eventually bringing her and her family to the spot to see where her uncle Bill died.

But I'm also thinking about something else Brian told me, which keeps nagging away in my brain. He said that he is 91, and that he was 13 when Bill's accident occurred, which would place it (according to my poor mental arithmetic) in 1943. But I know that the accident happened in the summer of 1941. It was a long time ago – more than 80 years – so maybe he's forgotten exactly how old he was back then. Turning into Orston and down towards the Durham Ox pub I ignore the nagging doubts and concentrate on finding Brian's house, desperate for some good news.

As it turns out, Brian's house is not that hard to find. The village is still as small as I remembered from my youth, and I park up in the lane just down from the Ox, take my notebook, pencil and phone up to the front door of the old cottage and ring the bell.

No answer.

I ring again, and wait, until I hear Brian call from over the way and realise I'm at the wrong house after all. But no matter. I head over to him: a small, lively nutbrown man, wearing baggy cords and a windcheater and leaning heavily on a walking stick. After the introductions, he is clearly very keen to get going to the crash site. I mention that it's looking like rain and ask if it's a walk or whether we should take the car. He says we'll need the car, but before I can get him into it, he's telling me again about the incident, the details as fresh and clear in his mind as they were when he was 13.

Startlingly, he tells me that the worst thing as he approached the crash site was the smell of the burning bodies. In that moment, listening to his description, I am carried there, imagining the experience of a young boy, what he's seen, and smelt: the war, in all its horror and brutality, in the shape of a huge aeroplane, falling out of the sky, exploding and burning in front of him, the image searing itself into his brain. He also tells me how a few years later he was walking across the same spot where the flaming wreckage had once lain and saw something small and white gleaming in the freshly ploughed earth. Picking it up, he brushed off the dirt and saw that it was a human tooth. *A real memento mori...*

'I don't know why, but I thought I ought to give it a proper burial,' he says, 'Which I did, in the back garden.' It's not a nice thing to remember, nor is it nice to relate to someone else, but he is obviously keen to tell me as much as he can, to get his story out.

'Can you remember anything else about the day it happened?' I ask, as the spots of rain start to fall more heavily.

'Yes, I remember it very well, like it were yesterday,' he says. 'I were walking home from the train, back from school in

Nottingham, and suddenly the whole sky were lit up with the light from this explosion-'

'You were coming back from school?' I ask. The faint nagging voice has suddenly become louder again. According to the letter from the RAF which Bill's mother received, the collision between the Oxford and the Wellington happened in the morning, at precisely 1125am (although the AIR27 report puts it at 1140 – but that may have been the time at which the station was informed). Either way, the crash happened in daylight, in the morning and in summer – June 1941.

'Oh no,' says Brian. 'This were dark, and it were December, I remember definitely because it weren't long before Christmas.'

Despite my efforts to keep the flame of hope alive, I already know that we are talking about two different accidents. I could go and look at the crash site anyway, but somehow it seems pointless, and as the spots of rain are now starting to show on Brian's windcheater, he agrees.

I help him back to his door, apologising for taking up his time, then hurry back to my car. Closing the door, I stare through the windscreen at the rain, and I can't help feeling a bit disappointed. No, more than that – I'm hugely disappointed, and I feel annoyed, let down, frustrated, and angry with myself - I really thought I was there, but I'm no further ahead. I desperately believed that I might have found the ending to Bill's story, but now I'm back to square one.

But on the drive back home, I remember Brian's story about a small boy finding a tooth, and giving it a decent burial, and I am overcome with guilt. I am being selfish. What right do I have to be annoyed or frustrated? *This* is not my story, or Bill's or that of Robson on Oxford T1334, or any of the Poles who died on Wellington R1017. This story belongs to another young man, the pilot of an unknown trainer that collided with another aircraft in the skies over Orston and crashed in flames by a Girl Guides' hut; the story of a young man whose life was unexpectedly brought to a violent end on a routine training flight just before Christmas, and even though I don't know his name, it is a powerful story, and one that deserves to be told, and remembered. *He died near this spot.* I owe it to Bill and all the others to keep on searching, and to tell their story.

Twenty-One

Only two days after Bohdan Kleczyński had reported four of his crews ready for combat, the men of 305 Squadron were in action.

The first operational sorties were flown by three of those crews on the night of 24/25 April 1941, their target the fuel tanks at Vlardingen, near Rotterdam. The target was considered to be relatively light, and not difficult to attack, and so a good raid for new crews to be tested on (or 'blooded' in the jargon), and the squadron's first operation was considered a success. Wellington R1017 did not take part. However, a little over a week later the aircraft was included in the squadron's second operation, on the German naval port of Emden. It was not flown by Flt Lt Stefanicki's crew, but one led by Sgt Jan Trembaczowski, and on her maiden operational flight R1017 successfully dropped her bombs on the target. Six Wellingtons took part in the attack and the squadron suffered its first loss when Wellington R1214 failed to return, with no news of whether the crew had been lost. The following morning, 3 May, crews were stood down to celebrate Poland's National Day, but the mood was understandably more sombre on this occasion, R1214's loss a sad reminder of the sacrifice and cost of war that the crews would continue to face.

Two nights later R1017 was once more on duty, and again Stefanicki's crew were not involved, presumably not yet regarded as being sufficiently ready for operations. Instead R1017 was captained by Sgt Ludwik Mołata's crew. Take off time was 2150, flying south over Rutland to Bridport, crossing the channel in bright moonlight and finding clear skies over the target, the port of Le Havre. The Wellingtons carried out straight and level bombing runs from 14,500 to 18,000 feet, after spending between 3 and 18 minutes over the target. In these early days of the bombing campaign operations were carried out in a much more improvised way than they would be later in the war. Crews were basically given the target, and map references to find it by conventional navigation techniques, then pretty much left to themselves as to how to get there and back. This was before the days of Pathfinder squadrons, target indicator flares and sophisticated radio-direction finding systems. On this occasion bomb bursts were seen, fires were started, and all the raiders returned, Sgt Mołata landing R1017 safely at 0250, a round trip of 5 hours.

R1017 was in action for a third time on the night of 6/7 May, returning to Le Havre, again flown by Sgt Trembaczowski, with Sgt Mołata flying as second pilot. R1017 landed safely back at Syerston at 0415, no doubt with Tadeusz Stefanicki and his crew desperately hoping their names would soon appear on the ops list.

On the following night seven aircraft flew from Syerston to bomb Bremen. R1017 was not among them this time, and all but one returned safely. However, on the squadron's next outing, R1017, this time crewed by all but one of the men who would die on June 12th, was included in the operation.

The first specific mention in the squadron logs of any of the crew who would be on board R1017 on June 12 1941 refers to Pilot Officer Aleksander Zirkwitz, who in February 1941 arrived at Syerston from No 4 Bombing and Gunnery School at West Freugh, on the west coast of Scotland, where he had completed training as an air gunner. On 30 January he had celebrated his birthday, probably in the bars of Stranraer, looking forward to rejoining his mates at Syerston. At 42 the man who would be the rear gunner on the fateful day over Elton would be the oldest man in the crew, but one who would prove to be something of a character, and popular on the station. The squadron *Chronicle* includes a charming caricature of Zirkwitz, making much of his prominent nose and curly black hair. Other than his character, the reason for his inclusion in the album may have been his advanced age – it was extremely unusual for a man of 42 to be flying operations, and many other men would have opted for the safer alternative of a ground job.

On 9 March, among others, Flying Officer Tadeusz Stefanicki was promoted to Acting Flight Lieutenant, and it is quite likely that he now began to assemble his crew: Kazimierz Mruk (second pilot), Marian Wojtowizc (navigator), Jerzy Krawczyk (wireless operator), Stanisław Kowalcze (front gunner) and Aleksander Zirkwitz (rear gunner). Although the crews of 305 squadron regularly rotated their roles and positions in aircraft, depending on availability and sickness etc, these seem to be the preferred roles of this crew, and were probably the positions they occupied when their aircraft collided with Bill's Oxford.

On 11 April we find the first mention in the operational log for Stanisław Kowalcze, 28, who, it is noted, 'returned from a navigation course at No 6 AONS (Air Observer Navigation School) Staverton, Gloucestershire.'

14 May was Stefanicki's 36th birthday. Although this could have been celebrated riotously in the mess, or in Newark or Nottingham, Tadeusz's mind was probably on his family back home in Poland. Born in Lvov[18] (in present-day Ukraine) he was the second oldest member of R1017's crew, and the only married man. He and his wife Janina (nee Krupa) had a son, Ryszard, born in 1936. Tadeusz's thoughts may have been mixed as he downed his drinks that night, a combination of happiness, pride and comradeship but also sadness, fear and concern for his family. Newspapers, radio and the newsreels at the Newark cinemas reported regularly on the sufferings of the Poles under the Nazi occupation. Of course it is almost certain that he will have been hoping that he and his crew would soon be flying operationally, able at last to get back into the war.

---

[18] Lvov was renamed Lviv in 1946 by the Soviets after they took control of western Ukraine; part of a deliberate policy to erase the Polish identity

And so three days after his birthday, on 17 May, Tadeusz Stefanicki's prayers were finally answered, and he was given the command of Wellington R1017, one of three aircraft from 305 Squadron along with five from other stations tasked for an operation against the harbour at Boulogne. The only man from his preferred crew who would not be flying that night was Aleksander Zirkwitz, his place being taken in the rear turret on this occasion by Flight Lieutenant Stanislaus Barzdo, and the reason why Zirkwitz was not on the crew list for the operation will become apparent later.

The crew of Wellington R1017 SM-K; clockwise from top left: Flt Lt T Stefanicki, Pilot; PO S Kowalcse, Obs/gunner; PO M Wojtowicz, Navigator; Sgt K Mruk, 2nd Pilot; Sgt J Krawczyk, Wireless Op; PO A Zirkwitz, Obs/gunner

There is no other experience that is quite like a day on operations, even though many of the tasks carried out will be just as the same as those performed every other day. It begins with the crew being notified in the early morning that they are 'on ops', followed by breakfast and then a short flight around the aerodrome. This Night Flying Test (NFT) is an opportunity for the crew to confirm that the aircraft is ready for the raid, checking instruments, engines, control surfaces, wireless, oxygen and guns while back at base the preparations for the raid are taking place, with target confirmed, and bomb and fuel loads worked out. There is a sense of nervous excitement among the crews, knowing that the next time they take off it will be on the way to a target, their first opportunity to get back at the Germans. This is what they came to England for, and all that training, boredom and bull in the cold and rainy British weather is finally paying off.

When the aircraft lands following its NFT, the ground crew immediately begins the job of going over any snags, or problems identified by the aircrew. There will be briefings about the target, probable and preferred methods of attack, routes there and back, weather reports, wireless codes and frequencies, and intelligence about flak and night fighter defences. In no time at all it is the evening, and the crew are off to the mess for their flying meal – bacon and eggs and lots of tea and coffee; flasks are filled, gambling debts settled, letters written and good luck charms collected before they change into their flying gear, pick up parachutes and are driven out to the dispersal point where their Wellington stands, all bombed and fuelled up, ready to go. Last cigarettes are smoked, notes from the briefings underlined and memorised, nervous jokes and laughter echoing across the quiet airfield as the sky darkens and there's a chill in the air. The smell of the grass suddenly seems sweeter, and the song of the blackbird more heartrending, as the men know they may never experience these sensations again. Watches are checked, and a little after ten word goes round that it's time, and the crew boards the Wellington, feeling the fear of the unknown. Some of these crewmen have flown operationally before, in Poland. For others it is their first experience of combat, but they are united in a determination to do their best and fight for Poland.

Strapped into their seats, the crew carry out final cockpit checks. Navigator Marian Wojtowicz arranges his maps, pencils and slide rule on his desk and the gunners settle themselves behind their Browning machine guns. In his seat behind the pilots, wireless operator Jerzy Krawczyk gets the message on the radio to start up, the engines burst into life, the chocks are pulled away and the big black 'Sooty Giant' wheels out towards the runway. Stefanicki and his second pilot Kazimierz Mruk glance from the instrument panel to the red lights around the airfield marking high buildings, aerials and the perimeter, their eyes now becoming accustomed to the growing dark. The engines roar for what seems a lifetime as the pilot waits... and waits. Finally, the green light comes on in the control van, Stefanicki opens the throttle, releases the brakes and the lumbering bomber moves off and down the runway. At 2235 R1017 lifts into the air and banks towards the southeast, destination Boulogne.

They soon begin to meet other aircraft that are part of the operation, and the main element leaves the Suffolk coast at Orfordness, flying out over the North Sea to the Belgian coast at Nieuwpoort, continuing in an almost straight line before passing to the south of Liege and swinging towards the target. Even in early summer, flying at height it is extremely cold in the Wellington, despite the crew's heated flying suits, warm boots and sheepskin jackets. But they have more important things to concentrate on, and no time to worry about their freezing fingers and toes. Some of them might have filled a flask with coffee, and there'll be sandwiches and a bag of dried fruit stuffed into pockets, but they save these for the return flight or the possibility of something untoward happening. The moon on the night of Saturday 17 May is entering its final quarter, and the absence of cloud lends a faint bluish tinge to the aircraft flying in tight vics of three. Although the other crews have great difficulty identifying Boulogne harbour, due to intense searchlight activity, Stefanicki finds the target, bombing it from between 17,000 and 18,000 feet, causing fires and a large explosion, probably from their 1,000 pounder.

There will have been shouts and celebrations as the aircraft turns to the west, but Stefanicki knows his crew have to remain alert and concentrated on the long flight home. The return leg is often the most dangerous part of an op, as by now the night fighters know where the bombers are, and are hunting... Compared to the bomber crews the German night fighter pilots would be relatively fresh and alert and would very often stalk a bomber all the way home to its station, launching a surprise attack when the relieved and excited crew was least expecting it.

R1017's ground crew will have been waiting, Aleksander Zirkwitz possibly among them, drinking coffee and nervously listening out for the sound of approaching engines. A huge searchlight would be turned on, pointing its beam directly up at the sky to act as a beacon for returning bombers, which circle the airfield waiting for permission to land, their green and red navigation lights twinkling in the deep black sky. At 0243 Flt Lt Stefanicki guides Wellington R1017 down, its wheels bounce on the runway before settling, and the ground crew sigh with relief.

With the engines finally turned off a silence descends around the dispersal point and the crew climb out of the bomber, laughing and lighting cigarettes. After telling the 'dear slobs'[19] about their night out they jump into a truck which takes them to the admin block and into the debrief. Gathered around a table with mugs of coffee and finally eating their sandwiches, the crew excitedly report the details of the operation to an intelligence officer, often a WAAF, telling them about the weather, defences on the way to and around the target, the success or otherwise of bombing and any flak and night fighter activity.

Then it's off to bed in their billets, trying to sleep while the raid plays over and over in their heads. Final letters to loved ones that were written before the op will be ripped up or

---

[19] The nickname affectionately given to ground crews by some Polish aircrew. *Bomber Aircraft of 305 Squadron*, by Lechosław Musiałkowski, Mushroom Model Publications 2014.

tucked into a drawer for the next time, and lucky charms replaced on shelves. For those who can't sleep, it's an hour or two in the mess, talking about what just happened or simply sitting and thinking, until the early fingers of dawn start to stretch across the morning sky.

Twenty-Two

High speed trains pass along this platform. Keep back from the platform edge behind the yellow line.

I'm standing on the northbound platform at Newark Northgate station, waiting for the early Newcastle train. The yellow crisscross markings running along the platform edge have never seemed significant to me before, but I find myself staring at them, and then at the yellow sign on the wall behind me. They put me in mind of the bright yellow paint job that I was applying to my 1/72 scale Oxford the other night. Until starting down this road I hadn't known that there was a special association with yellow and 'caution' – or maybe it was simply that the association was so obvious I never really thought about it - but now I can't avoid it. I look around and suddenly the world is full of potential hazards painted bright yellow to warn the unsuspecting to keep clear: warning signs, yellow handrails, sliding doors, the edges of the wheelchair ramp leaning against the waiting room, even a crane parked in the siding. Yellow, I now know, is the colour of warning, and the warning is clear – stay away!

So why didn't the pilots of the Wellington and Oxford see each other when they were flying on a collision course? Admittedly in its wartime camouflage the yellow would have been reduced to the trainer's undersides with the upper surfaces in a drab green and brown, and if the Oxford was flying directly towards the Wellington, with its relatively small cross-section, and possibly the sun behind it, the crew of the bomber couldn't have been expected to see it. And then there is the question of haze...

I remember a conversation about haze which I had recently with Megan Bowden, a friend who happens to fly aeroplanes. At the time she was working as a co-pilot, flying business flights on a Cessna Citation CJ4 from Oxford to Turkey and Croatia; normally her role covers radio and navigation duties, but when they're not carrying passengers she pilots the aircraft herself. The Citation is a sleek, powerful jet, flying at 45,000 feet at a speed of Mach.77, very different to anything Bill, Robson or the Polish airmen could ever have imagined, and she loves it. In her spare time she is involved in a Spitfire restoration project and indulging her real passion, flying the 'Wacky Wabbit', a North American T6 Harvard single-engine aeroplane of the type on which thousands of RAF pilots trained during the war.

I had contacted Megan about Bill's accident earlier in the year, hoping that she might be able to help me to understand a little more about the problem of haze, which had featured prominently in reports of the collision, and which I was pretty ignorant about. I had a basic definition, supplied by the Met Office – '*a suspension of extremely small, dry particles in the air, not water droplets. These particles are invisible to the naked eye, but sufficient to give the air an opalescent appearance,*' – but wanted to get a 'pilot's eye' view of the problem, and Megan was only too keen to help. We said we'd talk but for one reason or another it never happened; time passed and I began to think we might never speak at all. And then out of the blue, as it were, Megan sent me a video, showing the haze she had encountered on a flight from Turkey only that weekend. It put her in mind of our conversation, and we talked.

We started off by discussing the collision. I outlined the factors, such as I knew them: summer, daylight, the Wellingtons practising close formation flying at 900 feet, an unqualified crew in the Oxford coming in the opposite direction and the seemingly all-important element of haze. I told her that haze had been mentioned in the Squadron's Operational Log, and that the rear gunner of the lead Wellington reported the Oxford coming out of nowhere and colliding with R1017 before either pilot had time to do anything about it. So, the $60,000 question: could the accident have been caused by haze?

Megan winds back a little, explaining what she calls the 'Swiss cheese' theory of accidents. This comes into play when investigating and analysing how air accidents happen. Imagine you have several slices of Swiss cheese and rotate them on a central point, she says; the cheese slices represent barriers, safeguards or defences to prevent accidents from occurring. The holes in the cheese represent gaps or flaws in the barrier, and these holes are constantly moving, opening and closing. When all the holes align, a threat line can breach all the barriers and an accident is possible. So there's usually not just one cause.

Having done the kind of low-level flying both aircraft were engaged in herself, she said the main thing to remember is that the pilots and aircrew might not actually be spending a lot of time looking out for other aircraft. Flying at around 900 feet the crew of the Oxford are watching out for ground clues – main roads, such as the A52 which runs through Elton, navigation and turning points like crossroads, a church, woods or a river. You train your eyes to look down at the ground and up for other aircraft then back down again in a regular staccato rhythm. For the crew of the Wellington, which was on a formation flying exercise, this is slightly different but equally crucial: the pilot is probably focusing entirely on the other aircraft he's flying in formation with, relying on the leading aircraft to do the navigating and ground checking, while he follows the other's wingtip, anticipating turns or changes in height – if anything it's probably the second pilot and/or navigator who are sharing the roles of watching the ground and looking out for other aircraft. Flying at speed, a momentary distraction, with any one of them taking their eyes off the job, could be fatal.

I returned to the subject of haze, which I had thought was made up of dry particulates, but in her message accompanying the video Megan had described the effect of the sun glaring off 'water droplets' in the haze. I asked her to explain the confusion, and she told me that water molecules can attach themselves to the dry particulates, creating the effect of glare. Haze often appears towards the end of a period of high pressure accompanied by little wind. And it can be exacerbated by a number of things, such as industrial pollution; were there any factories close by where the accident occurred, she asked. Not really, I said, it's farming country. But Elton's not far from Newark, I suppose, and Grantham, both of which had some relatively heavy industry at the time – there was that German bomber raid on the ball bearing factory in Newark only a month earlier - also the Met report at Syerston, some 12 miles away, had emphasised haze, so maybe it was quite generalised that day. Megan told me the Trent area, being full of industrial towns and especially coal-fired electricity power stations, mines and factories (not to mention RAF Bomber stations), would be likely culprits for creating hazy conditions. And even dust thrown up by agricultural activity such as ploughing or stubble burning could impact the haze's effect.

Megan then described how the haze can form a dense horizontal layer, which when seen from above can look like a perfectly calm stretch of sea. She remembered how when on a training flight of her own, she had been in the situation of flying above haze and losing her way completely; not knowing how to get down, she suddenly saw the much clearer 'actual sea' through holes in the haze and was able to re-orientate herself. When the sun is in a particular direction the light can bounce off the haze, blinding a pilot. And *inside* the haze it's even worse - you lose the glare, but the effect can be much more disorientating; not as solid as flying through cloud, when you can't see anything, but 'Like flying through murky water'. Haze happens at all altitudes, so the Wellington and Oxford could have been flying 'in' the haze, staying at 900 feet to try and keep track of the ground features, with the pilots having that sensation of flying through murky water; or they could have been above it, in which case the glare of the sunlight bouncing off the water droplets would come into play.

Now I knew why haze had featured so prominently in the contemporary reports – it must have been responsible for the accident. '*Possibly*,' said Megan, 'But remember those other possible factors, the holes in the other slices of Swiss cheese.'

'So what are they?' I asked.

They could be anything, Megan said. What's going on in the cockpit? Are the pilot and crew talking (or even arguing) for instance, or does the pilot feel under particular pressure to perform? Is he feeling tired, ill, hungover, depressed, euphoric? Other factors to consider could include bugs - flying at relatively low height in midsummer the windscreen would be covered in squashed insects. Add that to a Perspex windscreen that probably has scratches on it, any of which could catch the light, magnifying the glare. And the Wellington's windscreen could also be picking up smuts and mess from the exhausts of the Wimpy in front. Even the goggles the pilots were issued with could cause problems with vision, as they were fairly primitive in 1941 and they might have worn sunglasses instead (I remembered a wonderful photo of a Polish bomber pilot from 305 Squadron wearing aviator shades). Megan reminded me of how the human element could come into play in a situation like this: what if, for instance, the pilot forgot, or mislaid, or broke his sunglasses? Then of course, there is the element of low-level flying, which Megan told me from her personal experience is much scarier and difficult than flying at altitude – everything happens so much more quickly, pilots have much less reaction time. So, she concluded, taking all these other possible factors into consideration, in a case like this, haze is only one of several possible factors that could have caused a fatal collision, but it remains a significant one...

The train is half-empty. Carrying a coffee and pastry I sit down by a window, pull my *A-Z of Gateshead* out of my haversack and begin to highlight certain points on the map. I'm travelling to Gateshead to try find out anything I can about Robson Newton. My attempts to generate some interest via the local media failed miserably, and other than the address where Robson lived with his father William, a postal clerk, and his mother Beatrice, I don't have much to go on. I've run off several hundred small flyers to pop through letter boxes around the immediate area where they lived in 1941, appealing for any information about the family. So far my investigations seem to suggest that this particular branch of the family died out a few years after Robson's death, so I'm not too optimistic.

The fact that in his will Robson Newton left over £750 to his father suggests the family weren't badly off, and I'm hoping to see that the house will confirm that. Although I've gone through Newcastle many times on the train, and passed what I now know is Gateshead, on the south side of the River Tyne, I've never actually been to the town before. I work out an itinerary, including war memorials, post offices and cemeteries, and getting off the train in Newcastle take a taxi to Devon Gardens and start leafleting, hoping I'll be able to finish before it starts to rain.

Devon Gardens is, unusually, two rows of houses facing each other across a narrow central path. Walking through gates and up and down garden paths is a long and repetitive job, and I make the most of trying to get a sense of the place as I push leaflets through letter boxes. The street is half-way up a hill, known locally as Low Fell, with views down onto parkland, although there are now many more buildings down below than there would have been when these Edwardian villas were built. Eventually I reach number 24 and pause for a moment at the gate before heading up the path. It's a well-kept double-fronted house, with impressive bay windows on the ground floor, original windows and what looks like it could be the original front door. Having written a special letter for the present owner, outlining my request for information in more detail, I knock on the door a few times but clearly no-one's in. Not surprising on a Saturday morning, I suppose. I can see from a few toys lying around that a family with young children live here, so my hope that it could be an elderly person who might possibly have known the Newtons seems optimistic.

I slip the envelope through the letter box, take a photograph from the gate, and carry on leafleting the rest of the houses. At the end of the street I'm taking some more photographs and gazing around, trying to get a sense of what the place would have been like in 1941, with fewer cars, and open fields where there are now modern houses, when I become aware of a man standing on his doorstep, clearly wondering who I am and what I'm doing. I realise that I probably look like I'm up to no good. I head over and apologise, giving him a flyer and explaining my mission. He's immediately interested. His parents lived in his house until they died, and they would have been around in the 1960s, but possibly not during the war. He hasn't any memories of anyone named Newton, as I expected, but he'll ask around, and he directs me to some houses where the older residents live. I think his real interest is in the mid-air collision, because he wants to know where it happened, and tells me that he has visited the Newark Air Museum. He asks me how long I'm planning to be in Gateshead and I tell him I'm catching a train home at teatime. 'Ah, just when we'll be turning out of St James Park – might see you then,' (he's going to watch Newcastle play Bournemouth). I wish him and the Toon Army all the best and head off.

After a couple of hours of delivering leaflets in the neighbouring streets, I'm tired, aching and thirsty, having covered around 200 pre-war properties. I've not met many people, but one woman has run up the street to tell me that her friend is from a large family of girls named Robson; I remember that Robson took his middle name from his mother, so that's a possibility, and she promises to ask a few questions. Another lady bemoans the lack of community here – neighbours don't know you, don't talk, just go to work, come home, keep themselves to themselves, not like the old days...

I spend the next few hours walking around Gateshead, checking out the war memorials, post offices and cemeteries, but with no luck, pretty much as I had expected. After sitting on a bench and eating lunch in Saltwell Park, watching the families enjoying their ice creams around the boating pond and tennis courts where I expect young Robson Newton will once have played, I head back into Newcastle, catching a bus for the station.

Has it all been a waste of time?

On the train home, watching the fields and houses flash by, remembering those happy families in Saltwell Park, I catch sight of my reflection in the window. I can't ignore the fact that I am sitting alone on a train, tearing up and down the country, head stuck firmly in the past, chasing answers to possibly unanswerable questions, when I should be living. Suddenly I am taken back to the last time I was doing something like this, when I was in Scotland, before the divorce. Once again I go cold, flushed with regret and shame about *Cultybraggan*. Is it going to be like that all over again?

Twenty-Three

There is a rusting collection of Second World War-era Nissen huts sitting on a flood plain surrounded by the imposing black Aberuchill Hills, a few miles from the village where we had settled when we moved to Scotland. I drove past it many times before my curiosity finally got the better of me and I reversed, turned down the lane and found myself sitting outside the gate to what appeared to be an old army camp.

A faded notice in the window of the deserted guard hut explained that this place was called Cultybraggan, and that it was the last surviving German Prisoner of War camp in Scotland. It certainly wasn't much to look at, but clearly very little had been done to it since the war apart from the addition of a firing range and, bizarrely, a nuclear bunker. There was a definite atmosphere about the place, a sense of ghosts (some restless perhaps?) and more than a hint of stories as yet undiscovered, waiting to be told, if only someone was interested enough to find them.

Not long after that I saw an article in the local paper about a former member of Hitler's SS, who had been held in Cultybraggan as a POW following his capture in Normandy. This German had recently died and in his will had left his entire personal estate, (running to several hundred thousand pounds) to the people of the neighbouring village, in gratitude for the kindness they had shown to him and other POWs all those years ago. After the war this man had befriended a local family who he got to know when he was working outside the camp, and their son, who was born after the war, was still living in the village...

I made contact with him and we met in a coffee shop to talk about the ex-SS man and his dad. He told me how well they got on together, eventually becoming close friends. It wasn't a unique story – many ex-POWs had become friendly with villagers, settling down and becoming locals themselves. It took a while but grudges were eventually put aside, resentments buried, and wrongs (on both sides) forgiven. Already an idea was forming itself in my brain that there was a story here, the starting point for a project that would tell the story of how the people of a small village and their one-time Nazi neighbours were thrown together and had to get on: themes of community, guilt and redemption were all there, waiting to be brought out. I set about tracking down surviving POWs who had stayed in the area, and their families, as well as those villagers who had developed particularly close relationships with them. Little did I know that Cultybraggan was to obsess me for the next three years.

Soon after settling in Scotland, we had set up a small independent film company, partly as a way of giving our sons some real hands-on practical experience in making films (they each had a sense that they might want to make careers in the media, like their parents), but also to give all of us a way of expressing our creativity. In place of the initial dream of creating a sort of holiday accommodation-cum-residential artist's studio, this might also create an income, and be a way of drawing closer as a family. For my then wife and me especially, sharing creative ideas could help us to rediscover what we once loved about each other and seemed to have lost; it might draw us more closely together as a couple, and as a family. That was the theory, anyway.

And so, working at evenings, weekends and on days off, we tracked down some amazing people and encouraged them to tell us their unique stories about Cultybraggan on camera. Some were locals who remembered the camp as children, others had been held as prisoners at the camp themselves. My sons set up the lighting, filmed and edited the interviews, and my wife, working largely as producer, organised shoots and directed her own segments. As the boys learned more they started planning and making their own projects, and she was working on hers. I was constantly reading and finding out more about Cultybraggan, chasing leads and setting up more and more interviews, travelling as far as the north of Scotland to interview people who had fascinating stories to tell. I was feeling more creative than I had been for a long time. This was the kind of work I wanted to do. I was free, and I was happy.

But as the project moved forward, each interview led to another strand of the story, each door opening to a room containing even more doors. *Cultybraggan* the film was growing, becoming bigger and ever more ambitious in scope, and as complications and challenges arose, and those resources became squeezed, my determination to make the film grew. Instead of being a happy, creative experience, filming and editing was turning into a grind, difficult, and stressful for all concerned. I couldn't work out why this change had come about, but focussed even more on the job, working ever harder to get *Cultybraggan* finished.

I was squeezing shoots and editing sessions into weekends and evenings, and all the time the finished film seemed to be moving further and further away from completion. The family went along with my obsession, knowing how much the film meant to me, even though they now had their own projects to work on, but as I was spending most of my time away from home, working on paid jobs, I wasn't always around to witness the strain and misery they were feeling. What should have been creative discussions became arguments; they would try to let me understand that working on the film wasn't fun anymore, but I couldn't see it, obsessed as I was by achieving the end result. How could it be my fault that the whole thing had become miserable and fraught, a chore rather than a pleasure for everyone involved? I was busting a gut, flying hither and yon – over to Ireland, down to England, back up to Scotland again – in order to get the film made – why was I being blamed for the awful atmosphere and the arguments? I refused to believe that my obsession with the film was the real problem.

Slowly and steadily I was becoming less of a father to my sons and a husband to my wife, and I simply couldn't see why. What had started out as a way of bringing us closer together had turned into the thing that helped force us apart. The tantalising prospect of being able to save the marriage was hanging there, within our grasp, and we lost it all because I was more concerned about making a film.

After the marriage finally crashed and burned, *Cultybraggan* was abandoned. I couldn't face the strain and tension involved in trying to complete the film on top of everything else the divorce was throwing up, and in the end I handed it, along with everything else I owned in the company, over to my ex-wife and sons. I assume it's lying unfinished on a shelf now, hundreds of files stored on a hard drive. But whenever I think about *Cultybraggan* I go cold, afraid to ask about the status of the project in case it brings up the old arguments, but also feeling guilty and ashamed of the way that I not only lost my family, but also let down all the people who gave their time, their stories, and their hopes to the project. I made them promises and left them with nothing. And after today, with nothing to show for a day spent in Gateshead, it feels like here I am now, doing exactly the same thing again.

I start thinking, as I do so often these days, about Guy Gibson. Wing Commander Guy Gibson, VC, for those who are not as interested in the Dam Busters as I am, was the RAF's most decorated flyer, and arguably the greatest hero of Bomber Command. Aged only 24 at the time he led the raid on the Ruhr dams, he had already flown an unbelievable 68 operations, and was all set to see out the rest of the war from behind a desk when he was asked to form 617 Squadron.

Now before I go any further, let's be clear: I'm in no way comparing myself to Guy Gibson as a man. He had more bravery, more mental strength and sheer guts to see a job through than I will ever have. I only use him as an example because he was famous, a man about whom many books have been written, a hero to many, a tyrant to others, and so I feel I have more of an understanding of his personality than I do the many thousands of equally brave bomber crews who lived and died during the Second World War. The interesting thing about Gibson, and what my mind was dwelling on now, was that he flew all those ops, completed his tour, and yet, just at the very moment when he could have said goodbye and gone on a much-needed holiday with his wife Eve, he accepted the dam-busting job. He had no idea what it was about because it was Top Secret. It was, he was told, also Highly Dangerous, for which read Probably Suicidal. There was enormous pressure on him to succeed. He knew that he was going to be responsible for the lives of dozens of aircrew, some of them old friends, and he knew that many of them would die for no other reason than that they willingly did what he told them to. He was under no obligation to do it, he had done his duty and already achieved as much as any man in his position could have hoped. He'd been told explicitly that he had the right to turn it down and walk away, just as any sane man would.

So why did he say 'Yes'? I think it was because for him the alternative was too horrendous to contemplate.

It's well known that Gibson's private and emotional life was to put it politely, complicated. He was not given to making many close friends, especially amongst his flying crew, and he had an extremely difficult relationship with his parents – an absent father and alcoholic mother – as well as his wife Eve. She was a glamorous showgirl who Gibson became infatuated with almost as quickly as he fell out of love with; their whirlwind wartime romance and marriage hit the domestic rocks as soon as Eve realized how miserable and lonely the life of a bomber pilot's wife really was. A tiny candlelit room above a Lincolnshire village pub held few attractions for a girl who was more used to the bright lights and fun of the West End. Maybe she also couldn't take living with a man whose thoughts always seemed to be somewhere else. Whatever, they separated, and when Gibson was faced with the choice between a cushy desk job or climbing back into the cockpit of a Lancaster for one last op, there was never going to be any contest.

Whether he was consciously aware of it or not, (and he may have told himself he was simply 'doing his duty') Gibson knew that going back to war gave him something to focus on. Every waking minute right up to his return from the dams (if he even made it) would be crammed with the task of working obsessively to solve the problem of how to get those bouncing bombs on their target. And he would be able to forget, or at least put to one side, the very real problems waiting for him at home.

I see Gibson, sitting at the controls of Lancaster G-George, racing through the moonlit sky at 250mph, skimming the treetops over Holland, heading for he knows not what. And although it's a world away on so many levels, I have this image of myself, metaphorically doing something similar. Like Gibson, when I start work on a project like this, or any job really, I feel that I'm progressing, moving forward. I don't always know what it is that I'm after - success, security, satisfaction, or just that less definable 'something' - but I am at least not standing still. And the 'life' problems - whatever they are - are behind me, out of sight, to be dealt with later.

The truth is, at exactly the moment when I think I am moving forward the hardest, I'm really running away.

Running from life, from the things I can't deal with, from the emptiness and pain, just like Gibson. When I'm haring around the Nottinghamshire countryside, trying to establish where an aircraft crashed 80 years ago, just like when I was making *Cultybraggan*, I am filling every day, every hour, from waking to sleeping, with 'the project'. I am happy, because I'm busy, and things are happening, I'm seeking and finding answers, and the world is making sense. I can't relax, because if I ever do allow myself to stop, and feel that I'm not moving forward, as has happened today, that's when I am forced to confront the emptiness, the darkness in me.

That's when I hear the inner voice again, asking those questions I can't or don't want to answer, and prefer not to think about. I don't like the person it shines a light on, I prefer to keep the truth about me in the shadows. I know that this is a pathological, destructive form of behaviour. But I carry on doing it, again and again, year after year, as the failures pile up behind me.

It's a truism that there is a fine line between creative and destructive behaviour. I know why I am obsessing about Leading Aircraftman William Wharton Parkinson, a man who I never knew, who I had never even heard of until a few months ago. It's not because I need to know the truth about his death, or that anyone else does, really; I'm not doing this for Fiona, or the families of the other men who died that day. This has nothing to do with altruism, maybe even less to do with creativity and art. I can walk away from Bill's story now, forget all about it – and nobody will think twice about it. Unlike *Cultybraggan*, I haven't gone far enough down the road to let a lot of people down if I turn around now. But I won't, because the alternative is worse. I'll be left to face the reality that I've failed again – that I didn't move down to England to be near my mother – I ran away from Scotland and my failed marriage, and I will probably never be able to mend that broken relationship with my family.

Just one more operation, one final raid…

Twenty-Four

The days have become swelteringly hot again. With nothing else to do I take myself on drives, sometimes alone, sometimes with Mum, bringing her up to date with my research. One lunchtime I get back to the flat to find a 'We tried to deliver' card on the mat. I go down to the Post Office, and pick the parcel up, realising immediately that it is from Fiona. I'd asked her not long ago if she had any personal items relating to her uncle Bill, and I guess this must be answer. Excited, I resist the temptation to open it straight away, and instead head to the marketplace.

Sitting in some shade with a coffee I set out my notepad and pen, take a sip of coffee, sit back and relax. This week the marketplace has been turned into Newark-by-the-sea; bizarre but comforting and enjoyable in a strange kind of way. In front of the Trumpton-style town hall there's a temporary beach, with clean sand, deckchairs, buckets and spades for the kids and even a tape loop of seagulls and gently crashing waves playing through loudspeakers. The place is full of families with happy children making sandcastles, eating ice-creams, and generally having fun. I'm fighting a rising swell of anxiety, which I can't quite put my finger on, although I know it's to do with the wasted day at Gateshead and all that it stirred up, and I finally open the parcel.

First, a note from Fiona:

Hi Ade,
Here we are – exactly as I found them in one of Dad's briefcases.
Hope it's helpful to have the originals.

I am extremely grateful to you for all your digging for details. It's great to have the gaps explained.
All the best,
Fiona x

The next thing I take out, entirely by chance, is a small manilla envelope, marked PRIORITY in large, unmissable capitals, and addressed to *Mrs G Parkinson, 9 Fountayne Rd*. I know what this is, of course, although I've never seen one in the flesh before, as it were. Looking at the back of the envelope I can see where it was opened, by fearful, trembling fingers. And inside, folded as it was over 80 years ago, is the telegram that no mother wants to receive, dated 12 June 1941:

10347 12TH CARTERTON OF OHMS PRIORITY 31

-IMPORTANT- MRS W PARKINSON 9 FOUNTAYNE ST GOOLE YORKS

REGRET TO INFORM YOU THAT YOUR SON 1067885 AC PARKINSON WW KILLED IN FLYING ACCIDENT STOP FURTHER PARTICULARS TO FOLLOW = AERONAUTICS CARTERTON

And that's it. I don't know where Mrs Parkinson would have been when she received the telegram. It will have arrived sometime on Thursday evening; perhaps she was having a late dinner with George, listening to stories about his day at the *Goole Times* as he passes a secret morsel to Raque, sitting patiently beside his chair. Or they could have been clearing the table for an evening of reading or listening to the radio together. Or perhaps, it being British Double Summer Time, and still light, Gertrude was out in the back garden, feeding the tomatoes and runner beans with the last of the washing-up water, exchanging a few words with a neighbour; mid-conversation, she looks up at the sound of aircraft high in the sky overhead, on their way from a bomber station to

Germany, thinking of her other son, 'Away down south, getting close to the end of his course now, according to his last letter, and it shouldn't be long before he gets his wings, fingers crossed.' Wherever she was, and whatever she was doing, having the envelope in my hand, with its simple tiny tear to show where it was opened, transports me back to the moment when Gertrude received the news she must have secretly been dreading, and the utter devastation she must have felt. No gentle introduction, no 'Take a seat Mrs Parkinson'. Just that stark PRIORITY marking to signal to her what was inside.

I notice that someone got the address wrong on the envelope: Gertrude lived on Fountayne *Street*, not *Road*, and she is referred to as both Mrs G and Mrs W Parkinson. There are also some pencilled additions, presumably made at a later point by Gertrude as she tried to make sense of what she had just found out: 'East Stoke 271,' which I take to be either the telephone number of the East Stoke Post Office, a mile or so along the Fosse Way from Syerston, or the station itself. And Bill's rank has been corrected, with an 'L', to *Leading* Aircraftman. More troubling I think, is an amendment to Bill's service number, which has in one place been mistyped, 1067883 instead of the correct 1067083. Someone, presumably Gertrude, has corrected the error. Could she have hoped, if even for just a fleeting moment, that someone down south had got it wrong and that it was not her Bill who had been killed but some other poor soul? But it can only have been a momentary hope, if hope it was at all. Possibly she just needed to make sure she had the correct number when talking to people for information. And this telegram would have quickly been followed by the letter confirming Bill's death, a photograph of which Fiona has already sent me, from the RAF Records Office at Gloucester. But the finality of this telegram, this tiny relic, one of just tens, possibly hundreds of thousands that will have been sent and received around Britain during the war, says Bill is dead, there's no getting away from the fact.

He was just 19. Not even killed in action, but on a training flight. His death was just an accident.

More communications follow, as the huge administrative machinery of the RAF in wartime swings into motion. Next is a letter of condolence, written the day after Bill's death, and which Gertrude will probably have received on Monday the 16th, the day before his funeral. Handwritten in blue ink on RAF headed notepaper, the letter is from RAF Brize Norton and reads:

Dear Mrs Parkinson,

I am writing to offer my sincerest sympathies in the death of your boy in a flying accident yesterday.

I hope it may be of some slight consolation to you to know that he was a very good lad and a promising pilot with the makings of a splendid NCO.

The accident which caused your son's death was a collision in the air near Nottingham in conditions of very low visibility where neither aircraft saw the other until it was too late to avoid disaster.

I beg you to realize that your son died for his country, just as though he had been killed in action. I am sure your loss will seem easier to bear if you think of it in this way.

Please accept, once again, my very deepest sympathies in your loss.

Yours sincerely,

Ronald H. Kershaw

(Group Capt. Ret.)

It's a simple, moving and above all I feel, *honest* letter, and may have brought Gertrude some comfort, as intended. Reading it I get the feeling that the writer genuinely liked Bill, again as was intended. Of course, the writer doesn't actually know for himself the details of the accident, he may not even have known LAC Parkinson, and is simply quoting from the accident report, a copy of which he will no doubt have received, sent down the wire to Brize Norton from Syerston, and reproduced in the AIR27 document Ian Shaw sent me.

Later I learn that the officer who wrote the letter, Group Captain Ronald Kershaw, Commanding Officer at Brize Norton, had been brought out of retirement, as many older airmen were, in order to supplement the enormous administrative burden of running the machinery of war, and something of a war hero himself. He had arrived at the station only the month before, and writing letters of condolence to bereaved families would have been just one of his responsibilities following the accident. There was also a letter to be written to the family of his co-pilot, Robson Newton, as well as the organising of sending officers and cadets from Brize Norton to Newark for one funeral and to Goole for another.

Similar administrative work was being carried out at RAF Syerston, from where another telegram was sent on 16 June, informing Gertrude that:

CORTEGE WILL ARRIVE 1.45 TOMORROW WITH BEARER PARTY IN ATTENDANCE

This telegram is not in its original envelope. Perhaps the communications were coming so thick and fast now that Gertrude did not have the time, or inclination, to think of saving envelopes. Indeed, far from being able to dwell on the death of her son, Gertrude will have had to think about his funeral, informing friends and relatives, as well as the RAF stations at Syerston and Brize Norton, of the location and time, and making arrangements with the funeral directors about the cars and flowers. Somewhere along the line she will have had the discussion about where the funeral was to take place. It is not unreasonable to suggest that the officers at Syerston, having charge of Bill's body, and already making arrangements for the burial of his co-pilot and the six Polish airmen at Newark Cemetery, will have assumed that Bill would be buried along with them. But for reasons of her own, Gertrude wanted her son's funeral to be in Goole, at home, where he could be buried alongside his father and sister.

Perhaps there was never any decision to make, as far as Gertrude was concerned; from Mum's description, she strikes me as being a strong woman, certainly someone who knew her own mind. If she wanted Bill to be buried at home, there was probably very little the RAF could do or say to change her mind. Or maybe the RAF were happy to go along with her wishes. Bill was, after all, a flyer, and even if he hadn't won his wings yet he was 'one of them' and had made the ultimate sacrifice. If asked, they would want someone to do the same for them, and for their mothers, wouldn't they?

A yellowing cutting from George's paper the *Goole Times* is the next item to emerge from the parcel, carrying the report of Bill's funeral, which took place on 17 June 1941. Under a headline announcing three local war casualties, the notice records the death of the twin son of Mrs and the late Rev W Parkinson, and goes on to give some brief biographical details of Bill, notably his birth in Hessle, five miles west of Hull, his education at Ashville College, Harrogate, where he was a keen sportsman, and his brief period of employment before volunteering for the RAF. Bill, before joining up, had worked for Messrs GW Townend and Co, Goole, from where a number of mourners had come to pay their respects, and had been a messenger in the Goole Auxiliary Fire Service (AFS), who had also sent representatives. Flowers were also presented by a 2nd Lt and Mrs Yealand, as well as George. Also present were Bill's commanding officer Group Captain Kershaw and officers in the RAF, NCOs and fellow cadets, and officers and senior NCOs at 'a Midland aerodrome'.[20]

Clearly a large number of officers, NCOs and cadets had made the journey, from both Syerston and Brize Norton, to pay their respects. Quite impressive, as the prominence the article is given in the newspaper also shows. Finally, in addition to representatives of the North Street Methodist Guild there was also a 'Mr and Mrs Bean' in attendance. This is something of a surprise for me – the Beans, (my father's side of the family) were not only (so far as I know) not Methodists, but they were also not yet connected to the Methodist church-

---

[20] Used with permission from the *Goole Times*.

going Wilsons of my mother's family, nor were they friendly with the Parkinsons. Now who were they..?

I replace the cutting in the envelope, and find a small white card, edged in black, from Gertrude and George, wishing to 'express our thanks for the sympathy you have shown us in our great sorrow', which would have been sent out to friends and family after the funeral. The envelope also contains a similar but larger card, sent from a grander address. This card, from Buckingham Palace, contains the note from the King that thousands of bereaved families would receive during the war:

> The Queen and I offer you our heartfelt sympathy in your great sorrow.
> We pray that your country's gratitude for a life so nobly given in its service may bring you some measure of consolation.
> George RI

More mundanely, there is also an official leaflet, telling the bereaved how to conduct themselves following their relative's death:

> CONFIDENTIAL NOTICE:
> The names of all who lose their lives or are wounded or reported missing while serving with the Royal Air Force will appear in the official casualty lists published from time to time in the Press.
> Any publication of the date, place or circumstances of a casualty, and particularly any reference to the unit concerned, might give valuable information to the enemy, and for this reason, only the name, rank and Service number are included in the official lists.
> Relatives are particularly requested, in the national interest, to ensure that any notices published privately do not disclose the date, place or circumstances of the casualty, or the unit.
> The Press have been asked to co-operate in ensuring that no information of value to the enemy is published.

Even, or particularly *at* times of great emotion and loss, everyone has to be reminded, in effect, to 'keep calm and carry on'. Don't allow your grief to spill over and let you say something you shouldn't, because behind every concerned and sympathetic neighbour there could lurk a German spy... I am reminded immediately of the stories of 'D Notices' that Uncle George used to tell when I was young. I see now that they had a personal significance for him, even then.

The package contains much more relating to Bill's death, the assorted administrative flotsam and jetsam of a death in wartime, where enquiries are made, answers given or queried, loose ends officially tied up, stamped, filed and put away; more of the kind of work that Group Captain Kershaw and his opposite number at Syerston would have been brought out of retirement to do. There are letters from various stations and offices, including Bill's certificate of service and discharge papers, showing that Bill volunteered with the RAFVR (Royal Air Force Volunteer Reserve) on 3 September 1940, and was mobilised three months later, which is when he would have begun his flying training, and his character and general conduct are given as 'very good'.

There is also correspondence from the RAF Benevolent Fund, notifying Gertrude about what benefits or assistance she was entitled to, and how to apply for them, and a letter dated 28 July 1941 from the Ministry of Pensions in Blackpool, informing her that her case 'has been carefully considered but, in view of [her] circumstances, it is regretted that it is not possible at present to award [her] a pension.' However, another letter, this time from the Air Ministry, dated 14 January 1946 (after the war) informs Gertrude that 'a War Gratuity is payable in respect of the Royal Air Force service of the above-named officer/airman'.

More poignantly perhaps, there are invoices and receipts, including a bill from Drury and Taylor, Solicitors, for £1, 5s and 1d 'for the death certificate of WW Parkinson deceased,' and another from Glews of Goole Ltd, Complete House Furnishers, Carpet Specialists etc, to cover 'funeral expenses including motor hearse and 3 cars, undertakers fee for arrangements totalling £14 and 14s, paid 23 June 1941.'

Strange that Gertrude should have bothered to keep this last receipt, along with all the other correspondence and mementoes.

Or perhaps it's not strange at all.

Twenty-Five

The walk along Station Road couldn't have taken more than fifteen minutes, but Bill was already drenched with sweat. The heavy suitcase he was carrying didn't help, but mostly it was the jacket, coat (and vest) which his mother had insisted on him wearing. Admittedly it had been pretty dull and chilly when he'd set off from Fountayne Street that morning, but by the time he'd travelled all the way across England the weather had changed dramatically, and the sun was now blazing down mercilessly. And the new shoes were killing his feet...

Tuesday September 3rd, 1940. Exactly one year since war had been declared. 18-year old William Parkinson was one of a long stream of young men coming from the train station and heading towards RAF Padgate, all carrying cases or rucksacks. Like them, he had received his call-up papers a week ago, in the final days of August, when the newspapers and wireless were full of the Battle of Britain being fought in the skies over southern England. He'd come home from his job at Townend's to find the house strangely quiet and a letter addressed to him sitting on the table. Knowing what it would be, he'd opened and read it quickly before noticing his mother standing in the kitchen doorway.

'I've to enlist next week. They've sent me a rail warrant to go to RAF Padgate, near Warrington.'

'Oh. That's not far from Liverpool. Your father preached there for a while.'

'I must tell George – where is he?'

'Out in the garden, watering the vegetables...'

'Playing with Raque more like!' Bill rushed past her towards the back door, calling for his brother. After a moment his mother picked up the letter and read it.

In the garden Raque lay disinterestedly in the early evening sun. 'When do you go?' asked George, putting down the watering can.

'The 3rd – Tuesday.'

'The RAF don't hang around, do they? So, you're going to learn to fly at last,' George said. 'Well, I'm delighted for you, really.'

'And you too, eh Raque – I bet you wish you were coming with me!' Bill knelt down to scratch the dog's ears.

'*I* do,' said George. 'Or rather I wish I was off to join the Navy as well – that's a *real* life for a chap, travelling, seeing the world; better than buzzing around in the sky hoping a wing doesn't drop off.'

'Sorry, George. You never know.'

'I think I'll stick to reporting about what you chaps get up to – much safer.' He thought for a moment. 'How'd Mother take it?'

'Seemed a bit down.'

'Yes. She knew what was in that letter as soon as the postman delivered it. Mother's bound to be a bit upset, but she'll get over it. You know she'd never stand in your way.'

'Yes. You know I sometimes think she'd like to have a go at Hitler herself.'

'Can you imagine that? One sight of her coming over the hill and Jerry'd turn and run! Anyway, I'll look after her, don't you worry.'

'Are you sure? I do feel a bit guilty leaving you alone.'

'Well don't. Just concentrate on what you Brylcreem boys are good at – bagging the girls!'

The next few days were a mad rush of sorting things out, handing in his notice at Townend's, saying goodbye to his friends at the AFS, writing letters to old school chums, and trying to work out what to pack. The night of September 2nd was a sleepless one for Bill, with a thousand thoughts whirring around in his brain. When he finally went downstairs to breakfast, there was a small brown paper package next to his plate. His mother came in from the kitchen, carrying the teapot.

'I thought you were never getting up, Billy,' she said. 'Your train leaves in less than an hour.'

'I'll be alright. What's this?'

'For you, a present. You can open it.'

He unwrapped the parcel, finding a copy of *A Pilgrim's Progress*. 'I know you've got your own copy but this was Father's, and he would have wanted you to have it.'

'Thanks, really.'

There was a pause. Gertrude turned away. 'Right, you better get that breakfast down you – it could be the last square meal you have for a long time. And I've made you some sandwiches and a flask of tea for the journey.'

George wasn't due into the office until the afternoon, as he was on nights, and had suggested they get a taxi to the station, but his mother insisted they walk, blaming the waste of petrol but secretly wanting as long with her boy as she could get.

Feeling a mixture of pride and sadness, Gertrude Parkinson locked the front door and joined her sons at the gate. With Raque running ahead they walked down Fountayne Street towards the river, Gertrude giving passing neighbours only the merest of nods as they wished Bill good luck. Bill himself showed no such reserve, waving and smiling broadly to anyone and everyone, and Gertrude was relieved when the family crossed the Hook Road to go up the river embankment and walk along the Ouse into town.

A silence hung over the group, and they looked out at the steamers and barges moving steadily along the river or tied up at the North and Victoria piers. Small 'coggie' boats moved steadily this way and that, their oars dipping silently in the brown water. Further upriver there were more masts and the cranes of the docks, and the sound of hooters, distant clanking and the shouts of men drifting over on the early morning breeze. Each had their private thoughts, and if there was any talking it was about Raque, who chased around George in circles some way behind.

When the embankment ran out, just where the river snaked round from the south side of the town, they crossed the road again, going up North Street, passing the Methodist Chapel where George and Bill's father had preached before they moved to Fountayne Street. They crossed the road near the Clock Tower and went up the Boothferry Road, past the *Goole Times* offices and finally reached the train station, just in time to see the Sheffield train pull up in a cloud of steam and squealing brakes.

'I'll get your case on the train,' said George, leaving Bill and his mother alone on the platform. She looked at her son, and smiled, showing her pride in him at last.

'Just take care of yourself, you hear me?'

'I will,' he said, and gave her a hug.

There was a shriek of a whistle, and the slamming of carriage doors, and George stepped off the train. 'Come on, you clot, or you'll miss it!'

Bill smiled and shook George's hand. 'Bye George.'

'Good luck Bill.'

'Thanks. I'll be back as soon as I can.' There was another whistle. Bill gave Raque a final scruff around the ears, got a lick in return and climbed onto the train. His mother stepped forward and held his hand for a moment. 'Don't forget to write.'

'I won't. Goodbye. Bye George! Bye Raque!'

The train pulled slowly out of the station, and through the clouds of steam George was sure he saw his mother wipe away a tear, the first time he had seen her get emotional in public since Margaret's funeral.

Bill felt a slight twinge of guilt as he found his carriage and settled onto the seat. Looking out of the window at the huge, white, water tower and the cranes at the docks, which soon gave way to warehouses and then the wide, flat expanse of farmland, he realised he was going to miss the place, but was glad he hadn't really let his mother see that. He hadn't said the things he'd wanted to either, the words he felt one was supposed to say on occasions like this. If anything, he was relieved to get away from all the hugs and the fuss, to be able at last to focus on what had been filling his thoughts all week – he was starting a new life, the life he'd been looking forward to since Hitler had kicked things off in Poland. Like many other lads of his age, he had signed up at the Employment Exchange to volunteer for the RAF as soon as he was 18. He'd been given a brief medical, sat some aptitude tests and told he would be considered for Pilot/Air Observer training when the RAF needed him; until then he should go home and get on with life. Now, almost before he could take it all in, he was heading off to join the Royal Air Force! He would write home tonight, once he'd settled in at Padgate, telling Mum and George all about the place and what he'd done and who he'd met, and making sure they knew he was thinking of them.

At each station stop he saw more men joining the train, following the now familiar ritual of farewell enacted with parents, wives and sometimes children, and soon the train was packed. At one station he noticed a young man getting a long kiss from a pretty girl who definitely was *not* his sister. Shame *he* didn't have a girl to write home to. But George was probably right – the RAF uniform and wings did seem to have an effect on girls, maybe it wouldn't be too long before he'd meet that someone special. He had noticed one or two of the office girls at Townend's who sported sweetheart brooches, gold RAF wings that indicated they were waiting for their boy to come home. That sounded rather fun.

Squeezed in the crowded carriage he tried to read his book, but the words weren't going in, he was just too excited. Then he came across an illustration that had thrilled and fascinated him when he first read *A Pilgrim's Progress* as a boy: Christian in the Valley of the Shadow of Death, armour clad, with a spear, and watching the hideous dragons, serpents and devils flying around in the flame- and smoke-filled sky. And the familiar words, '*Though I walk through the valley of the shadow of death, I will fear no evil, for Thou art with me.*'

As they approached Liverpool he noticed tell-tale signs of bomb damage, and a pall of smoke hanging in the air. The city had been recently bombed and would experience another fifteen raids during September.

By the time the train pulled into Padgate Station it was heaving with recruits, jamming the corridors. He managed to jostle his way through the crowd along the platform, looking for a sign to RAF Padgate but eventually just going along with the noisy, sweaty, smoking crowd, and followed them up Station Road on the short walk to the station entrance.

At first sight RAF Padgate was not particularly impressive – just a wire fence, and a couple of sentry boxes either side of a red and white barrier pole, beyond which there was a collection of buildings and huts. He stood in the long queue for what seemed an age, waiting to show his papers and identity card to the guards, and then followed the rest of the recruits as they formed up in ranks before entering the camp. As he marched between the low huts and buildings, past parade grounds and assault courses, he stole sideways glances at the squads of young men in blue uniforms with packs and steel helmets, feeling proud to know that he was at last on the road to becoming one of them – the boys in blue.

One thing puzzled him, however. Where on earth were they hiding the aeroplanes?

RAF Padgate, Bill soon discovered, was less an aerodrome and more of a reception centre for new recruits and volunteers from all over the country. There were no aeroplanes, and this was only the first stage in his new career in the RAF. The making of a pilot, even in the early days of the war, was a long and complicated business, starting with enlistment and four brutal weeks of basic training. At Padgate he and thousands of other recruits would have their first contact with the RAF. He was be allocated an iron bed in a hut with at least twenty other men, given a severe haircut, and issued with a basic kit including bedding, mess kit, steel helmet, greatcoat, gas mask, holdalls, domestic kit, several brushes (boot blacking and polishing, brass, clothes, hair and shaving, for the use of) and a PT kit. He also signed for his 'best blues' service uniform: jacket, trousers, cap, white insert to denote Under Training, shirts, tie, boots, socks, vest and pants, all to be marked with his service number. He was also told in no uncertain terms that it was his responsibility to keep each item spotlessly clean and to be laid out for the daily inspections. Then it was off at the double to the sick bay for medical checks (eyes, ears, teeth and private parts – 'strip, cough and bend over'), inoculations against diphtheria, typhoid and smallpox, basic physical examination - height six foot one and a bit, chest thirty inches, weight ten stone dead. Unsurprisingly, given his prowess at all things sporty, Bill was passed 'Fit Aircrew A1'.

It seemed like hours before he was fed and when he was sent to the mess there was more queuing before getting a plateful of something 'hot and filling' that reminded him of the worst days at Ashville. But Padgate was less like a boys' boarding school and more like a borstal, with the constant orders, shouting, marching, and the ever-present smell of boiled cabbage and testosterone. Wolfing down their food for fear of being late for whatever their corporal had in store for them in the afternoon, Bill and the others swapped horror stories about RAF Basic Training, the dreadful punishments corporals could inflict on their victims, the fleas, lice and VD, and about lads being killed in accidents and how it was all covered up because Churchill didn't want to lower morale. Bill looked wide-eyed at the others, wondering just what he had got himself into, but sure that he could take it. 'Just like Ashville,' he said, and the tension was relieved. Almost.

If only it *was* like Ashville. As each day dawned the reality became worse. Over the next four weeks Aircraftman Second Class WW Parkinson, service number 1067083, and 'the lowest form of bleeding life on God's earth,' according to his corporal, would face a daily routine of early rising, inspections, fatigues, hard physical exercise, even tougher than anything ever devised by the worst games master at Ashville, training drills and more inspections. He was always being sent *here*, told to go *there*, always at the double, always in the wrong place, always late, always being yelled at. No, Bill thought, next to RAF Padgate, Ashville College was a holiday camp. If he or any of the other recruits had any thoughts that volunteering for the RAF was an act of heroism, or in any way romantic, their experience of Padgate would certainly disabuse them of that. In fact, their corporal seemed to be doing everything in his power to make the RAF, and their place in it, as unpleasant as possible.

And he still hadn't come close to an aeroplane. He thought he saw one, once - an Avro Anson, which he recognised from a photograph he'd cut out of a newspaper and pasted into his scrapbook. Hearing the engines he had looked up eagerly before the aircraft disappeared in some clouds, and his corporal yelled into his ear at him for not paying attention to whatever he was supposed to be doing. But eventually, after a month of marching, running, polishing and being shouted at, all for the princely sum of 3 shillings a day (plus 6d war pay) Bill was 'mobilised', which meant he had passed Basic Training, was now Leading Aircraftman Parkinson, and was able to enjoy a couple of weeks' leave before reporting to his next posting – RAF Torquay.

'Oh, Torquay is lovely. Palm trees, lovely beaches and hotels.'

Mum is telling me about her honeymoon, which she and my dad spent in Torquay in the late fifties. Terrified of being seen by crowds of shoppers she insisted on getting married early in the morning, on a weekday rather than the usual Saturday, and walked down the steps of Carlisle Terrace Methodist Church with barely an eye being turned in the street.

Shortly after the wedding reception they left the church hall and caught the train for the southwest. Dad had done his two years National Service in the RAF on air-sea rescue launches stationed at Fowey in Cornwall and remembered the lovely seaside resorts all around the area; Mum found an advert for a hotel in the *Methodist Recorder*, and remembers the journey took 'hours and hours'. The newlyweds had forgotten to take the sandwiches her mother had packed for the journey, but when they arrived at the hotel, very late, very tired and very hungry, the owner (in very un-Basil Fawlty fashion) cooked them a wedding breakfast. He also offered to drive them over to Plymouth to see the reconstruction of the Pilgrim's ship *Mayflower*, which was in the harbour, and the weather was lovely (even in March) so everything turned out well.

My parents' wedding, Goole, March 28, 1957 (Bean family)

RAF Torquay, which LAC WW Parkinson was posted to in mid-October 1940, was a very different affair. For a start, the resort had been shut since the declaration of war, barrage ballons hung over the town, barbed wire was stretched across the beaches, and machine gun nests, pillboxes and large coastal guns lay in wait for any potential German invasion force. Secondly, it was even less of an RAF station than Padgate had been. The RAF had simply taken advantage of the numerous empty hotels in the town and made it the centre for Initial Training of aircrew: thousands of pilots, observers, wireless operators and air gunners would pass through their doors during the war.

After a similar lengthy rail journey as the one my mum and dad took 17 years later, Bill and the other recruits were picked up in a truck at the station, driven to their hotel and told to sort out their beds. They were given a meal, told to report for lectures in the morning and had the evening to themselves. So this is where we finally learn about flying, Bill thought, at last I'll have something to write home about. But in the event, Initial Training was all theory – days filled with lessons, lectures and demonstrations, book reading, homework, exercises. This was where Bill and his fellow u/t pilots learned about the principles of flight - lift, velocity, control surfaces, airframes, engines; there was also aircraft recognition (friendly and enemy), meteorology, navigation, weapons training; it went on and on. There were talks and slide shows by instructors on the most intricate and arcane details about aircraft handling, and more interestingly, some films about the bombers in current service with the RAF – the Hampden, Blenheim, Whitley and Wellington – and hushed talk about the new bigger and faster bombers that were coming down the line: the Stirling, the Halifax and the Manchester.

Reveille was at 0630 with breakfast at 0700. Then first parade at 0730, followed by training (with a half hour break for tea and a smoke) and dinner at 1245. 45 minutes later it was second parade of the day, with more training or exercise continuing until 1800. Tea was at 1815 and lights out at 2230 hours.[21]

This schedule was less punishing that that at Padgate, but still didn't leave much time for relaxation. Any free time they did have would be taken up with reading, listening to the wireless and exploring Torquay's pubs (although the strict Methodist William Parkinson probably wouldn't have strayed into those dens of iniquity). Bill still found the time to write letters home, and to read those from George, his mother and school friends.

---

[21] Details from website *Aircraft Q Failed to Return* (see Bibliography)

Gertrude was interested in his health, if he was eating enough, and whether he was able to get to chapel (there was a church parade every Sunday morning). She asked how he was getting on with *A Pilgrim's Progress*, but to his shame Bill hadn't had a chance to get any further than the first chapter – his head always seemed to be reeling from the day's lessons or full of preparation for tomorrow's class.

George asked if he'd been in a plane yet? Bill replied that he still hadn't seen any and reminded George not to call them *planes* – he'd already been bawled out by a fearsome instructor who shouted at him, 'It's not a plane. It's an *aero*plane or an aircraft!' But he was doing what he wanted and if he was honest he wasn't really missing home. The flying would come later, in the form of ten weeks of Elementary Flying School, but only if he passed his exams at Torquay and that meant keeping his head down and cramming.

On 30 October Bill celebrated his 19th birthday with fish and chips sitting on the sea front, in the cold biting wind. November brought the dreadful news in the papers of the Coventry Blitz on the 14th, and a week later more of the same in Birmingham. George wrote to Bill about the recent War Weapons Week, in which Goole had raised three times its initial target of £50,000, and the hoo-hah that followed when it was revealed in the *Goole Times* that the Borough Council was found not to have donated 'a single penny' to the fund. The Treasurer Mr EW Dulson explained that the Council was overdrawn at the bank at the moment. George said his mother was 'hopping mad.' Bill laughed at the thought, knowing exactly how Gertrude would have reacted.

There were no Remembrance Day commemorations in Goole that Armistice Day. No parade, no flags, no two-minute silence, just a wreath laid at the cenotaph. Later that same day a German aircraft machine-gunned a bus and train before bombing several farm buildings just outside the town. No-one was hurt. More dramatically, in the early hours of 16 November a Handley Page Hampden of 50 Squadron flying from RAF Lindolme crashed in flames in Dunhill Road on the west side of the town, near to the Boothferry Road School. No civilians were injured but three of the crew were killed, the fourth being rescued by Dunhill Road resident and part-time fireman Edwin Richardson and PC Alfred Dunn, who risked the flames and exploding ammunition to pull the flyer clear.

Evidently Bill did keep his head down while he was at Torquay because he passed out of No 7 Intensive Training Wing around Christmas 1940. Possibly while he was at home in Goole he received the news that he was to be posted to RAF Sealand to begin Elementary Training. The New Year was celebrated soberly at Fountayne Street. 1941 was to be a momentous year for William Parkinson.

Twenty-Six

'Some of the brighter ones among you may have noticed that the RAF has not let you anywhere near one of its aeroplanes yet. That is because his Majesty's aircraft are very expensive and he would be upset if you broke one. Today, however, all that changes. From now on you lucky people will live, eat, breathe and dream aeroplanes, beginning with this little beauty - the de Havilland Tiger Moth.' The flying instructor indicated the aircraft behind him and a couple of dozen u/t pilots looked in fascination at the flimsy biplane.

In the 1930s it was decided that civilian-run flying schools would be responsible for basic training and the RAF would cover the more advanced training of pilots. There were 20 Elementary Flying Training Schools (EFTS) at the outbreak of war and the one to which Bill had been posted, RAF Sealand near Queensferry, Flintshire, was taken over by the military in 1916. RCFS Shotwick, as it was then known, became a centre for training by the newly formed Royal Flying Corps, flying Sopwith Camels and SE5as, which were reported as 'falling out of the sky', there were so many accidents. At least 17 aircraft were lost and 8 pilots killed in the first 6 months of its operation. In 1924 it changed its name to RAF Scaland to avoid confusion with RAF Scopwith in Lincolnshire (now RAF Digby) as too many letters (and pilots) were being sent there by mistake.

19EFTS, to which both William Parkinson and Robson Newton were posted in February 1941, was only transferred to RAF Sealand at the end of January 1941, so they and their fellow cadets would have been part of the first or early intake.[22] Bill and Robson may have met before – they were both at RAF Padgate and RAF Torquay at the same time, but it isn't known whether they knew each other then, other than perhaps by sight. Sometime during their training at Sealand, or later at Brize Norton they would come to spend more time with each other, possibly because of their shared Methodist background, or more likely, simply because they got on well. Robson Newton, from Gateshead in the northeast, was 7 years older than Bill, and had probably seen a bit more of the world, so perhaps there was something of a reassuring big brother figure about the handsome Geordie. However, it is equally possible that their flight on Oxford T1334 on 12 June 1941 was the first time they met. We just don't know.

As the flying instructor had promised on that first day, Bill's world now revolved around flying. Each of the cadets were soon taken up in a Tiger Moth by an instructor to give them a sense of being in the air, experiencing climbs, dives, banking, loops, stalls and spins. Those who were sick were told to get straight back up again until they felt better. If they didn't get over their airsickness (and many didn't) they were quickly posted elsewhere, to train for another RAF trade. Some hid their airsickness, desperate to get their wings. Those who took to flying without any side-effects now began to put the theory they had learned at RAF Torquay into practice, partly in a Link Trainer (a simple mechanically-operated wooden cockpit that simulated flight at its most basic level, resembling the ride you'd find at a funfair or parked outside a supermarket), and gradually clocking up more hours in the dual control Tiger Moth until they could be trusted to start up, take off, do a circuit and bump before landing with the instructor merely observing. After that they were entrusted to fly the aircraft solo, which could be both exhilarating and terrifying.

I can imagine the excitement with which Bill must have written home about his first solo flight, even though I am sure he will have tried to maintain a certain insouciance about it.

---

[22] RAF Sealand continued in RAF service until 2006 when it was closed and sold off. It is now known as MOD Sealand.

In addition to learning how to fly, the cadets were also beginning to adopt the RAF's affected coolness about their extremely dangerous jobs, something that would serve them well on operations. In return his mother may have told him about the situation at home, which can't have been easy with Goole being an important inland port. German bombs fell ever closer to Goole at the end of February and the government distributed leaflets informing the population of what to do in the event of a German invasion. People were told that if an invasion occurred and the fighting was some distance away, they should carry on as normal, going to work, shopping and attending school, leaving the roads free for troop movements. Should the fighting draw close to home they were instructed to stay indoors or in their shelters, putting all cars, lorries and motorbikes out of action when told to by the police. If they or their families and homes were at risk from enemy soldiers, they had the right to do 'what was necessary' to protect them. With all this tension and fear in the air, knowing that Bill was closer to getting his wings may have brought some comfort and hope to the Parkinson family.

Once they had completed a successful solo flight though, Bill and the other cadets were expected to improve their skills, logging dozens of hours on the trainer. Finally, after 10 weeks of intensive flying, and after sitting and passing more exams Bill was posted to No 2 Service Flying Training School, stationed at RAF Brize Norton, in Oxfordshire.

Bill may have been lucky enough to snatch a week or two of leave before his final posting because he didn't arrive at Brize Norton until 19 April. If he did get to spend some precious time at home he may have gone with George to watch *Flight Angels* with Ralph Bellamy, Virginia Bruce and Jane Wyman at the Cinema Palace on the corner of Boothferry Road. Bill would be able to watch this Hollywood drama about commercial airline pilots and air stewardesses from a new perspective now that he could fly himself.

What is almost certain is that this period of leave would have been the last time that Gertrude Parkinson saw her son alive.

RAF Brize Norton was a brand-spanking new aerodrome built, like Syerston, during the late 1930s. The station officially opened on 13 August 1937 and is now the largest RAF Station in the UK, home to the RAF's Strategic and Tactical Air Transport and Air-to-Air Refuelling capabilities. Then it was full of cadets learning to fly.

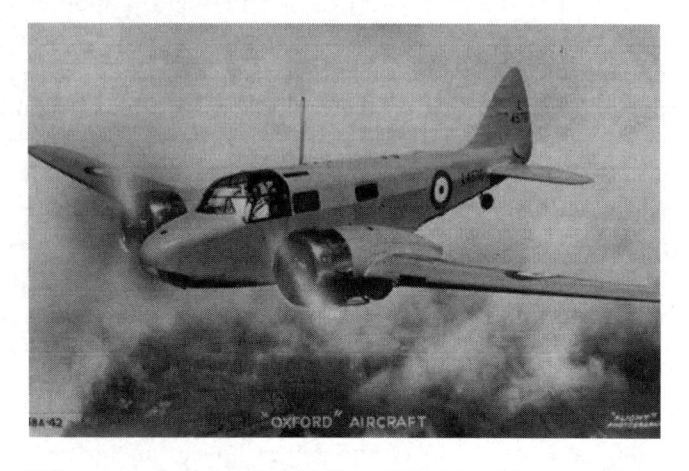

Bill's postcard of the Oxford from RAF Brize Norton 1941 – the type of aircraft he was flying on 12 June 1941 (Fiona Reid)

Among the possessions that Fiona showed me when researching this book was a postcard, a black and white photo of an Airspeed Oxford 11, from Brize Norton. This was the aircraft which Bill and his fellow u/t pilots were training on in order to learn how to handle a large two- or possibly four-engine bomber. The twin engines and retractable undercarriage took some getting used to, but the relative simplicity of the Ox-box, together with its greater speed and ceiling meant they were getting much closer to flying the real thing. They would clock up many hours over their twelve-week course, and any non-flying time was filled with more classes, lectures, and drills. At the time of his death on 12 June 1941, when Bill would have been only a few weeks away from completing his flight training, he had logged a total of 54 solo flying hours, including 26½ on the Oxford 11. If they had not crashed over Elton, they could have expected to pass out of 2SFTS with their wings around the end of June, ready to join Bomber Command.

Twenty-Seven

After the success of their attack on the Boulogne docks on the night of 17/18 May, there would be 10 days of heel-kicking frustration before Flight Lieutenant Tadeusz Stefanicki and the crew of R1017 made their second operational flight. For 305 Squadron's eleventh operation of the war, the target was again Boulogne, but this time Aleksander Zirkwitz took his place in the rear turret. This was Stefanicki's crew as he wanted it, and they would stick together until the sunny morning just over two weeks later, when they would be involved in the mid-air collision with my uncle George's brother Bill in Oxford T1334.

Part of a much bigger operation involving aircraft from other stations across the group, the three aircraft from 305 Squadron took off into clear dark skies between 2240 and 2245, arriving over the French coast to find, as happened so often, haze and fog obscuring the target. Nevertheless, all three made their bombing runs at between 15,000 and 17,400 feet, each seeing their six 500lb bombs and two SBCs (small bomb containers) burst on the western side of the dock. A large fire was reported as they left the target, and all returned safely, with Stefanicki touching R1017 down at 0300.

Two nights later, on 30 May, the crew celebrated the 28th birthday of their front gunner, Stanisław Kowalcze. Born in Łętownia, Poland in 1913, Pilot Officer Kowalcze was a handsome man, with strong features and piercing eyes. His birthday was another opportunity for the crew to bond, to build close relationships in the good times which would be tested during the bad. There was some sadness to mar the celebrations, as the crews remembered the crews of the two

Wellingtons that had so far failed to return from operations: R1214 SM-N, captained by Pilot Officer Jozef Nogal, which had been listed as Failed To Return following the raid on Emden on the night of 2/3 May, and R1322 SM-F, piloted by Sergeant Jan Dorman, last seen during the operation against Bremen on 8/9 May. Nothing had been heard of either aircraft or crew since the operations, and toasts and silent prayers were offered in the hope that they had escaped their stricken aircraft and would soon return, possibly rescued by the resistance in occupied Holland. But as the return flights from the targets were largely over the hostile environment of the North Sea, the possibility of this happening for either aircraft seemed slim.

June opened with Stefanicki's crew taking part in a raid on Duisburg on the 2nd, along with six other aircraft from the squadron. This time, the industrial haze in the Ruhr obscured large areas of the target and after 'stooging around' for some time, none of the crews was able to positively identify it. This, together with poor weather encountered on the return, ended up with Stefanicki becoming lost, and short of fuel he was forced to make an emergency landing at Horsham, St Faith, (now Norwich Airport), before refuelling and returning to Syerston early the following morning.

Coincidentally, another Wellington, R1696, flown by the 'B' Flight Commander Squadron Leader Ścibior, encountered similar difficulties, being forced to land and refuel at RAF Debden, a fighter station near Saffron Walden. Although nobody could be aware of the significance at the time, Ścibior's aircraft would be the one flying in close formation with R1017 on the training flight over Elton on 12 June, narrowly avoiding disaster itself.

On 3 June there were no operations flown from Syerston, but news was finally received concerning Flying Officer Nogal and the crew of Wellington SM-N. The aircraft had been shot down by a night fighter over Budel, Holland, and the German authorities confirmed that four of the crew (pilot Józef Nogal, observer Aleksander Jastrzębski, second pilot Tomasz Kasprzyk and radio operator Tadeusz Żuk) were safe, held as POWs in a German stalag. However, the other two crew members, (Wacław Malak and Ryszkiewicz Mieczysław) were confirmed as dead. Although there was relief that four of the crew were safe, if captured, the loss of the navigator and rear gunner were the first confirmed deaths for the squadron to deal with, and came as a huge shock to the crews, Stefanicki's included. What the crews didn't know, was that the other missing aircraft, R1322, captained by Sgt Dorman, which failed to return on the night 8/9 May had also been shot down, with the loss of all on board; news of this loss would not arrive at the squadron until much later; after, in fact, the deaths of Tadeusz Stefanicki and his crew.

The next day was overcast and cloudy, reflecting the dour mood around the airfield, and drizzle in the afternoon kept the aircraft on the ground. There was, in the words of the Squadron Operational Log, 'Nothing to report'. The next few days were similar – fog, drizzle, rain and more fog. Newspapers were read, cigarettes smoked, stories swapped, memories of home rekindled and shared. It was a miserable weekend all round.

The mood was probably lightened somewhat on Monday with the celebration of Jerzy Krawczyk's 24th birthday. The wireless operator/gunner was a popular member of Stefanicki's crew and faced with a choice of celebrating in the mess, in Newark or Nottingham, may well have opted for the latter. The clear-up following a devastating raid on the city a month earlier was well under way, and the crew may well have wanted to revisit some old haunts. Celebrations over, Wednesday 11 June also gave the crews something to focus their minds on as Syerston was honoured with a second visit within months by Air Marshal Sir Richard Peirse, head of Bomber Command.

The Air Marshal's visit coincided with a change of thinking within Bomber Command. The relative ineffectiveness of small-scale, supposedly 'precision' attacks on military and industrial targets was by now clear to all. Flying aircraft with limited range and bombloads, using unsophisticated bombsights and basic navigational aids, in difficult weather conditions and up against an impressive German air-defence system, their results were not good, to say the least. Peirse's crews were also hamstrung by a policy that still strove to avoid unnecessary civilian casualties. But attitudes had hardened within Churchill's cabinet and in the country; new aircraft such as the Lancaster, with longer range and bigger bombloads were in development, as were more advanced navigational aids, which would allow the RAF to strike at new targets, deeper into Germany, and with a new ferocity. Instead of being limited to military and industrial targets such as docks, railway yards and weapons factories (which it was impossible to hit with any accuracy anyway), Bomber Command would soon be given a freer rein to strike hard, and repeatedly, at larger urban areas. Having seen Warsaw attacked mercilessly in the early days of Hitler's invasion and witnessing the deliberate policy of terrorising and targeting civilians by the Luftwaffe, the crews of 305 Squadron would have had few qualms about giving German civilians a taste of their own medicine.

However, this change of policy was still some months down the line. It would require the new Lancaster, and a new head of Bomber Command to carry the policy through. Sir Arthur 'Bomber' Harris would not replace Peirse until early 1942, but his commitment and determination to make the Germans 'reap the whirlwind' would transform the air war. It would also, inevitably, call on the crews to make a greater sacrifice, flying more dangerous sorties at higher risk, and it was possibly with this in mind that a morale-boosting visit by the soon to be ex-head of Bomber Command was planned. With their desire to get back at the Germans being so deep and heartfelt, it was probably an escalation in fighting that the men in Tadeusz Stefanicki's crew would have wanted to be part of. Unfortunately, they would not be seeing those changes. The bright, sunny day that dawned the next morning was Thursday June 12th.

Twenty-Eight

Even before I am properly awake I sense that there is something very different about this morning. Instead of the usual noisy traffic, footsteps and voices, the world outside is quiet and still, as if everybody has forgotten to get up, sleeping under some magic spell.

I peer through the blinds and see that Newark is covered in a thick, almost impenetrable mist. Even though it is still summer, when I open the door I am met by cold air, and the street is suffused in an eerie half-light which gives a surreal sheen to everything. There are cars and people outside, but any sounds they make are muffled. Visibility has reduced to a couple of hundred feet and I can't even see the buildings at the end of the street.

Driving through the town, and out onto the Fosse, I head south, noticing again the strange half-light caused by the mist. Cars and lorries have their headlights on, but it doesn't seem to be slowing them down. This, I know, is not haze, but mist, probably rolled in from the Trent, but it makes me think about the conditions that were reported in 305 Squadron's Operational Log on the morning of 12 June 1941, and what Megan Bowden described to me. Getting more of a sense of what it would be like to fly in anything approaching these conditions, I see that even driving at 70mph, three times slower than the Wellington would have been cruising, electricity pylons and even trees emerge quickly out of nowhere. No wonder the pilots didn't have time to take avoiding action when they each saw the other aircraft hurtling towards them – if they even did.

Back to the present. I park the car in Elton, just around the corner from the small medieval parish church of St Michael and All Angels. The mist has burned off now, leaving a crushingly beautiful late summer morning, and I'm getting on with things. The anxieties of recent days are forgotten again, pushed once more to the back of my brain, for another day, when I've sorted this out. Determined not to fail in my mission to find out what happened to William Parkinson, I decided last night to do another mail drop. I've got a handful of leaflets appealing for information about the collision, which I ran off last night, and as there are only a couple of dozen houses in the village I shouldn't be too long. I'm not expecting that a leaflet will be picked up by someone who actually knows anything about the accident, let alone remembers it personally, but they might know someone who mentions it to someone else who might know someone...

A handful of people are up and about in the village: the postie of course, in his red Postman Pat van, always keeping just ahead of me; a dad driving his daughters to a riding school, all kitted out in jodhpurs and boots, and at one house a woman who it turns out is an historian and is fascinated by my story. She's relatively new to the area (the story of these villages it seems) so doesn't know anything herself but wishes me luck, suggesting the people at the farm behind the old pub might be able to help.

Back in the car I head across the A52 to leaflet the houses and flats that were converted from the old Manor Arms pub and the farm behind it. The farm doesn't appear to have a letter box, so I head for the nearest building to it – an old white house, early 20th century, which doesn't have a letter box either. I look all round, without success. They've not even got one of those black metal boxes with a post-horn on it that everyone seems to have these days. I'm about to give up and move on when I rethink – I fold the leaflet in half then in half again and jam it into the narrow gap in the doorway above the handle, before carrying on. I walk down the road towards Orston until the houses run out, leaving me with plenty of leaflets left over, then head back towards the car, passing the old white house again. Hurrying past, I glance down the path and see a woman standing at the open door, looking intensely at the leaflet that I stuck in her door. She is probably my age, wearing jeans, riding boots and a scruffy old polo top, and looks every bit a farmer straight out of Central Casting.

I could pass on, but don't. Instead, I go back to the gate and call, just as she's heading inside, apologising for leaving the leaflet in the door jamb but I couldn't find a letter box. But she's not annoyed. Angela Copley, who lives at the farm, asks me a bit more about the crashed aircraft and I tell her what I know. 'You should have been here six months ago,' she tells me. Her father died recently, and he and his friend (also recently gone) lived here all their lives, knew everything and everybody about the place and would have talked to me until the cows came home about the crash, and much more besides.

'If anyone knew anything about it, they would,' she says. 'Sorry.'

She's about to close the door, but obviously senses my disappointment, and hangs on, racking her brain. There are some older folk up the road in Orston – have I tried Brian Gunn? I tell Angela about my meeting with Brian, and how I thought I was onto something until we realised we were talking about different crashes. 'You could try Sutton,' she says, gesturing in the other direction. 'Just past Elton. You never know, there might be someone down there who can help. Good luck.'

Sutton (or Sutton-cum-Granby, to give it its full title today) is even smaller than Elton, with a population of only around 60, so it doesn't take me long to cover the few old red brick houses that used to be farmworker's cottages, now mostly occupied by Marketing and IT workers who work from home or commute each day to Nottingham, Grantham and London. But by now, job done, I'm starting to feel that familiar sense of anticlimax returning. Has any of this been worth it?

Unsure what to do now, I head home. Half an hour later, I've barely closed the front door behind me when my mobile rings. I look at the number and it's one I don't recognise. My instinct is to let it go to answerphone when something tells me to pick up. I hit the green button and speak: 'Hello?'

The voice at the other end answers breathlessly: 'Hello is that Adrian? My name is Robert Brown, from Sutton-cum-Granby. I know where your Wellington bomber crashed.'

Twenty-Nine

It must a local thing. Or it could be country folk in general. Just like Brian Gunn, Robert didn't give me an address, more a rough idea of where he lived, simply describing 'The house with the Virginia creeper,' adding 'You'll soon find it.'

He was right. I pull into the narrow drive next to the cottage which is covered in Virginia creeper, walk round the back and ring the bell, remembering what I'd noticed when I delivered the leaflet here only an hour or so before: a garden full of neat rows of tomatoes and runner beans, chickens in a wire-covered run to one side, and beyond the small orchard a perfect view of Belvoir Castle. I am reminded of the dozens, possibly hundreds of watercolours my dad had done of that castle. Mum used to say he couldn't drive past the place without stopping to do a quick sketch or take a photograph. 'Every time I look at it, it's different,' he'd say, 'The light, the sky, clouds, the fields, always different.'

No answer. A pigeon calls from high up on a roof, and from down the road I can hear a lawnmower start up. I ring the bell again, put my nose to the grimy, cobwebbed window and peer into the porch full of the detritus of a long life lived in the country – tools, plant pots, an old waterproof hanging on a nail. Still no answer. But I can hear the sound of a radio coming from further inside, so I knock on the window.

'Alright!' comes the reply. The radio is silenced, I hear someone moving around and eventually the door opens. I'm greeted by a round, ruddy face, white hair and fuzzy chops, and bright blue eyes. I put out my hand and smile, 'Robert? It's Adrian.'

Inside, I'm surprised at how tiny the cottage is. It's like the Tardis in reverse. As I perch on the edge of a sofa, fighting for space with the coats and newspapers piled on it, Robert leans back comfortably in his armchair and informs me that his family have lived in this house and the one next to it for generations. He tells me when it was built (he has the original deeds, on vellum no less), about the thickness of the walls, and the unique *Blue Lias* rock that was used in its construction. He has lived in Sutton-cum-Granby for longer than anyone else and is the proud author of a small book about the village, full of stories about its history and characters. He remembers the war very well, and the bombers flying out of nearby Langar airfield for Germany: 'We had double summertime then so it was light until about eleven o'clock at night, and I can remember seeing and hearing 'em like a swarm of bees, going round and round as they gathered for the raids, then all of a sudden they'd be gone, and it would be quiet again.'

Then he's off telling me about the time when he was helping with the haymaking and they saw a fighter plane make a forced landing at a spot called Jericho Covert. His uncle told them to take their pitchforks, in case he was 'a bleddy Jerry', but when they got closer they could see the roundels on the fuselage, and it was a Spitfire. The pilot was still inside the cockpit, calling for help; his legs were gone, and he couldn't get out. 'Anyway, we got him onto a cart and my mum put her coat on him because he was shivering, even in the heat of the summer, and the RAF boys arrived in a truck and put him on a stretcher and drove off, with my mum's coat still over the pilot.' A few days later the same truck turned up and an NCO handed his mum her coat. The pilot had wanted to make sure she got it back. Robert never knew if he survived.

I bring Robert round to the reason for my visit, and he is immediately on the defensive: 'What's your angle on this Wellington crash then?' he asks. 'Why do you want to know what I saw?'

I tell him about my uncle's brother Bill, explain that I have done some research into the accident, that I think both aircraft crashed in this area but am trying to pinpoint exactly where. I'm being a bit cagey, because I don't want to lead him at all in my questioning – we are talking about something that happened a long time ago, when he was only 9 years old, and if his memory is weak he could very easily tell me what he thinks I want to hear. I have a long list of questions designed to jog his memory and help paint a picture for me of what happened, but I needn't have bothered because this isn't like an interview – Robert's soon asking *me* all the questions, and before I know it, he's describing the Saturday morning in June 1941 when he and his pal went to the Wellington crash site, and –

'Hang on a moment please, Robert,' I say. I take out my mobile and ask if he minds me recording the conversation.

'What do you want to record me for? Is this for a programme?' He eyes me suspiciously. I explain that I want to be able to get all the details, and it's easy to forget things, and ask him to start again at the beginning. But before he does, he insists on calling his friend Mike Fox, who he has known since they were at infant school together, so that Mike can 'back him up'. Mike is the pal who was with Robert on the day they went to see the crash site. Robert puts the phone on loudspeaker and we have a curious three-way conversation as he tells Mike all about me, and the two friends go back in time to a hot summer's day during the war when they went treasure-hunting.

Normally, on a Saturday in summer the boys would have been bird-nesting or catching bullies in the stream, but that morning they decided to go to Barnes' Field in Elton, to see if they could find some bullets. The Wellington had come down in the field a couple of days before, Robert said, and everyone in the village had been talking about it, but no-one could get near because there was a heavy guard posted round the clock while the wreckage was cleared away. Anyway, the soldiers had gone now, and they could go into the field and look for ammunition. So off the boys went, on their bikes, cycling through Elton and sneaking into Barnes' Field, where they saw the blackened patch of ground where the Wellington had burned. Mike said he thought it had hit a tree just before it crashed, but Robert wasn't sure. The 'carcass' had been removed, and the field appeared to have been cleared of any pieces of wreckage, but the boys were determined to find their treasure, and searched the scorched earth with care. Eventually, with their backs aching from bending over and scouring the field in the heat of the midday sun, they found some small bits and pieces of aluminium, and a handful of bullets, which had somehow been missed by the recovery operation. And he found a St Christopher as well…

I almost have to catch my breath, Robert has mentioned this so casually. 'You found a St Christopher's medallion?'

'Yes,' Robert says, 'It was lying there in the grass. I saw it glinting in the sun and picked it up.'

'It must have belonged to a member of the crew,' I say. What I'm really thinking is *does he still have it?* and *will he let me see it?*

Robert looks a bit shamefaced. He doesn't know what happened to the St Christopher. Maybe he lost it, or gave it away, or swapped it for something that was of far more interest to a 9-year old boy; whatever happened to it, he never realised the significance of what he had found until he was older, and although he has searched high and low for it, it has definitely gone. Both Robert and Mike go quiet, thinking back to that innocent summer's day, and eventually Mike makes his apologies, saying he has to go. Before he hangs up, Robert tells him that I have promised to buy them both a meal at a restaurant of their choice for being so helpful with this book I'm writing. I haven't, it's the first I've heard about it, but I can't help admiring his cheek, and have to agree. While Robert and Mike say their goodbyes, I choose this moment to get my OS map out and ask Robert to show me where this Barnes' Field is. I tell him about my recent visit to the Becks Plantation, which is where I think one of the aircraft crashed – could that be it? Robert has never heard of the Becks Plantation, or Beckswood, but he knows where both the

Wellington and the Oxford came down. In fact, he says, he can show me to within 50 feet of where the Wellington crashed, because he stood on the exact spot as a boy, and he also knows roughly where the Oxford came down - that's got to be worth a free dinner, hasn't it?

I can hardly believe it. The spot that Robert is pointing to is close to the edge of a field that runs alongside the A52, a couple of hundred yards west of Elton. More precisely, it is no more than 50 feet from the road which I have travelled up and down, on my bike and later in a car, hundreds of times. I have driven within stone-throwing distance of it four times today! Even though there is nothing to indicate that a bomber ever crashed here, I can't help experiencing the same thrill of excitement that those two boys must have felt when they had leant their bikes up against the gate post and peered into Barnes' Field all those years ago.

That gate is open today, and we take a few steps into the perimeter of the field, which is covered with rough stubble – it looks as though the wheat has been recently harvested – so the earth is clearly visible. From where I am standing, there doesn't appear to be any sort of dip or hollow that might suggest the presence of a crater where an aircraft once crashed - I had imagined that a large, two-engine bomber like a Wellington would make some sort of an impression on the ground. But the reports of the collision describe 'the Oxford striking the Wellington at the Astro-dome carrying away its tail unit'. Without its tail section the Wellington turns from something that can fly through the air like a bird, into nothing more than an enormous lump of un-aerodynamic metal and fabric. Rather than diving into the ground at full speed, as I had imagined, the Wellington may simply have gone into a flat spin, fallen like a stone and effectively 'pancaked' onto the field.

Robert is nervous about going too far into the field; he doesn't know who owns this land now, and the innate schoolboy fear of the angry farmer (coupled with a proper respect for the countryside) means he isn't taking any risks. Much as I want to walk the couple of hundred yards along the edge of the field and actually stand on the crash site, I respect Robert's caution. It shouldn't be difficult to find out who owns the land and contact them for permission to come back.

'What do you want to come back for?' says Robert. 'You know where the Welly landed now, don't you?' I don't realise it at the time, but there's something in what the old boy is saying.

Robert Brown in Barnes' Field, the village of Elton behind him. Wellington R1017 crashed 20 yards from the road on the left, just before the incline. Becks Plantation, where the Oxford crashed, lies beyond the trees to the right (Author)

I stand there and look up into the bright blue sky, with its *Simpsons*-style puffy white clouds, then down to the wide yellow-and-brown expanse of stubble stretching before me. The sky would probably have looked like this on the morning of the accident. Taking a moment, I close my eyes and say a short prayer in my head for the men who died here. Suddenly it all seems very close. After all this time, wandering down so many blind alleys, I have found it - this is what I have been searching for. At least, this is where the *Wellington* crashed, I can be fairly certain, if Robert's memory is to be trusted, which I am sure it is. I could, if I wanted, just stand here for a few minutes, happy to share a unique moment with an old man who last stood here over 80 years ago, holding a silver St Christopher and some bullets in his grubby little hands, and move on. As Robert says, his blue eyes twinkling, *I know where the Welly landed now*. All I have to do now is to see where the Oxford crashed, and my journey is over.

I thank Robert for bringing me here, and ask if he would mind if I take his photo with the crash site behind him. 'For the book?' he asks, cheekily. 'Maybe, but for me too,' I reply.

Photos taken, we drive back into Elton and turn up the Redmile road, following the route I took all those weeks ago when I was first trying to locate 'Beckswood'. He points to his left, telling me that beyond the tall hedge is where the Oxford came down. 'That's on Gillian's land,' I say, 'That's the Becks Plantation, where I was recently.' Robert says they never knew it by that name, it was always 'the Gildings' to him and Mike; but whatever it's called, that's definitely where the Oxford crashed. I make a mental note to talk to Gillian again, and contact her metal detectorist, Tony; then seeing that Robert is looking tired, I turn the car round and head back to his cottage.

Having seen Robert to his door I'm about to go when he asks me if I'd like to come in for a drink; I say thanks, but no, I'm driving. Not alcohol, he says, dismissively; he doesn't touch the stuff. He says he had his first and last taste of beer at the Manvers Arms in Granby in 1951; it was horrible and he's never touched a drop since. He's offering me some squash - it's been a long, hot afternoon. Instinctively, I want to say no; a sense of anticlimax after finding the crash site, and the knowledge that I've been so close to where all those men died has left me feeling a little down. Or perhaps, having got what I came for, I've got nothing more to say, and want to run away, and carry on with the investigation. But something makes me accept his offer; I duck my head and go inside.

Handing me some squash in a mug, Robert leads me into his back room, which is stuffed from floor to ceiling with the most amazing collection of musical instruments: organs, accordions, guitars, mandolins, ukeleles, banjos and piles and piles of sheet music. We clear some space to sit and spend the next couple of hours chatting. Robert is a talker, but also a great listener; he wants to know all about me and my family, and within a few minutes we have established links. He knows some of the people my parents worked with, and their friends, including Sally Butler, daughter of Mrs Butler who ran the Butchers shop in Bingham when I was a boy. I remembered going in there with my mother to buy sausages for our tea and chitterlings for Dad, and noticing the ever-present coppery smell of blood, and that it was always freezing cold in there, even in the summer. Sometimes I'd catch a glimpse of a metal bucket, full of blood, beneath the counter, saved for making black puddings. If we were in the shop at the end of the day we'd see Mrs Butler through a cloud of steam as she poured scalding hot water over the bloody chopping blocks, and scrubbed the pale wood with a big bristly brush, her hands red from the cold (or the blood – I couldn't tell which). Now Sally is as old as her mother was then; the butcher's has become a coffee shop, and I go there on breaks from my research and writing, and until recently Sally used to come round to the house to do my mum's hair in the kitchen.

We talk about the other Bingham shops, back in the day when I was a boy and the place was still a small village; the old Tip Top bakery, Mees Electrical (which my parents swore by as the only place to buy anything electrical, from an AA battery to a television), the old Handicentre shop that sold tools, gardening equipment and, more importantly to me, had shelves full of Airfix, Revell and Frog kits. We remember Mr Smith, who ran the Rural Studies department at my local comprehensive, a series of sheds containing pigs, sheep and chickens, which we all took lessons in, and which didn't seem at all unusual at the time. Robert and I seem to have lots in common; it even turns out that from time to time he used to play the organ at the Bingham Methodist chapel, and would have done so when I was at Sunday school. As if to prove the point he sits at one of his keyboards and starts playing an old hymn tune, and I have to admit that although I feel this is all a bit strange, I'm quite enjoying sitting here in the cool, drinking squash and listening to Robert play.

The subject of my recent divorce comes up, and unlike most people (including me) who move quickly on, Robert wants to know what happened, what she was like, whether there was anyone else involved, how we get on now, and how I feel about it all. Surprisingly, I open up, revealing things I probably haven't told many of my closest friends. He asks me if I wish I could go back to how things were, which I find a strange question, as a divorce is pretty final, until I realise that he's actually thinking about his own marriage. He tells me about his lovely wife, who he lost a few years ago. They'd had a wonderful marriage, he said, and were the best of friends. One evening, feeling tired, he'd gone up to bed early, and came down in the morning to find her cold and motionless in her chair. It's still raw; he clearly still feels the dreadful loss, and some guilt, though I say he doesn't need to.

Through the small windows I can see that the light is beginning to fade, but we carry on talking; he wants to know about my book, and tells me about the book he has written, a history of Sutton-cum-Granby, which I can find in the Newark library.[23] We talk about our health, and ghosts, about his musical instruments and his collection of watches and clocks, and even his healing hands, which I worry he's going to try on me, but I manage to swerve that one. This is so bloody weird, two men who only met a few hours ago, talking about their most intimate thoughts and feelings. A little voice in my head is telling me I should go, but I'm happy to stay, drink tea and eat biscuits, feeling relaxed and without a care in the world.

---

[23] *Memoirs of my Village Sutton-cum-Granby*, Robert Brown. 2007

When I do eventually leave, Robert stalls me by filling a watering can and insisting I go on a tour of the garden, where he shows me his veg patch, the orchard, and his beloved chickens. Finally, I insist that I must go, and we say our goodbyes with a handshake.

'It's a lovely night,' he says, looking up. Then, quietly, he asks if I think we will meet again? I sense that he knows I am likely to forget all about him now I have got what I want.

'Yes,' I say, 'I'll come back and chat, to let you know what happens. And I'll invite you to the book launch, if I ever write the damn thing.' I get a brief glimpse of his cheeky face and eyes, hiding under that tatty Panama. We shake again, and I get into the car and pull into the road.

Driving up the quiet, narrow lane towards Elton, with the low sun slanting its orange rays through the trees, a weight seems to have been lifted from my shoulders. I feel energised, motivated, I have a direction and purpose once more. It looks like I have found the crash sites, obviously, but I think it's more than that, and yet I can't quite put my finger on it. At the crossroads on the A52 I turn left and go down the hill, past Barnes' Field and the spot where I now believe the Wellington crashed. Something seems to have changed, something indefinable, and surprisingly it's less to do with crashed aeroplanes and more to do with me and a lonely old man.

Thirty

'There's nothing in that field. I've already swept it and haven't found any bits of aeroplane.'

We are sitting at Tony Young's kitchen table, in a cottage which by coincidence is only a few hundred yards from the spot where Robert Brown insists the Wellington came down. He places a mug of tea in front of me, and I suddenly feel very foolish. Have I got this completely wrong?

Following my meeting with Robert, I had asked Gillian if she would put me in touch with the man who had done the metal detecting on her land, and she happily gave me Tony's number. I had also asked if she knew who owned the land Robert called Barnes' Field, but she didn't know. I did a bit of Googling to try and find the landowner but no success, and in desperation knocked on Angela Copley's door, the lady who had suggested I letter drop Sutton-cum-Granby, leading me to Robert. Angela kindly pointed me in the direction of a farm a few miles away, on the other side of Bingham and after several unanswered letters I managed to speak to the owner Adam Fisher on the phone. Of course he knew Tony, having given him permission to sweep the field in the past, and was more than happy to let us go there again, so long as we didn't do any digging. I assured him that wasn't our intention. Farmers are rightly protective of their crops.

Back at Tony's, he is telling me how he got into metal detecting, something which has always fascinated me, but about which I know precious little. My knowledge of metal detecting is limited to reports of hoards of Saxon and Viking gold being unearthed in farmer's fields, and more recently, from the wonderfully addictive television series with

Mackenzie Crook and Toby Jones. Like me, Tony was drawn to the idea of finding treasure, but with him it was more the notion that history was lying perhaps just inches below the surface that fascinated him. We are in agreement on that one, sharing a sense of wonder at another world existing in parallel with our own. He shows me some finds, small brooches, coins and so on, and confesses that he dreams of finding a Roman settlement in the area – he is sure there is one nearby and that he'll come across evidence one day. I ask him about the identity bracelet that he found on Gillian's land, bearing the inscription *Toby Dec 1939*, and ask if he can remember where he found it. He can't remember precisely, but knows it was just to the east of St Michael's church, so only a little to the east of a direct line that you can draw between the Becks Plantation and the spot where Robert says the Wellington crashed. My mind is racing: could there have been a collision in the sky somewhere over the church, and the bracelet fell to the ground directly below before the aircraft crashed 700 yards apart? But I know I am leaping ahead, and anyway, this is where Tony reveals that he has already swept not only the area around the Becks Plantation but also Barnes' Field, with no evidence of any aircraft crashes.

I bring Tony up to date with the witness report of the rear gunner on Wellington R1696, and tell him I believe Robert, and his friend Mike, who both swear that what they are saying is true.

He pulls a face: '80 years ago. It's a long time. The memory plays tricks.' I agree, it is a long shot, but it is all I have to go on; I know it is a lot to ask, but would he be prepared to give it another go, starting with Barnes' Field?

Tony thinks about it. The detecting season is short, he says, and we're right at the end of it. It all depends on being able to get access to the field before the next sowing. But he's up for it.

A few days later I am standing by the gate to Barnes' Field, with Robert and Mike, two pals who came here in June 1941 looking for bullets, just as we are today. Mike has driven Robert over from the cottage, and we are waiting for Tony to come down from his house, which we can see from here. It is a lovely, bright, but slightly breezy late summer afternoon. There is a feeling in the air of autumn approaching, and I have a sense that time is running out if we are to find any evidence.

Mike points to a house just the other side of the Nottingham to Grantham road where he lived during the war, and remembers how he was at school in nearby Bottesford the day of the crash, and all the children heard the noise of sirens and vehicles, but didn't find out what the fuss was about until home-time. The road was full of military vehicles, soldiers and airmen, the Home Guard and Police, and clearly something major had gone on. The wreckage of the Wellington had already been cleared away, or was covered in tarpaulins, he can't remember which, but soon everyone in the village was talking about the awful mid-air collision between a bomber and a trainer, which had crashed near the village. After doing his National Service as a mechanic in the RAF, Mike had returned to the village and now has some land near Newark. Mike and Robert talk every day, often ringing each other at breakfast, or in the evening, and they go out for drives in Mike's 4x4. Mike's health isn't good. He's always puffing, says Robert, who is worried about his old friend.

We look up and see Tony walking towards us, looking, as all metal detectorists seem to, like a refugee from an army surplus store. I feel rather inadequate in my jeans and trainers. Introductions are made, and from the 4x4 Robert and Mike point towards where they remember the Wellington had burned, a couple of hundred yards away, about twenty yards in from the edge of the field, just before the beginning of the incline. I show Tony a map which I have drawn, marking the fence posts running along the edge of the field, the trees and road signs by the A52, and the beginning of the incline, ready to mark anything that he finds. It's time to start.

Robert and Mike remain in the 4x4 while Tony and I set off around the edge of the field, and I tell Tony when we have reached what I think is the spot. Straight away Tony strides into the field, but I hang back at the perimeter as he starts sweeping the area. Almost immediately there is a squeak from the metal detector, and Tony crouches down, poking over the surface with his trowel. My heart races – *he's found something already*. Slowly Tony stands, rubbing the soil from the small object he's found. I can't help calling from the side of the field, like an excited kid, 'What have you found?'

He turns. 'A nail - rubbish,' and puts it in his bag so that he doesn't come across it again later. And so the process continues for another 15 or 20 minutes; Tony sweeps, he hears a squeak, higher or lower in pitch and volume depending on what he has detected (iron nails sound very different to silver coins, apparently, and even the way a coin is lying can produce a different sound), he crouches, scrapes, picks something up, pops it in his bag and moves on. There's a kind of rhythm to it all, and I can see that it must be quite mindful, rather like the fishing I used to do as a kid, on the ponds just up the road.

Feeling like a bit of a spare part, I look up into the sky, and try to picture what must have happened all those years ago. With the positions of the two crash sites in mind, I imagine the two Wellingtons, possibly flying towards Elton church from the direction of Belvoir Castle, and the Oxford coming in the opposite direction, heading south; the collision, when it happened, could have taken place over in the direction of St Michaels and All Angels church, a few hundred yards away, with the Oxford falling to the ground just over the ridge, and the Wellington hitting the ground in front of me, exploding on impact. I think of the people living in the big house on the hill, the Tomlinson's, who Mike's dad worked for and who would have seen and heard the crash. If they had a telephone they would have called the local police, who probably contacted the main office at RAF Syerston. (RAF Bottesford is nearer to Elton, only 3 miles down the road towards Grantham, but the station didn't come into service until September 1941. RAF Langar is only 5 miles away but wasn't operational until 1942. Personnel may have come from Bottesford and Langar to help, or alerted Syerston, but it seems uncertain whether emergency or recovery crews from either would have been available to assist in June 1941).

There's another squawk from the metal detector; a loud one. I turn and see Tony bending down. He picks something up and heads towards me.

My heart is racing; has he really found something interesting? He opens his bag and shows me the contents: some nails, bolts and bits of rusty metal that he says are Victorian farm implements, screwed up tinfoil, squashed drinks cans; nothing he thinks will be of interest to me. We are looking for aircraft alloy, light aluminium rather than heavy iron or steel. He says that when they cleared the site in 1941 the RAF would have swept the area thoroughly, not wanting to leave anything behind that could be dangerous, and the other problem is that the Wellington's aluminium frame would probably have been destroyed in the heat of the fire. The likelihood of us finding anything conclusive is very small.

But he's not giving up. He says he's going to try further up the hill. Without wanting to look like I'm telling Tony how to do his job, I remind him that Robin and Mike were very specific about the Wellington landing on the flat, *before* the incline, not up there. He points out, correctly, that if there was an explosion, small pieces of wreckage could have been thrown some distance away, and he heads off up the hill, sweeping as he goes. What he says makes sense, and he's the expert. Perhaps he hadn't searched the area up the hill when he swept the field years before?

I look over at the 4x4, and remember Robert and Mike, waiting patiently. They must be wondering what is going on...

'He hasn't found anything,' I say, leaning in at the window on Robert's side.

'That's 'cos he's looking in the wrong place,' says Robert, grumpily. 'I said the Welly landed *before* the incline, not up the hill. He's wasting his time if he looks up there, in't he Mike?'

Mike isn't so sure. He's been thinking, and the more he has thought about it the less convinced he is that Robert's memory is correct. The Wellington could have crashed by the road, where we were looking, but it could have been the other side of the field, or even the *next* field, it was a long time ago...

'Perhaps Robert has got a better memory than me,' he says. 'I don't really remember.'

'Well, I do,' says Robert. 'It were where I said. I told you.'

My heart sinks. This is becoming embarrassing. Maybe I shouldn't have taken Robert at his word. I allowed my excitement to get the better of me, as usual. We are talking about a day 81 years ago, just an ordinary summer day, when two naughty boys ran into a field on the lookout for treasure. They had no need to commit the exact spot to memory. All they were interested in was finding bullets, and quickly, before the farmer caught them. The field would have been ploughed soon afterwards, grass or crops would have hidden the crash site from view, and the crashed aircraft was forgotten. This is why I needed to bring Tony and his metal detector, which Robert thought was unnecessary. I look back at the tiny figure of Tony, away on the hill, sweeping left and right. Science, in the form of a metal detector, will always trump memory, and imagination, and hope. This makes sense, but at this particular moment it's not a very comforting thought. Perhaps it has all been a waste of time. But I can't allow myself to think that, not after all the work I've done. Trying not to show my frustration, and staying positive, I head back around the edge of the field towards Tony.

'Not looking good,' he says. He's found a few more bits and pieces – a rusty hinge, more nails, and something that looks like a button, but nothing to write home about. I tell him that Robert and Mike are still convinced he's looking in the wrong place, and turn to look at the 4x4. But it's not there. The old boys have gone home.

'Well, I can stay until five,' says Tony, 'then I've got to go into West Bridgford for a curry with the wife. Let's go back down and give it one last go.'

We trudge back down the hill. I am feeling awful now. There's a hollow, gnawing feeling in my stomach. I am sure that this whole day has been a waste of time, and I'm not sure that I want to go on after this. And yet, there is still a little voice that says *keep trying*. Just like when we went fishing, and we'd spend all day without a bite; *just one more cast*, we'd think, *in that patch just by the reeds, or under that branch*. Just one more cast... Or as Guy Gibson would say, *one last op*.

We approach the rough area that Robert initially identified. I point to a spot about 20 yards from the edge of the field, hoping that this is where Robert was describing. Suddenly the brown stubbly expanse all looks the same. Tony paces out twenty yards into the field and looks back at me. I give him the thumbs up. I can tell what he's thinking - that this is exactly where we were earlier, and therefore a waste of time. For something to do I get the map out of my pocket, unfold it, and mark the spot – directly opposite the third tree on the other side of the A52. Tony begins sweeping. There's a squeak almost immediately. He bends down and picks something up, looking at it for what seems an eternity, turning it over in his fingers, before eventually putting it in his bag. More rubbish...

Only a few seconds later there is another sound, one I haven't heard before. I can't tell whether it is louder, or higher, or lower than the other sounds, but it is *definitely different*. Tony crouches down, and there's suddenly an alertness, an energy in the way he moves that makes the hairs come up on the back of my neck. Without standing, he turns and calls, 'Want to have a look at this?'

I actually *run* across the field. He's still crouching down when I get to him, and he holds out his hand. In his palm is a small, grey pointed object, about an inch long and a quarter of an inch in diameter.

'A bullet,' he says. I pick it up and am surprised by its weight. Yes, it's a bullet alright, there are even faint machine marks running around the base of it. In my pocket I have a key ring, attached to which is a .303 round that I bought from the Metheringham Airfield gift shop a while ago. The Browning machine guns on a Wellington fired .303 rounds. I show it Tony, barely able to breathe. They are identical.

'.303 Browning machine gun bullet,' I say, trying to sound like I know what I'm talking about. My heart is pounding in my chest, and I can't suppress a smile. Tony, on the other hand, remains calm. I stay out there as he begins sweeping again, and less than a minute later there's another squeak, different in pitch again. He has found a small, hollow, metal tube, about a couple of inches long. He rubs the dirt off it with a cloth, revealing a brass cartridge case, the kind that would have held a bullet like the one we have just found. The top half is jagged, as if it has been blown apart, perhaps when the heat of the fire exploded the charge inside.

Tony and I look at each other. The bullet itself was inconclusive. It could have ended up here after being fired from an aircraft. But to find a cartridge case nearby...

In an area no larger than a few square yards Tony finds more material: some electrical bits and pieces, another cartridge case, then another bullet, and finally, a small, light grey piece of aluminium, three inches long, one edge of which shows where it has been torn violently apart, with abrasions that can only have been made by a massive impact.

We are both smiling now; big broad, beaming smiles of relief, and genuine excitement. This is how young Robert and Mike probably were in the summer of '41. It is nearly five, and Tony needs to go if he's to make that curry date, and I'm happy to end things here, having found what we were looking for. Kindly, Tony offers to return and carry out some more sweeps, but I am more concerned to see if we can find the Oxford site, as the season for detecting is coming to an end and time is running out. I don't really need to find more treasure here, it is enough for me to know that we have definitely found the spot where the Wellington crashed.

With a shared sense that we have achieved something pretty amazing today, we agree to meet up again towards the end of the week and say goodbye. It's time to give the old boys their reward.

Teasingly, I have made Robert and Mike wait until they are sitting at the restaurant table. We order food, raise our glasses – lemonade and limes for the old boys and a pint for me, and I make a toast – *to us!* They still don't know what happened after they left Tony and me at Barnes' Field but must be guessing that we were successful.

I take a small, clear plastic wallet out of my pocket and the contents rattle onto the table: two lead bullets, and two brass cartridge cases. They are excited, but not as excited as I had possibly expected them to be. I suppose they've seen these things before... Well, obviously they *have* – that day they scoured Barnes' Field for their own treasure. I show them my keyring with the .303 round hanging on a chain, and they can see that yes, we are talking Browning machine gun bullets. Robert remembers the bullets they found, and he describes how the lead had oozed out of some of the cases, melted by the heat of the fire, he thought.

As we demolish our roast dinners, I say something silly about it being Fate that brought us to this point. What do you mean? they ask. Well, *if* it hadn't been for my mum mentioning my Uncle George's brother, *if* I hadn't decided to do that letter drop, and *if* Angela Copley hadn't told me to try Sutton-cum-Granby, *if* Robert hadn't read the letter, and *if*, after more than eighty years, he and Mike hadn't been able to remember exactly where that bomber crashed, we wouldn't be here now, would we? The mystery of the mid-air collision that killed those eight men would remain a forgotten footnote in an archive. How many people, like me, have driven past that spot on their way to work, or to the shops, or to school, and not had an inkling of the bit of history that happened just the other side of that hedge? Robert and Mike nod in agreement.

Now, we just need to find the spot where the Oxford crashed, and the story will be complete...

Before I know it, they have cleared their plates. Either I've been talking too much, or they eat faster than I do. Either way, the old boys are keen to get home. It's already getting dark outside. They are grateful for the meal, but I am more grateful for what they have given me, which I can never put a price on. We finish our drinks, I escort them out to the car park, now bathed in the soft orange glow of a summer sunset, and we say our goodbyes.

Thirty-One

The laptop pings, notifying me of the long-awaited arrival of the AIR81 File in my inbox. It has been so long since I ordered it from the National Archives that I had almost forgotten about it. I immediately stop what I am doing, download the file and print it off.

The Air Ministry File AIR81/6855 is a collection of RAF records and correspondence relating to the crash and represents possibly the most complete account I will get of the official version of what happened on the morning of 12 June 1941. I don't know exactly what details the documents will contain, but hope that questions about where the aircraft crashed, and how, and maybe even why, will be answered. They may also tell me whether any kind of an inquiry was held into the incident, and possibly provide pointers to more family connections. Having located the precise crash site for the Wellington in Barnes' Field, I hope they will help to pinpoint more exactly where the Oxford came down. Since talking to Robert I have been on cloud nine, boring anyone who will listen with my theories about the collision, carried along by a kind of excited momentum that seems to assume that we will be equally successful in finding the Oxford crash site. The one person I haven't yet shared the news with is Fiona. Although she knows about my first meeting with Robert and his confident assertion about where the Wellington crashed, the fact that I don't yet know exactly where the Oxford ended up has made me hold back from sharing the news about our recent find.

Since coming down from my high of discovering the Wellington site I have only clues as to the location of the

Oxford's final resting place: the note in the 305 Squadron Operational Log that the two aircraft landed '700 yards apart', and Robert's vague but still confident memory that 'The Oxford landed *over there*', somewhere in Gillian's field to the west of the Becks Plantation. Other than that, I have no real indication of precisely where Bill's aircraft might have come down. Hence my fear about disappointing her, and the hope I am placing in AIR81/6855 that it will give us something more solid to go on...

The file – all 39 pages of it – is an illustration of the huge administrative effort that went into running a highly industrialised war. More than 55,000 men and women died while serving with Bomber Command in World War Two. Just trying to imagine the bureaucracy involved in dealing with all those deaths is pretty mind-blowing.

The first item I download – the Casualty Notice Sheet - is a checklist of all the various departments and offices to be circulated and actions to be completed, in the correct sequence, so the RAF could officially sign off the deaths of the eight men involved. These include Signal or Note Received (of the incident), Action Sheet Prepared, Verification (Officers), Telegrams (Next of Kin/Others), Liaison Officer, File, Journal, Master Cards, Circulation List, Accounts, Pensions, Death Book, Missing Book, Benevolent Fund and Royal Letter. Clearly it was important that nothing would be omitted or forgotten when clearing up the administrative fallout from the accident.

There are also Burial Returns, requiring confirmation about the whereabouts of personal effects and notes confirming the allocation of war graves, the deceased's religion and asking whether a cross or other marker would be required, and so on. Interestingly, they show that although the Polish crew were all buried on the 15 June, LAC Robson Newton, who was interred only a few feet away, was actually buried in a separate ceremony the following day.

There are copies of notes confirming the deaths of all 8 men, noting that the next of kin of the Polish aircrew have not been informed; this would presumably be left to the Polish Government in Exile, however they might be able to manage that. Also, later correspondence from the Polish Embassy dating from 1948, requesting death certificates so that families back in Poland could settle legal issues. In one case, in a letter dated 28 November 1960, Sgt Jerzy Krawczyk's unnamed sister is noted as enquiring about 'whether the deceased was married and if so what was the last address of his wife known to the Air Ministry,' (opening up the question of whether Jerzy might have formed a strong romantic relationship with a girl in England, and whether the family back home knew about it...) A handwritten note at the bottom of the letter indicates that the N/K (Next of Kin) is recorded as Sgt Krawczyk's mother Bronislawa Krawczyk.

A medical note records that Pilot Officer A Zirkwitz was treated at Nottingham Hospital for *otitis media*, a minor middle ear infection, only a few days before the accident. This seems to be a rather mundane and irrelevant item in relation to PO Zirkwitz's death, but it presumably was a document lying around at Syerston and some clerk decided to slip it into the file just in case. It's a reminder that these names represent real people, whose day to day lives were taken up by simple problems such as an ear infection. It also explains, I realise, what it was that prevented Alexy from joining the crew in his rear turret on the night of 17/18 May when R1017 bombed Boulogne. There is also a large handwritten note, presumably the result of some confusion and/or embarrassment, reminding any user of the file of the correct spelling of the surname of PO Kowalcze. Some typist had obviously been a bit hasty and mis-spelt his name. This is not something that applied only to the Poles, with names that must have been unusual and unfamiliar to the RAF clerks typing up records: there are several copies of notes in which details such as the serial number of the Oxford are incorrectly typed, then corrected and re-sent, as well as the names and initials of Bill's co-pilot, who is named incorrectly as *H*R Newton before the correct *W*R Newton is reissued. I remember that Gertrude

Parkinson, when she received the news of Bill's death via telegram, saw not only her initials and address typed wrongly but also the service number of her dead son incorrectly typed. The sheer number of cases of accidents, crashes and deaths to be dealt with, and the rush to get information from A to B as quickly and efficiently as possible, inevitably invites mistakes.

The file also contains some technical documents, dealing with the history and state of the aircraft involved (aircraft and engine serial numbers etc), and the details of the crash as it was found when the recovery teams and investigators arrived at Elton. Also, copies of two telegrams *en clair* (ie not written in code and therefore *urgent*) which were sent from RAF Syerston on the day of the crash, notifying other offices and stations about the crash. The first telegram covers the Oxford, which Bill was flying, identifying it incorrectly as X1334, and I see that Bill is identified as PILOT. William Robson, again incorrectly identified as WR STON, is not listed in that way, so am I to assume that he was flying as second pilot or navigator? The telegram is explicit in stating that NEXT OF KIN NOT REPEAT NOT INFORMED, and as this message was sent at 1630hrs I can assume that the telegram Gertrude Parkinson received notifying her of her son's death arrived at her house later that evening.

The second telegram refers to the Wellington R1017 from 305 Squadron based at RAF Syerston, listing the crew, and stating that machine gun ammunition was present at the crash site. There is no mention of any bombs, as I expected, as the Wellington was not involved in an operation at the time of the collision and wasn't carrying bombs (thankfully – it doesn't do to imagine the damage a fully-loaded bomber would have done to a tiny village). Finally, 58 Maintenance Unit, based in Newark, is informed of the crash in order that they can organise the recovery of the wrecked aircraft. 58MU was situated near the Lincoln Road, where the Yorke Drive estate now stands, and after the accident the wreckage of the Wellington and Oxford would have been brought here for salvage. The unit also had a hangar behind Newark Castle

Station, close to where the Waitrose now stands, for receipt and despatch of aircraft and parts.

Both reports state that the accident occurred at 1125, that it was a mid-air collision in conditions of haze, with a 7/10 covering of low cloud, and that ACCIDENTS BRANCH INQUIRY NOT REPEAT NOT REQUIRED. There seems to be little doubt, as supported by the eye-witness account of the rear gunner in Wellington R1696, that the collision was a dreadful accident which could not be avoided, and blame was not being apportioned. This should be good news for the families of the crewmen, and particularly for Fiona, who I only recently burdened with the news that seven other men died with her uncle Bill. But the real gold dust contained in the AIR81 File, at least as far as I am concerned, is that the telegrams include locations and grid references for the crash sites. The Oxford is recorded as crashing at ELTON MAP REF SHEET 54 230577 APPROX 800 YARDS ELTON CROSSROADS NEAR BECKSWOOD. The Wellington crash site, with a little less detail, is given as ELTON NOTTS SHEET 54 226586.

This is great - actual map references for the precise crash sites of both aircraft! Without really stopping to think, I unfold my Ordnance Survey Map which covers the Elton area and look up the grid references. But neither reference works. If I remember the instructions my geography teacher drilled into me (along the corridor then up the stairs) my OS Explorer 260 map places the Elton crossroads at a completely different grid reference: 767389. Not only that, the grid references given in the telegrams, 230577 for the Oxford and 226586 for the Wellington, do not even appear on my map.

I look again at the telegrams, more closely this time, and see the words SHEET 54. I've never heard of this before, but go online and type in *SHEET 54* – and then add *RAF*, to make sure, hoping to find out more. Sure enough, it turns out that the RAF had their own wartime maps, designed to help crews navigate around the country, with unique grid references. SHEET 54 covered the area in which this particular incident happened, so the grid references should show me exactly where both aircraft crashed. If only I can get my hands on a copy of SHEET 54... Maybe some kind soul has uploaded a copy, or posted a link to an auction site where I might find one for sale - but no luck. I know I'm a complete amateur when it comes to aviation research but am quickly learning about the places to go for answers, and fire off emails to RAF Syerston, Cranwell, Hendon and the National Archives. Someone in one of these offices is bound to have access to those maps. Until then, frankly, I feel like I am at a dead end. Which is unfortunate, because next week my cousin Fiona is visiting my mother.

Thirty-Two

For days now I have felt what I can only describe as a certain sense of foreboding. Dark, unsettling and inescapable, this feeling of anxiety is there each morning, growing in intensity as it follows me around during the day, refusing to go and still lurking ominously when I go to bed at night. The thing hangs over me like a presence, upsetting my attempts to be happy, and if for a few moments I do manage to forget its existence, it taps me on the shoulder, or whispers softly in my ear, reminding me: *'You've failed,'* it seems to say, cruelly.

Driving home from work one darkening autumn afternoon I know this anxiety must be down to the dead end I seem to have hit in my search for the Oxford crash site. My appeals for help with SHEET 54 have so far produced no results. Undeterred, I contact some of the people I have met and who have helped me try to piece together Bill's story: Ian Shaw, the Polish Air Force expert who I met at the Newark Air Museum; Tim Chamberlain, the local historian and bookseller who I met at the East Kirkby Air Show; and Squadron Leader Mark Williams at RAF Syerston, all without success. Nobody seems to even know about these mysterious RAF maps. But my sense of foreboding can't only be because of the dead end looming ahead of me – there is always the possibility that I can find another way of locating the place where Bill's aeroplane had crashed – so what is it? I already know the answer - it is the fact that I am about to meet Fiona – my cousin and Bill's niece. She and her husband Mike are on a short end-of-summer tour catching up with relatives and friends and have arranged to call in at Mum's en route further north, drop off some Bill-related items which were too bulky to post, and catch up on the latest news about his story. They'll have had tea with Mum, and then taken her to the local restaurant which I am now pulling up outside. Not feeling at all in the mood for this, I get out of the car and grab my bag and head up the steps.

This meeting should be a cause for celebration, of a sort, as I will be able to tell Fiona all about Barnes' Field and show her what we found just lying on the surface, proof that I am getting somewhere after all this time. But I've hit that dead end with SHEET 54, and what was always the real goal of my journey – finding the crash site for her Uncle Bill's Oxford, however ghoulish that seems now – looks no nearer to happening. I'm sure it's the fear of disappointing Fiona that's making me feel so edgy and nervous.

But these anxieties are put to one side when I walk into the bistro to find Fiona and Mike sitting with Mum. They greet me with hugs and kisses, clearly having had a lovely afternoon already, and are glad I was able to make it. Before I even have chance to sit down, Fiona is telling me how surprised she was when I first emailed her about Bill, and how she feels honoured that I am doing all this work to find out what really happened to a member of her family. And she is delighted that I am writing a book about it too – she and Mike can't wait to read it! How is it coming along?

I'm a little taken aback, perhaps by her enthusiasm, and perhaps because this is the first time we have met in many years, and it feels a little strange to be happening in these unusual circumstances. That conversation Mum and I had about RAF Syerston all those months ago started me on an all-consuming journey I never expected to make, and I certainly had no idea that at the end of this long, hot summer I'd be showing Fiona a handful of documents detailing the crash and some dirty old machine gun bullets.

They've already ordered, so I quickly make my choice and start to tell the story, beginning with my first conversation with Robert and him showing me the spot in Barnes' Field where he remembered the Wellington had crashed. I tell it much as I have told it before, to Mum, or Martin, or friends at work and members of the writers' group, when I have been able to speak with unbounded enthusiasm, doing a more than passable imitation of Robert's broad Nottinghamshire accent, and the reception has been equally fascinated. But this time my telling of the story is difficult, disjointed; my delivery is faltering and feels (to me at least) somehow unconvincing. I feel as if I'm performing, and the story itself feels false. For whatever reason, my heart isn't in it, and I wish I could be at home, alone, reading my books or working on my 1/72 scale Wellington.

I show her the bullets and fragment of aluminium, explaining that I think the metal will have come from somewhere on the front of the Wellington – the leading edge of a wing, engine nacelles or the nose perhaps, where the metal tended to be thicker – and notice her reaction is one of interest certainly, but measured, and not what you'd call *fascinated*.

Maybe this is just proof that I've become obsessed about Bill's story for no real reason, and that really it's nothing special, certainly not as remarkable as I've been making it. Things which seem hugely significant to me, as an interested observer, maybe don't to someone who is closer to it. Their relationship to the story is inevitably going to be more personal, more unpredictable, less rational.

And then I realise the awful truth. Although I'm talking about the Wellington, she is obviously thinking about the Oxford, which her Uncle Bill was sitting in, and what he must have experienced on that dreadful day.

Pushing on, still trying to emphasise the drama of it all, I talk about the finds that have since been lost, or which don't seem to have an explanation: the St Christopher which the 9-year old Robert found that day lying in the scorched, blackened earth, and which he has since lost; and the silver bracelet with the unusual inscription, which Tony's metal detector discovered only a few years ago and now hangs in a frame on Gillian Robert's office wall. I ask Fiona if the name

Toby and the date December 1939 mean anything to her. Fiona says quietly that they don't.

I move on to the eye-witness report contained in the Squadron Log which Ian Shaw sent me, describing the collision as seen by the rear gunner on Wellington R1696, and explaining that the two stricken aircraft came down some 700 yards apart from each other. I outline the contents of the AIR81 File, deliberately avoiding the references to the burnt-out wreckages of the Oxford and Wellington, and the identification of the dead by ID Tags, focussing instead on the telegrams sent on the day of the accident which state that there would be no need for an Accidents Branch Inquiry – emphasising that the official line at the time was that nobody involved should be blamed for what happened.

It is subtle, almost invisible and, I am sure, unconscious, but to me at least, Fiona's shocked reaction to the word 'blamed' is undeniable. I am not sure that Mike or my mum notice it, but I do, and I immediately feel I have to explain myself, saying that I wondered whether the family might have worried about the question of blame, especially when eight men's lives were lost. I blurt out something facile about the likely attitude of the crash investigators, and of the other crews of 305 Squadron, to whom it might have seemed obvious that in a collision involving an operational crew and one that was inexperienced, the finger of blame would probably point in the direction of those piloting the trainer, however unfairly, and so to me at least it is good news that no-one was found to be responsible for the accident...

Immediately a strange, uncomfortable mood descends on the party, for which I know I must be responsible. Again I have raised a subject, the question of blame, which Fiona has probably never thought about, but which seems obvious to me coming at it from my direction. I am aware that I have said the wrong thing, but don't say anything to address the situation. Instead, it is left to Fiona to rescue the evening, moving on to ask about the Oxford site, and I have to admit to her that I have run up against what I hope is merely a temporary brick wall, explaining about the RAF wartime maps and SHEET 54. I feel (and probably appear) terribly down, depressed and negative as I skirt around the issue, unable to disguise my sense of failure in not being able to deliver what I (and I assume, Fiona and Mike) had expected - the crash site of Bill's aircraft. Mike comes up with some helpful suggestions about how we might track down a copy of SHEET 54, but which I have already tried. He also mentions a friend of theirs who is a well-known writer on military history, and might be able to help open some doors, but instead of receiving the offer with open arms I am merely lukewarm. In my present mood, the idea just makes me feel more inadequate and amateur.

Maybe it's just because I don't want to feel or appear stupid and helpless, but now I feel like I'm on trial for my failure to deliver. Not that anyone is doing anything to make me feel that *at all* – it's my own inadequacy and lack of self-confidence, combined with my insensitivity towards people's feelings and need for control. The guilt about *Cultybraggan* returns with a vengeance. I just want to get away, to the safety of doing my own research in isolation, like that young teenager hidden away in his bedroom making models of Lancaster bombers when he should have been out there in the real world. Ignoring my odd behaviour, Mike says he'll mention the maps to his friend anyway and see if he can come up with anything.

Fiona remembers the box containing some more items relating to Bill which she has left at Mum's house (some scrapbooks, drawings, school and family photos). I say I'll scan them and send them back straight away, but she insists the parcel would be too large and too heavy, and also there is the worry about their personal value. I agree to hang onto it until they return, or as they suggest several times, when I visit them. I mutter something about it being difficult finding the time, especially with the book hanging over me, and I notice Mike glances at his watch, aware that they have to be making tracks if they are to get to their hotel in Lincoln. They are planning to make a visit to the International Bomber Command Centre, which I told them has a dramatic central memorial containing all the names of the more than 55,000 members of Bomber Command who died during World War Two, including those of the Polish airmen on board Wellington R1017 but sadly not of her uncle and his co-pilot, who were not yet fully qualified when they died in the service of their country, and therefore not qualified to be memorialised.

Gathered outside in the still-warm evening, I can't escape the feeling of awkwardness. Standing by our cars, we hug and say our goodbyes, and I see a tear in Fiona's eye. I think her sadness comes from seeing Mum, her mother's sister, and possibly regret that as cousins we never saw more of each other when we were younger. If I can salvage anything from today it is that at least Bill's death has brought us back together.

Back at Mum's, she and I sort through the items which Fiona has left, me listening as each triggers more memories for her. She turns the pages of some scrapbooks kept by Bill and George when they were at school and in the early years of the war, filled with cut-out and pasted-in cartoons of Hitler and Goering, air raid shelters and rationing, as well as more serious articles about the progress of the war. There are photographs and cuttings describing decisive battles and actions, the men and the weapons involved, including fighter and bomber aircraft, and their crews; Bill's work, possibly. He, like me, was presumably interested in aircraft as a youngster; their design, appearance, performance, armament – everything about them. How he must have yearned to get up there behind the controls of the romantic, exciting-looking aircraft filling the newspaper pages, including the Wellington. The Royal Navy, its fleet of battleships and destroyers, and the engagements it fought, also feature heavily in the other scrapbook. Fiona had mentioned that George always regretted not being able to join the Navy during the war due to his childhood polio, so maybe this was his, articles carefully cut out on the kitchen table when his mother had finished with the newspaper. Then I see a page which is a cutaway of the *Daily Telegraph's* London office and printworks, with descriptions of the way a newspaper is produced, and this seems to confirm my suspicion that this scrapbook belonged to a young man with ideas of becoming a journalist, archiving information, facts and opinion for future articles.

Bill (top) and George (Fiona Reid)

As well as the scrapbooks there are children's paintings, and letters, and a number of photographs of the Parkinson family, dating from the 1930s I guess, which no doubt would have held pride of place on the walls and sideboard at Fountayne Street. There's a portrait of Gertrude, looking as formidable as I had expected, and some family groups, including Bill's father William and older sister Margaret, both of whom had already passed away when he was killed. There are also delightful photographs of the twins together, at various ages, including one probably taken when they were around 18 if the ciggies are anything to go by; both are smiling and happy, reflecting how close the twins were in those innocent, carefree days just before the war.

More photographs show Bill in the various rugby and hockey teams he played in at Ashville College during the pre-war years. Arms firmly crossed, back straight, fresh-faced and confident, he and his team-mates smile for the camera, flanked by their proud masters. How many of those boys would, like Bill, not live to see the end of a war which at this point could have seemed no more than a vague possibility on some dim future horizon? Ashville was a 'boys only' school in Harrogate, run on strict Methodist grounds. Methodist preachers were expected to move regularly around the country, enriching the circuit with their sermons and ministry, and so William and Gertrude must have felt it was preferable for the boys to have their education undisturbed by remaining in the one school (and the Methodist church were also ready to assist with the fees). I had called the college when beginning my research, wondering if perhaps they had any photographs or records of Billy and George, and the librarian and archivist Dr Pavneet Kaur kindly sent me copies of the *Ashville Magazine* which mentioned both boys in the various activities they were involved in.

Fiona had also sent me the boys' diaries for 1938, when they would have been aged sixteen and in their final year at Ashville. The small Letts Schoolboys Diaries could not be more contrasting in revealing elements of George and Bill's characters and interests. For a start, George's diary is meticulously completed for the whole year, with entries for every day, no matter how brief. Bill's runs from the beginning of the year but ends abruptly on 26 February and remains blank for the rest of the year, when he was either too busy, or forgot. Up until that point his diary entries seem to concentrate mostly on the fights he got into, and on his active sports schedule, whereas George with his gammy leg has to settle for acting as scorer. Bill also has a clear passion for things technical, particularly radios: 'Bought an HF [High Frequency] valve,' 'Sold Worthington a transformer for 10d,' and 'Mended Coulson's wireless. OK.' Both boys record the anniversary of their father's death on 15 February the previous year. The Reverend William Parkinson had died suddenly at the manse on Victoria Street that night, at the age of 50. Apparently suffering an epileptic fit, he had been writing a sermon, while his daughter Margaret was in the chapel schoolroom at the rear of the manse, helping to decorate it for the annual bazaar. The boys' mother Gertrude had found him sitting by the fire, apparently unwell, and called the doctor, but by the time he arrived it was too late.

Reading his diary entries, my hunch that George had already decided on a career in journalism is confirmed: 'Foreign affairs very shaky, rumours of rebellions, war, fights, dictators in Rumania (sic) Greece, Germany, Spain,' he writes, and 'Watched some sports tests and knocked a ball about with Unwin. Lost the ball. Caught a frog. Saw a wren's nest and a blackbird's. Saw some young magpies. Made up the scorebook and wrote up a report on the match. Magazines distributed.' Towards the end of 1938, he notes 'Listened to Hitler's speech,' and 'Arrived at the GT [*Goole Times*] in spite of my nervousness. Had a talk with the editor and was introduced to the other reporters. Did shorthand most of the afternoon, helped mother at night. Margaret ill.' The boy's sister had been ill for most of 1938, spending ever-increasing amounts of time in Leeds General Infirmary. One diary entry has George recording that one evening he listened on the radio to a Gracie

Fields concert from the Albert Hall, with Margaret upstairs in bed listening through the open door. Sadly, she would die in the spring of 1939 following an operation. Death, it seemed, was never far from the Parkinson family.

Last among the things Fiona has left is a small, anonymous-looking, brown cardboard box, a little smaller than a cigarette packet, which contains a medal. This is the 1939-45 War Medal which will have been sent to his mother after the war. Never to be worn by the man it was awarded to, and with the ribbon still unattached, the medal is in its original greaseproof paper envelope, together with the printed citation:

> *The Under-Secretary of State for Air presents his compliments and by Command of the Air Council has the honour to transmit the enclosed medal granted for service in the war of 1939-45. The Council share your sorrow that* LEADING AIRCRAFTMAN W.W. PARKINSON *in respect of whose service it is awarded did not live to receive it.*

Like the telegram containing news of Bill's death, this is another physical reminder of how hard the loss of her son must have hit poor Gertrude, as it will have hit Robson Newton's parents, and so many other families (although not, I assume, the families of the Poles, who may have remained ignorant of their fate until after the war.) With those words echoing in her brain, I imagine Gertrude looking at the medal for a long time, remembering her beloved Billy, before closing the box and putting it away.

It is only now, as I write these words, trying to make sense of what happened, that I finally understand why Fiona was upset, what that tear in her eye meant when we parted. All summer I have really been thinking about me. But this is not my story.

Since starting on the journey to discover what happened to Bill, and without necessarily being consciously aware of it, I was forgetting the actual people, like Fiona, directly connected to the dead men *whose story this is*. Meeting Fiona was the first time I had actually spoken to someone to whom the story has a direct personal, emotional or blood connection. One of the men who died in that dreadful accident, who was probably at the aircraft's controls in those horrendous last few seconds, was Fiona's uncle, her father's twin brother. She missed seeing him as she grew up and knew him only as the fresh-faced lad in the photo on the sideboard, all smiles and ciggy in hand, or the uniformed boy who died a hero's death in the war. How could I not realise how she must be feeling when confronted with the evidence of his death? Evidence which I have found and shown her.

And it's not just blood, even though that is important and magical and mysterious in the way it affects us; it is the accumulation of all those years of memory, the stories told (or not told) about Bill, and the awareness, painfully acute at times, of how awful the experience was for her grandmother Gertrude, and her father George. The dispassionate, objective search for 'the truth' about what happened to Bill and the others that day, has driven me, dominating my waking and sleeping hours for months, but not in any way that can be comparable to what Fiona and the other relatives of the dead men have been through.

And not just them, of course, because although they as family were close, tied by bonds which cannot be truly understood by those who stand outside, there are many others who were directly or indirectly involved in the accident: the villagers who first heard or saw the collision high above Elton, and may have watched the aircraft fall helplessly to the ground; the men in the rescue trucks speeding along the A52 in the direction of the columns of black smoke, dreading what would meet them on arrival; the Erks who were given the task of recovering the bodies; the ground- and aircrews back at Syerston, the cooks and the women from the NAAFI and YMCA tea wagons who would notice the absence of a familiar face or two in the queue; the young men at Brize Norton, waiting for the return of their fellow cadets before being given the news that they would never see them again; the officers tasked with the job of writing the letters of condolence to the families of the two Pilots Under Training; the Warrant Officers and NCOs who escorted LAC WW Parkinson's body to Goole and stood awkwardly in the family home while his mother served tea and sandwiches; the proud Polish flyers who stood to attention around the gravesides at Newark cemetery, and fought back the tears as the Last Post was played on the bugle and the coffins of six brave Polish comrades were lowered into the ground.

My desire for control, and frustration with being unable to provide a 'good' ending for 'my' story are as nothing compared to what all those people went through (and some are still going through). As a writer, whether dealing with fiction or real life, I shape and structure events, thoughts and emotions, foregrounding and highlighting some and conveniently consigning others to the shadows. In real life, this is called selective memory, or denial of reality (neither of which is a particularly attractive or positive attribute), but in storytelling it is essential. Bill's story, which I thought was giving some order and structure to my life, enabling me to understand *what happened*, has turned into a dark obsession. And the writing of the book, which I'm now doing from some distance, is revealing things about me which I have hitherto denied or resisted. Like the scattered fragments from the crash, they are now coming up to the surface and their interpretation reveals terrible things that happened in the past, and sense needs to be made of them if the story is to mean anything.

Thirty-Three

'Me and Lucy were inseparable. Always together. We even wore the same clothes. If Lucy bought a nice dress, I'd get one just like it and if I had a pair of shoes she liked she'd buy a pair just the same. And we were so *silly*...'

Mum is recalling her best friend, Lucy, who Mum grew up with in Goole. They remained best friends until Lucy passed away a few years ago and were so close I grew up calling her 'Auntie' Lucy, although she was not a relation. I'd gone round to see Mum for a cup of tea, and found her in a slightly agitated state, worried that things were getting on top of her. She has always been very good at sorting and filing correspondence (bank statements, bills, etc) and ran the show where those things were concerned when Dad was around, but recently things seem to have got a bit out of hand. She shows me a large pile of letters from the bank, the insurance company, utilities and subscriptions, some opened, others untouched, which would normally have been dealt with, filed in order and kept up to date for easy reference. I offer to go through the pile and sort them out.

'Thank you. It seems so much harder to keep on top of now. Just show me anything I need to attend to and chuck away what's not needed.'

It doesn't take long to go through the pile, and Mum's sense of relief is palpable. It had clearly been getting to her and it's another sign that she needs more help. I bring her another cup of tea and steer the conversation back round to Goole, and what life was like back in the day. Immediately she's off, remembering stories about her teenage years, her first jobs as a typist at the Hospital and at Goole Steam, and the fun times she had with Lucy in the late 40s and early 50s. 'We were always off on trips to the seaside – Blackpool, Morecambe and Scarborough, and even on the Hull ferry to Bruges or Ghent. And we used to go on fabulous weekend trips to London, all the time, to see the big shows in the West End. We'd save up, and I would write a letter to the theatre asking for two seats, enclosing a postal order, and the same with the hotel...'

'Which hotel did you stay in?' I ask.

'Oooh now... it was on The Strand, I remember that, a huge building...' I scroll through a few Strand hotels on my phone and show her some pictures. 'That's the one,' she says, looking at the Strand Palace Hotel, with its distinctive Art Deco design. 'It was lovely. Very posh.'

'And which shows did you go to see, can you remember?' Of course she can: 'All the big ones, the musicals. *Oklahoma*, *Carousel*, *South Pacific*, over from America, they were fantastic.'

'It seems quite a daring thing for a teenager to have done,' I say. 'Getting a train all the way down to postwar London and going up West.'

'Well things were different then,' she says, 'But me and Lucy were so daft in those days, I'm surprised we didn't get into more trouble sometimes.' Mum then tells me a story about how the two of them were sitting on a bench on the platform at Goole Station, all ready for their trip to London, and laughing away at something so much that their train came in and went out again without them even noticing.

'A guard came up to us and he said, "You two have missed your train, haven't you?" We said we hadn't, but he said, "You have, it's just come in, right in front of you and you didn't even notice, you were that busy yakking." Well that just set us off again, and we didn't know what to do, but the guard thought we were as daft as brushes, so he told us to go over to the other platform, get the train to Hull, then come back on the London train. "But don't get off at Goole, you hear?"'

Lucy and Mum, around 1948 (Bean family)

She is almost crying with laughter as she remembers the moment with her dear friend. Then she's off again, remembering one time when she and Lucy, aged about 15 or 16, were in 'Miss Dew's Benefit Shoe Shop on Boothferry Road. That's where we went to get our shoes, and we were in there one day trying some on when Raque came wandering in...'

'He came into the shoe shop?'

'I told you, he went everywhere in Goole, he was always wandering in and out of places, everyone knew him, and George just laughed when you told him about it. "Good old Raque," he said. Anyway, this day me and Lucy were in there when he came in, sniffing around with his nose to the floor and he came up to the tall mirror Miss Dew had, for trying on shoes you know, and when Raque suddenly saw himself he jumped *so high*! You've never seen anything like it!'

And we're back onto Bill's story, with me asking her more questions about the other places she used to go to during the war, the parks and cafes and so on, and Mum remembering everything so clearly. 'If only I could remember the simple things,' she says, 'Like how to sort those statements, or how to work the television.'

Heading home through the villages I think about how vulnerable Mum suddenly seems. It seems to have galloped up without me noticing, or preferring not to notice. Each time I visit, her short-term memory seems to be even worse, and of course she is aware of it, which is upsetting for her. 'I don't want people to think I'm doolally,' she says, when any of us makes the suggestion that she might be happier or safer in a care home. It's something she keeps putting to the back of her mind, unwilling to face the inevitable. But it's something my brothers and I are going to have to deal with at some time.

Taking a different route just for the hell of it, I pass through the village of Screveton, a few miles to the north of Elton, and notice a granite memorial at the corner of a field. There's a metal plaque on the stone and I'm sure I saw the outline of a Lancaster on it. Parking up, I walk back towards the memorial, noticing a couple of 20-foot-high figures constructed from straw in the nearby field. Reading the plaque confirms that this is the memorial the grey-haired lady at the Newark Air Museum was talking about back in May. The memorial is to the eleven men who died in a mid-air collision between a Lancaster from RAF Syerston, and an Oxford from RAF Wymeswold in April 1944. Driving home I've forgotten about Mum and her fading memory, thinking instead about the practicalities of erecting a memorial to Bill and the other aircrew.

Later that night, when I am at home, wasting the evening watching Saturday night TV, the phone rings. It's a number I don't recognise but I answer it anyway.

'Is that Adrian? You don't know me, but my name's Dave Flint and I was given your number by Shaun Noble. He thought we should meet.'

Shaun Noble was the name of the man who had supplied the photograph of Jerzy Krawczyk to 'Kryztek's List'. He had received the email I'd sent months ago, and although I had not heard anything back, Dave tells me that Shaun (who has been busy) told him about me.

We meet in my local, the Fox and Crown, an unspoilt old Newark pub opposite St Mary Magdalene church, and only recently re-opened following the pandemic. Dave looks to be around my age, possibly older, and over a pint of Elsie Mo he cautiously checks me out, wanting to know where I'm coming from. We soon establish a rapport, having a common interest in aeroplanes. Dave tells me that his dad was in the RAF during the war, but had failed the wireless operator's exam on enlistment, and ended up in a ground job. Dave is thankful for this – if his dad had been aircrew he probably wouldn't have survived, and Dave wouldn't be enjoying a pint now.

Credentials established, Dave pulls out a folder and gets down to business – Jerzy Krawczyk – telling me that he had made contact with the wireless operator's family back in the early 1990s. It all happened quite by accident – he had been taking his son on a bike ride through the Newark cemetery, and going past the Polish war graves he saw some flowers and a note lying beside one of the headstones, which happened to be that of Jerzy Krawczyk. The note was an appeal for anyone with information about Jerzy to contact a Barbara Tyminski in

Poland. His interest piqued because of his curiosity about these things, Dave got in touch, using a local translator to help, and discovered that the note had been left by Marta Machnikowska, Barbara's daughter, who in turn was the daughter of Jerzy Krawczyk's sister Halina. Dave and Marta, who lives in Łódź, Poland, where her husband Ryzard is a professor at the University, began a correspondence, but Barabara died soon afterwards, and Dave was able to confirm that none of the family who actually knew Jerzy or would have been alive during the war are now living.

Dave met Marta and Ryzard when they visited Oxford, and Marta shared some letters and photos of Jerzy, copies of which Dave now gives to me. One is of Jerzy and a friend, both in uniform, smiling as they sit astride a motorbike, clearly posed in a photographic studio (most likely in Blackpool, given the POLAND flashes on their shoulders) and sent home to his family.

The other photographs are more personal, showing Jerzy with a pretty girl, again I assume taken in Blackpool. In the first, Jerzy and the girl are walking down a town street, Jerzy in uniform again, and the girl wearing a well-cut dark suit and sweater. In another, possibly taken on or near the beach as they appear to have sand on their shoes, Jerzy has his arms around the girl, holding her tight, and both are smiling and laughing for the camera. The fact that Jerzy sent the photos to Poland suggests this was more than just a passing fling and ties up with the letter referring to an enquiry from Jerzy's sister (presumably Halina) lying in the AIR81 File, enquiring as to whether Jerzy was married at the time of his death. Dave tells me that according to Marta the girl was called Joan Bailey, and that she was from Keighley in Yorkshire, but that's about as much as he knows. It seems it was one of those many wartime romances cut short by tragedy and forgotten by history.

Dave had done some research into Jerzy's military career as well as the crash and had also discovered that he had an earlier brush with death before joining 305 Squadron. In October 1940, he was part of a night flight on an Avro Anson of No. 6

Jerzy Krawczyk (left) and pal, Blackpool, 1940 (Krawczyk family)

Air Observer Navigation School when the aircraft hit a barrage balloon cable over Southampton. The aircraft crashed into a house in the city, resulting in the death of the pilot. Jerzy and two other men were injured but survived.

Jerzy Krawczyk and Joan Bailey, Blackpool 1940
(Krawczyk family)

Dave was fascinated to hear that I had managed to establish exactly where the Wellington had crashed and said that he would love to take Paula to see the site for herself.

'Paula?' I asked.

'Yes,' he replied. 'Paula is Marta's cousin. She and her family live in the UK – would you like her number?'

Thirty-Four

'It's kind of incredible that after all these years I think we considered it a closed chapter in the family story and then out of nowhere...'

Paula Pietrzak places a cup of coffee on the dining table in her house, which despite being a modern build has the appearance and feel of an Eastern European apartment: lots of family photographs, oil paintings of the old country, ornaments in glass cabinets and books everywhere. Half the table is taken up with an enormous incomplete jigsaw. She has just picked me up from the station, and despite her friendliness and charm seems a bit nervous and edgy. In the car Paula had told me that her husband Piotr had recently gone into hospital, and she apologised that we may not have as much time to talk as we'd like because she's hoping to visit him later. The jigsaw, she tells me is her way of focussing and forgetting about her troubles.

Paula, it turns out, lives in a small town only a few minutes' drive from Padgate, the RAF Station where William Parkinson and Robson Newton had done their Basic Training in 1940. She begins by telling me how she met Dave Flint. Since moving to England she had heard about Dave from Marta, but didn't actually meet him until she visited Jerzy's grave in Newark and posted a message on social media about it. Dave saw the message, responded and they exchanged messages before finally meeting, when Dave showed her the file containing his research into Jerzy (who she tells me was known to the family as Jurek).

Paula remembers that there were always stories about the war and the family's involvement in it when she was a little girl. The family (including Halina, her sister Elisa, and children Jurek, Tadeusz, Saturnin and Janusch) lived close to Warsaw city centre, at 40 Koszykowa Street and later at 17 Zakroczymska Street, on the west side of the river Vistula. Jerzy was a handsome man, 1.8 metres tall, with light hair and complexion, and blue eyes. He was born in Ternopil, in present-day Ukraine, and after completing his compulsory military service in the 1st Air Regiment in Warsaw from 1935 to 1937, he gained his glider pilot's licence and became an instructor at the Military Gliding Centre in Ustjanowa, southern Poland. He was mobilised just before the invasion, serving as an aircraft mechanic but left Poland in late September, travelling to Paris via Romania and Italy. He was evacuated to England on the 24 June 1940, and assigned to the No 5 Air Observers School at RAF Jurby on the Isle of Man, before being posted to No 18 OTU (Operational Training Unit) at Bramcote in December. He joined 305 Squadron at Syerston on 20 January, 1941.

Only three of the children survived the war. Tadeusz was killed whilst fighting with the Polish resistance, the youngest Janusch died in a car accident, and of course Jerzy was lost while serving with the RAF. Paula remembers as a little child seeing the photo of Jerzy standing on the chest of drawers in her grandparent's room, along with one of his fiancée Joan...

'Fiancée? So Jerzy and Joan were engaged?' I ask, remembering the photos Dave had shown me of Jerzy with a girl.

'Yes,' she replies, 'but we never knew very much about Joan other than that she died quite elderly, possibly in the 1980s. She got married apparently, some ten years after Jurek's death, so that was kind of romantic, and sad of course.' I realise that there is a missing beat to the story of what happened after the crash. At some point following Jerzy's death a member of the squadron must have telephoned Joan to break the bad news, or he may have left a letter to be sent to her in the event of his death. I wonder is there anything else Paula can tell me about how the Polish airmen in Britain communicated with their families back in Poland?

Paula tells me that in the early years of the war the Germans allowed some limited communication through the Red Cross, and that several letters and parcels arrived from England including some food and a small doll, which the family back in Poland still have. The doll was intended, she believes, for her auntie who was born in 1934, and who Jerzy would have known. Dave Flint has shown me an article written by Marianna Machnikowska (Marta's daughter) that appeared in a magazine in which she tells Jerzy's story as it was told to her by her grandmother. The family believe that he was going to bring the doll back after the war and give it to Marianna's grandmother. 'He always took this doll with him when on his flights,' she writes. 'There is a legend that it was with him also during the plane crash in which he died. The doll flattened as a result of the fall from a great height. Someone found it and sent it back to Poland. Now the doll is at my home and it is the only witness that could tell the whole story and explain what really happened on that tragic day. But unfortunately it can't speak.'[24]

More unusually perhaps, the family also received some parachute silk, reportedly from Jerzy's own parachute. Parachute silk was considered a very valuable fabric because it was good quality material, and this piece was eventually used to make a First Holy Communion dress for Paula's auntie Magda, and two years later the same dress was worn by her auntie Joanna. Paula thinks the parcel containing the silk and the doll (along with notification of Jerzy's death) was sent by the Red Cross, and must have been kept by Elisa (Jerzy's other sister) in the village where she lived, somewhere between Warsaw and Łódź, because after the failed Uprising in 1944 Jerzy's mother and father were transported to a concentration camp just outside the capital, and 'As they escaped with just

---

[24] From the article *The Story of a Doll*, published in GAPA Aircraft History Magazine, Issue No 23, August 2017

one suitcase, a parachute would probably not be the first necessity to take with them.'

Marianna Machnikowska with Jerzy Krawczyk's doll
(Machnikowska family)

I wonder how much of either story is entirely true – it is unlikely the doll was blown away from the crash, unless it was found on Jerzy's body, if he was thrown away from the explosion and escaped the fire. And the same goes for the parachute, which he was probably not wearing at the time, and would have only clipped on in the event of an evacuation, which of course didn't happen; it was more likely something he had obtained knowing how much the family would appreciate it. But family legends are important.[25]

The First Holy Communion dress, made from parachute silk
(Machnikowska family)

---

[25] Parachute silk was expensive. An u/t pilot at RAF Brize Norton who had his parachute stolen had to pay back £40 from his LAC's weekly salary of around £1 per week. *Aircrew* by Bruce Lewis, Cassell 1991.

The family also have a letter from Joan to Jerzy, probably contained in the same package delivered by the Red Cross, in which she writes:

My dear Jerzy,

Thank you for your letter which I received yesterday. I am very glad you finally got my letter, and Ralph's and Jack's. Thanks for writing me some more Polish words out... Nellie wrote to your friend but he did not write back. This week I will start going to evening college for French, afterwards I will study German. I want to learn Polish but they do not [teach it?].

Today is Sunday, and Jack, Mum and I have been to Church Harvest Thanksgiving. It was very lovely. I hope you are still well. Give my respects please to your friend who was boating with us in Stanley Park. I think of you also every night, and never forget to pray for you. When I am alone I always think of you, I know you will be too busy to write very much to me, but try to write if it is only a page.

I have nothing more to write now, look after yourself darling. Goodbye for now, your ever-loving baby Joan. I have not put kisses because you did not – why?

Joan ends the letter with the common wartime sign-off I.T.A.L.Y, an acronym which was often written on the back of the envelope and meant either 'I Trust And Love You' or 'I'm Thinking About Loving You'.

So what did the family know about the circumstances of Jerzy's death?

'We knew that when he died it wasn't in action, we knew it was in some kind of training,' says Paula. 'It was quite unclear, I remember it was a story about checking the plane after some repairs? I believe that they had two new crew members on the bomber, so they just wanted to fly a little bit as a new crew together.' (This could have Aleksander Zirkwitz, who had been missing operations because of his ear infection, and Kazimierz Mruk, who usually flew second pilot but according to one source flew as first pilot on the fatal flight.)

Paula's recollection is suddenly interrupted by her phone. She reads the text and puts the phone down, telling me it's from the hospital where her husband Piotr is. I immediately apologise and say that we should finish now and continue the conversation some other time but she is adamant that she wants to tell me her story now. She takes a moment or two to gather her thoughts, remembering where she was. 'We knew that Jurek had trained as a navigator and wireless operator, and before the war he was a gliding instructor. I'm not sure if he evacuated together with the army. A lot of Poles, as soon as the Russians entered from the east, when it became clear that western countries were not coming to help, which you know all Poland waited for, they just escaped through the southern border. I think Jurek went through Italy then France and then to England so it was quite a complicated, long route. They kind of followed events really, so I think France was probably the prime destination but again as soon as they learned that France was giving up then it was only Britain left so that was the obvious destination.'

Paula is surprised when I ask her if Jerzy was regarded by the family as a hero.

'Yes, absolutely, of course! You know there was no questioning of anyone's actions during the war, it was obvious to most Polish people that action was needed, and I think that Warsaw was quite a special place when it comes to the resistance and fighting so everyone was a hero in Warsaw. If Warsaw broken, then Poland broken.'

She doesn't have many stories about Tadeusz's involvement in the resistance, because it was all very secret, but she knows that he was fighting with the AK (Home Army), the largest group among several factions, and linked directly to the Polish Government-in-Exile in London. 'It was very political, unbelievably political. The second biggest faction was AL (People's Army) which was supported by Soviets. Really Russia wanted to crush Poland as well, at least morally, psychologically. That was the plan.' All she knows about Tadeusz's death is that, 'Some evening in 1944, it was before the uprising so probably around summertime, someone came and told them that Tadeusz died in action trying to sabotage a train. My great grandma went to the kitchen probably to make him a cup of tea or give him something to eat and when she came back the window was open and the man was gone, so that was probably as much detail as he dared to share, and that's all we know. Tadeusz doesn't have a grave, I think he has some kind of symbolic grave with my grandmother's family in Warsaw with an inscription on the stone.'

I remember a conversation I had with Ian Shaw in the Newark Air Museum, when he described the fierce fighting spirit of the Polish aircrews. 'It was a generation which grew in special times,' Paula says. 'For nearly two hundred years Poland was fought over and dominated by Germany, Russia and the Austro-Hungarian Empire. Then in 1918 Poland gained independence, it was a massive happiness having the country back, there was a lot of political mess which people tend to forget but this newly-gained pride in a very short period of rebuilding the country was very significant, so the generation had something to be proud of and when the war followed it was all translated into this massive heroism.'

Mindful of Putin's 'Special Operation' ongoing in the Ukraine, I ask her what the mood is like in Poland now?

'When Russia attacked Ukraine there was a big fear in Poland. But I am really amazed with Poles, because we were never great friends with Ukrainians, but support was tremendous. I don't know how it will turn out. I am scared because everything is in the hands of a madman so it is unpredictable. And now America is involved so it is different from the war. Massive united forces on one side and crazy on the other. To be honest I try not to think about it on a daily basis, I have got enough to think about.'

Shortly after meeting Dave, we had driven out to Barnes' Field and I showed him where the Wellington had come down. He had asked if I would mind if he showed the site to Paula because the family were coming over to Newark to visit

Jerzy's grave soon. Unfortunately I was going to be out of the country then, working, but I had no problem with that. He later sent me photographs of the family standing at the edge of the field, on a sunny day, much as the day when I first visited it with Robert Brown, and also at Jerzy's grave. I wondered if she could tell me how she had felt about visiting the crash site.

'The moment when we learnt about you and your uncle, I cried,' she said. 'It was not exactly sad, it was you know very moving. I was exactly where I am sitting now, my husband was sat here and I read him the email and I cried because, I don't know, it sounded so incredible like a story from a movie really, not from real life.'

Piotr, Paula and Neirin Pietrzak in Barnes' Field. (David Flint)

I take a small tin out of my bag and open it, showing Paula the bullets, cartridge cases and fragment of shattered metal that I had found at the crash site. She is absolutely silent and her eyes fill with tears as she turns the bullets and metal in her fingers, feeling their power. It is as if I am showing her some ancient relics, which in a sense I suppose I am. She doesn't know what to say; or does, put can't yet put her feelings into words.

She shows me her photos of the painted stones that her family had left on Jerzy's grave, and which Dave remembered seeing – painted in bright colours, one a portrait of Jerzy, another with the UK and Polish flags, one in the shape of a Wellington's fuselage with cockpit and roundels painted on. Her pride in them is unmistakeable.

I remark that it is odd that my family doesn't seem to know anything like as much about Bill as hers does about Jerzy. Paula also thought it strange, but put it down to 'English reserve', saying that 'It was something that you Brits seemed to find harder to talk about.'

It feels like we have talked enough, and I know that Paula needs to get to the hospital to see Piotr. She offers to drive me back to the station, and on the way I ask her about how she had come to the UK.

She says she had wanted to escape from Poland for some time, finding it 'very stifling.' She first made enquiries about working abroad after the Berlin Wall came down in November 1989, initially looking at France, which didn't work out, before hearing from some friends about other Poles who were settling in the UK. She made some enquiries with an agency about finding work and was told all she could expect to get was warehouse packing jobs, for which she was obviously vastly over-qualified, but it would be a start. Her plan was to come over, find a job and somewhere to live, then bring the family to join her. The agency identified two possible locations for her – Leeds and Warrington. Leeds, they said, was a university city, and Warrington 'a seaside resort'. She liked the idea of a city full of students but preferred the idea of living by the sea and arrived in Warrington in the middle of the night after a 30-hour coach drive. She was surprised at what she found, Warrington not looking at all like the seaside resort she'd been expecting, but relieved because she could at least hear the roar of the sea. Laughing, she tells me that in the morning when she drew back the hotel curtains she realised that this was in fact the roar of the M6.

She worked hard, brought over the family (her husband Piotr and two daughters) and soon they had a son, Neirin, born in the UK. Paula admires the Welsh for their independence of spirit. Making their new life work was a matter of all or nothing for Paula – 'No one foot in UK, one foot in Poland,' for her. They wanted to be totally integrated, so tended to steer clear of Polish community groups, and says that she had always thought of Jurek as a bridge for her between Poland and the UK.

At the train station we say goodbye, promising to meet again, maybe for a reunion or memorial. Watching her drive away I felt admiration, both for the way she and her family had fought to make their move to Britain work, and for the way she was dealing with her current difficulties. There was something about her no-nonsense, down-to-earth attitude towards them that made me feel I perhaps understood Jerzy and his crewmates a bit better now.

Thirty-Five

The afternoon is slightly overcast. A colourless, watery grey sky stretches above the flat expanse of dull brown earth. Aside from the dry rustle of dead leaves in the few skeletal trees, all I can hear is the distant caw-caw of rooks, rising and falling against the cold, gusting wind. There is a definite chill in the air, reminding me, if I needed reminding, that the year is finally drawing to a close; the summer has gone and autumn is almost past too.

Not being one of those who enjoy the heat, autumn is normally my favourite season, but today I wish I could claw back just a few weeks of precious summer, which once seemed to stretch out neverendingly, full of promise and potential, and now has run away so quickly. A hundred yards or so across the recently cropped field, almost invisible against the Becks Plantation in his camouflage gear, Tony is methodically sweeping the earth with his metal detector. As the wind is blowing in the wrong direction I can't hear any beeps or whines, but I doubt that he's found any treasure anyway.

There seems to be an element of sad desperation (well, maybe more resignation on Tony's part) in what we are doing. If I'm honest, I believe neither of us really think that we will find anything today; we don't even know for sure if we are looking in the right place to find where Bill's Oxford crashed 80 years ago. In the absence of SHEET 54, I'd spent the previous few weeks walking around the edge of the field, or at my desk, trying to work out where the spot might be. It was not promising. I had been really lucky with the Wellington – Robert Brown had remembered exactly where he had searched the scorched earth for bullets back in 1941. But I'd had no such luck with the Oxford, and as it was the aeroplane Bill had been flying, I was feeling anxious that after all this time I might not actually be able to find the most important thing, as far as I was concerned. Admittedly I had Robert's assertion that 'the Oxford came down in that field by the Gildings', but he was indicating a huge field. Slightly more hopefully I had the AIR81 Accident File and the 305 Squadron Operational Log which put the Oxford as crashing at '800 yards from Elton Crossroads near Beckswood,' and 700 yards from the Wellington. I had used this information to make a rough calculation and drawn two arcs, one about 700 yards from the Wellington crash site in Barnes' Field, and the other 800 yards from the crossroads, and where they intersected I drew a circle. This is where I was hoping the Oxford had crashed.

As Tony doesn't seem to be having any luck I walk around the edge of the field, hoping for inspiration. Looking over a low hedge I see another field which seems fairly featureless, apart from a small area of hardstanding just south of the hedge, which some farm vehicles are parked on. I suppose the concrete could cover a hole made by a crashed aircraft, but the hardstanding is some way off from the area I'd marked and which Tony has now finished sweeping, so probably not a candidate for searching.

We wander back, looking again over the next field, which is to the northwest of the woods, in the direction of the Wellington crash site but less than the distance specified in the AIR81 report. Tony feels that it is worth searching, as it is clear of crops and other features, but I am doubtful as it is further away from the Becks Plantation – if the Oxford had ended up in that field why wouldn't the reports have said the crash was near Sutton Lane?

I can sense Tony's frustration that we don't really know where we are supposed to be looking, despite my basic calculations. Trying to sound confident, I explain my dilemma again: I have the two map references in the AIR81 File but need the actual RAF Map (SHEET 54) if they are to be of any use. Worse, I've had no positive replies from any of the sources

I've contacted, and I feel frustrated and really stupid having to admit that we may never get hold of it.

While he drinks a warming cup of coffee, Tony tries to cheer me up by showing me the items he has found – more bottle tops, a Victorian cap badge, a few things that look like they could have been part of a buckle or some farm machinery, a tiny cog, and various other unidentifiable bits of metal. I lay them out on the car bonnet and photograph them alongside a ruler, just in case, and then the rain starts. Tidying the finds away into a box, I ask Tony if there is any chance of us coming back and maybe trying the field to the northwest, even though I hold out little hope that we'll find anything there. Tony says there is really very little chance of squeezing in another session before the field is reseeded and winter sets in for good - Gillian, the landowner, and her gamekeeper, are very strict about when they will let people onto the land.

After all this time we are going to have to give up until next year. Tony can see the look of undisguised disappointment on my face. There is just one more afternoon when he could be available, he says, next Friday afternoon, if he shifts a few things around in his diary - could I be free then? Could I? Of course! I'd been planning to work from home that day but I can make any time he wants. So we make it a date, me delighted that I have one last window of opportunity, and as the rain falls ever more heavily, we get into our cars and head off.

That evening, I download my photographs of Tony's finds and email them to the Lincolnshire Aircraft Recovery Group, or LARG, as they call themselves. They have a fantastic collection of recovered aircraft parts at East Kirby and I hope that their expert eyes might recognise something of interest.

The Friday morning of the search doesn't start well. The skies are leaden, full of cloud, and the chill in the air suggests more rain may be on the way, which is a problem. However, I don't have much time to think about that – my morning is full of work at my desk, finishing prep for the shoot that starts on

Monday. Emails and phone calls keep interrupting my work, as people in Scotland ask about this plan or this shot, with last minute changes of schedule and so on. Always, however, at the back of my mind is that clock ticking away – my date with Tony at 3pm at Becks Plantation. Then an email arrives from Tony, who's also at work, and has some bad news.

It turns out that the field is rented out to a tenant, and it's been seeded – Tony doesn't want to scupper his chances in the future by clumping all over the tenant's field, but he hasn't got the tenant's number. Can I contact Gillian? Yes, I say, no problem. And what's the weather like over my way? he asks. It's looking pretty gloomy where he is. He asks me to keep an eye out and let him know and, 'We'll see about this afternoon.' I talk to Gillian and she tells me the tenant is away at the moment but confirms all the fields are seeded now. Then, hearing the silence at my end, she says she's happy to let us look at the field so long as we use our common sense. Phew.

I return to my prep. Then, not long before lunch, there's a phone call from Mum, panicking because her washing machine's on the blink and she hasn't been able to wash anything for a week. She wants me to ring the manufacturers. I want to ask why she hasn't mentioned this before when now it's become a major emergency just at the worst time for me, but I bite my tongue. Instead, I promise to drop by in the afternoon en route to or from Elton. But she is worried, saying she has the instruction manuals and guarantee there, so maybe she should ring the number on the guarantee herself..?

I tell her I'll come over *now*. And I do, after sending a last-minute flurry of emails to the production office and reassuring myself that I can finish everything else I need to do over the weekend before heading to Glasgow on Sunday. I drive to Bingham, my head full of the sweep we are planning, constantly looking up at the ever-darkening sky. I think I see a few isolated spots of rain on the windscreen, hoping it's nothing more than that. Within a minute of looking at the washing machine I've identified the problem – it's the childlock, inadvertently activated – the door clicks open, and Mum's delighted. We load up the machine and set off her washing. I have to head off after a cuppa, and looking up it now feels that the worst of the weather has maybe passed.

Back at home there's an email on the laptop from Louise Bush at LARG. They have looked at the photographs I sent them and are very sorry but can't positively identify anything. But that doesn't matter – I put any disappointment behind me. This afternoon Tony and I will be able to look for the Oxford crash site.

I look at my watch. Half past two. Time to finish work – I've done enough, and anything else that comes up last minute I can deal with by email tonight.

I wander into the kitchen to make a cup of coffee and look out of the window. It's raining. No question about it – real, heavy, wet *rain*. Bugger. The street is full of people running, trying to escape the rain which is now hammering on the pavement. As if it will make any difference, I open the front door, and the smell of fresh rain hits me, as well as the sound.

I have to email Tony, and even at this last minute I try to sugarcoat it, still hoping that it might only be a passing shower. But it's no good. He gets straight back – it's chucking it down in West Bridgford, he says, there's no way we can search in this. We have to leave it. I email back, saying that's fine.

But it's not. I feel like I've been punched in the gut. The shutter has finally come down on our hopes for finding anything this year. That's it until next spring at the very earliest.

Thirty-Six

The year is in its dying days, and my journey, as far as searching for the Oxford's crash site is concerned, has already come to an end. What do I do to fill my days? I try to write the book, but I had always hoped there would be a positive ending to my story, which makes it difficult. I haven't found the crash site of Bill's Oxford, so what's the point of telling a story without an ending?

Quickly, more quickly than the nights are drawing in, a kind of melancholia settles around me. I feel guilty about the failure to deliver, after all I'd promised myself and others, Fiona, especially. The memory of *Cultybraggan*, coinciding as it did with the end of my marriage, is at the heart of it I know, and I can't erase the feeling of hopelessness from my mind. All I have to look forward to now is another lonely winter in Newark, dealing with another failure.

Then one day I get an email. It's from the RAF Museum at Hendon, and it comes with an attachment – a chap called Andrew Dennis has read my email and scanned SHEET 54 for me! I stare at the map as if it holds the key to buried treasure – there's Bingham, and Elton (just simple Elton, no On-The-Hill in 1940), and the Becks Plantation is there, but unnamed, which confirms my theory that some RAF officer on the scene just wrote down the name he was given by a local – 'Beck's Wood', which became Beckswood in the report. Checking the grid references in the crash report I can now find the indisputable point where Bill's Oxford crashed, measured and marked out precisely by the RAF recovery team and investigating officers from Syerston immediately after the accident.

I can't believe it. The point I'm now looking at, the very point on the map where the Oxford crashed, is very close to the intersection of the arcs that I had drawn with my rough calculation, only a few tens of yards nearer the woods than the spot where we looked last week.

So now I know exactly where to look. Except I can't look. The metal detecting season has closed and Gillian's gamekeeper doesn't want the fields (and more importantly his precious pheasants) disturbed. Tony is settled in for the winter, dreaming of finding his ancient Roman settlement. We won't be able to meet up again until the spring at the very earliest. And I still have a book to write.

The field where the Oxford crashed, looking southeast with The Becks Plantation centre. (Author)

I go for a walk around St Mary's churchyard, thinking. Once again, the future looks bleak. I sit down on a bench in the old graveyard, the one, I remember, where I sat earlier in the year, waiting to see the BBMF Lancaster fly over Newark, thinking that the situation was a bit like someone waiting for a lover, who is late for a meeting. Along with the sweep over the marketplace by that Spitfire on my first day in my new home it was a moment that convinced me I'd made the right decision in coming to live in Newark. Sometimes you just know a thing is right.

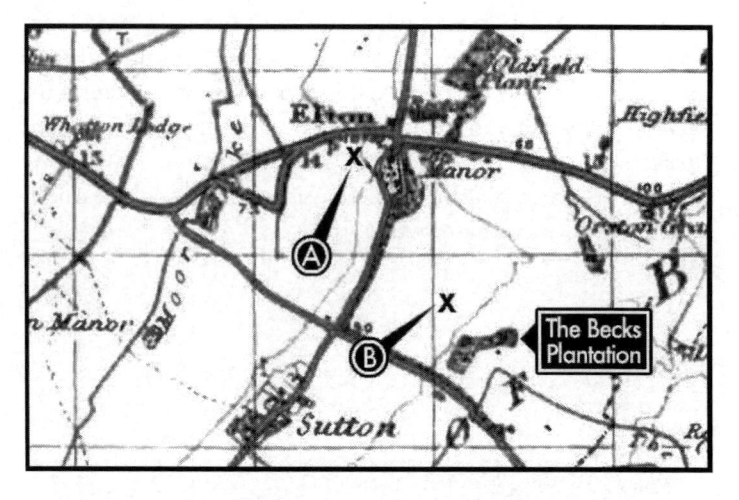

The crash sites. The Wellington (A) and Oxford (B). The A52 Nottingham to Grantham road runs L-R through Elton (RAF Museum Hendon)

And then the realisation hit me: why am I worrying? I now know the exact points where both the Wellington and the Oxford came down. If I had been able to get my hands on SHEET 54 right at the beginning of the journey, I'd have been happy enough just to be able to stand at the edge of Gillian's field and point to the area just to the west of the Becks Plantation knowing that's where Bill's plane crashed. Which is exactly what I can do now. I can stand at the gate and look back over my shoulder, to where the Wellington came down, then gaze up into the sky somewhere over Elton church and say, with confidence, that this is where it happened.

Thirty-Seven

Thursday June 12 1941.

It was over a week since the raid on Duisburg. Since then, life at RAF Syerston had been dull and tedious, with no operations and only limited flying due to the miserable British summer weather; low thick cloud, drizzle and rain kept the Wellingtons on the ground. The Wimpys' engines and turrets were safely covered by tarpaulins, while the ground crews sat in their huts around pot-bellied stoves, drinking mugs of tea and playing cards while the rain hammered against the corrugated iron roofs. But having had a taste of combat, the crew of R1017 were becoming increasingly frustrated. Although Squadron Leader Kleczyński had laid on extra lectures and instructional films to keep the squadron occupied, there was almost a feeling among the crews that they were past that now – they'd had a taste of operations and being shot at and didn't need to sit through yet more lectures on night fighter recognition, or practise evacuation and dinghy drills. They kicked their heels in the flight office and the mess, smoking and reading novels or magazines, whatever was to hand. Even the *Newark Advertiser* and the *Nottingham Evening Post*, normally only glanced at for information about where the next dance was being held, were read from front to back. Some had braved the rain to go into Newark to watch Vivien Leigh and Robert Taylor in *Waterloo Bridge* at the Kinema, followed by a dance at the Corn Exchange, and the visit on the 11th by the OCC Bomber Command Sir Richard Peirse had livened things up a little, but they yearned to see more action.

Away from Syerston, at I Group Headquarters in Hucknall there was action, of a sort. For a couple of days now reports had suggested an imminent change in the weather situation over Britain and Europe. Maps were consulted and plans discussed for mounting more raids on German targets as soon as the weather would allow. Coded telegrams had already been sent out to stations across 1 Group ordering crews and aircraft to be on standby for a Maximum Effort. The first real hint that the crews might be about to return to operations came on Wednesday evening, in the mess after the OCC's visit, when Squadron Leader Ścibior, commander of B Flight, tipped Stefanicki the wink, telling him to make sure his lads got an early night...

A little over a hundred miles south of Syerston, just west of Oxford, the last notes of the Reveille echoed around RAF Brize Norton. 19-year old Leading Aircraftman William 'Bill' Parkinson turned over on his iron bed, trying to snatch a few minutes extra sleep, but there was no point – the corporal would soon be slamming around, encouraging them to rise and shine in his own special way, and Bill's brain was already thinking about the day ahead.

He pulled himself up and sat on the edge of the bed, rubbing the sleep out of his eyes and trying to remember what he was down for today. All around him the other occupants of Hut 7 were doing the same, the noise of coughs and farts mixed with the odd word or grunt as they tried to wake up. The last few weeks at Brize Norton had been exhausting – the days packed with lectures and demonstrations, and the evenings spent cramming for the tests that seemed to happen every day. They were flying a lot too – Bill had amassed 54 hours in his logbook, 26½ of them flying solo on the Oxford. He'd been lucky enough to go up in one a few times with a decent instructor who didn't yell and roll his eyes at every little mistake, like Albrighton, his usual instructor. He didn't really seem to get on with the young Flight Lieutenant, who at only 23 was already a DFC and a veteran of a full tour on

Hampdens and Wellingtons. But Bill liked the Oxford. It was a tidy little aeroplane, not easy to fly but with the twin Cheetah engines packing quite a punch, so sitting at the controls it was easy to imagine himself as the pilot of a bomber, which after all, was what this was all about.

Then he remembered. Today was a Cross Country Navigation Exercise. Of course, at this stage in their training the cadets of No 1 Squadron 2SFTS were flying almost every day, but this was a bit different. He grabbed his towel and soap and headed out to the ablutions.

'Easy there boy, *easy*.'

The young girl spoke calmly, and pulled back on the reins, reassuring the old, red horse as a long stream of trucks sped past them, on their way to the aerodrome. The last one in the convoy sounded its horn as it passed, and old Lancelot jumped again, his horseshoes clattering on the metalled road. 'Bloody idiots. Anyone would think there was a war on,' said the girl, repeating one of her dad's favourite phrases.

Betty Kinch, who had missed her breakfast after sleeping through the 4.30 alarm, was in no mood for speeding drivers, war or no war. It was a little before seven o'clock in the morning and she had already been up for over two hours, getting the cows in, helping with the milking and loading the churns onto the cart before setting off down the road to Syerston. Every morning since last December, when the airfield had opened and the place was suddenly full of men in uniforms speaking in strange accents, she had repeated the pattern. At least now summer was here, the days were lighter and warmer, and the mile and a half drive from the farm to the 'drome was worth getting out of bed early for. She loved the smell of the milkweed and cow parsley in the verges, especially on a pleasant morning like this, and the calls of the peewits as they flapped crazily over the fields.

Another big truck rumbled past the cart, an enormous camouflage-painted tanker, full of petrol for the planes, she guessed. They seemed to be flying all the time now, endlessly taking off and circling round the 'drome, appearing suddenly out of nowhere with a huge roar, and swooping low over the fields. They were frightening and exciting at the same time. She thought they looked like pregnant sticklebacks, and Dad said their big bellies were full of bombs, so she was right, they were like the sticklebacks, in a way. Over the last few weeks the planes had done a lot more flying at night, taking off in numbers in the evening and coming back in the early hours, just in time to wake her for the milking. Dropping their bombs on Germany, Dad said.

Betty had left school at 14 in the summer of '40, and already she'd seen a lot of change around Syerston. Before the aerodrome came all of this was farmland, good solid pasture, according to her dad, whose family had been tenant farmers here for donkey's years. And then one day, as she was walking to school, she had noticed some men had turned up in a lorry, setting up strange things like cameras on tripods, which they peered through across the fields, waving their arms, shouting numbers and pacing out distances; they were still there when she walked home again in the afternoon, writing things down in notebooks and hunched over huge maps, which they weighted down with stones to stop them blowing away in the wind. She entered the farmhouse kitchen to find Dad sitting at the table, with what her ma called 'one of his moods' on him. Mr Hobbes from the estate had been round to tell them that the government were buying some of the land, right up to the river, more than half the fields he rented. Mr Hobbes wasn't happy either, what with him not *asking* if they could buy it, mind, or if the estate would *consider* selling, *they were buying it*, and immediately, on Air Ministry orders, no questions. There was no haggling over price either - they told the estate what they were paying and that was it. *But why?* her dad had asked. What does the government want with my land? They're going to build an airfield, Mr Hobbes said. Well, my cows might have sommat to say about that, her Dad replied – all them bleddy aeroplanes zooming all over the place – it'll put them off their milking. Sorry, Mr Hobbes had said. Still, better than having Jerry march in here and take it all away from us, eh?

And Dad couldn't really argue with that. He'd lost his brother in the last war against Germany, Ma said, and if building an aerodrome put Hitler off starting another war, well that had to be a good thing.

They had reached the aerodrome now, and Lancelot turned in towards the entrance before stopping a few yards from the red and white striped barrier. He knew the routine well by now: after a few moments a guard would wander out of the hut, say, 'Morning,' to the girl and her horse, and cast a quick look over the milk churns sitting on the cart, making a note of their number on his clipboard. Back in December, when the officer from the aerodrome had called round to ask Dad if he could supply the canteen with a regular supply of milk, it had seemed like poor recompense for the loss of his fields, but there was a war on, and the extra money came in handy. Apparently, there were getting on for a thousand men on the 'drome, and they all needed their cups of tea. Betty couldn't work out why the guard always counted the number of churns on the way in and then out again, until her Mum had told her that there had been some trouble with the black market, and that 'them Poles' had been up to their tricks again.

Satisfied, the guard said, 'Alright let her through,' and waved to his colleague to raise the barrier. The daily routine repeated, Lancelot started up again, the girl smiled and gave a little wave to the good-looking guard, and the milk cart slowly wound its way past the great green-and-black camouflaged hangars, towards the airfield kitchens. A couple of WAAFs smiled at her as they passed, and she thought they looked very glamorous, although she knew her dad didn't approve of them, having seen WAAFs drinking and smoking until all hours in The Boot and Shoe. She could tell from the signs of activity around the airfield that something was up, which didn't bode well – if there was a raid on tonight they'd be flying around all day doing last minute checks and her dad would be cursing them for disturbing his milkers with 'their bleddy noise.' But there was nothing she could do about that.

George Parkinson, Bill's twin brother, picked the newspaper up from the hallway floor and wandered through to the breakfast table.

'Breakfast's nearly ready, George,' said his mother, placing a pot of tea on the table.

'Thanks,' he said, quickly scanning the front page as he sat down. *RAFs heaviest Rhur attack... Duisburg and Dusseldorf main objectives... attacks also made on the docks at Rotterdam and Boulogne...*

His mother went back into the kitchen. 'We're out of sugar I'm afraid – no more until the weekend.'

'Don't worry. I'll wait until I get to work. They always have some in the journalists' office. They hoard it for bribing policemen and judges with.' *...British success in North Africa... towns in the north-east, west midlands and the south bombed...*

Gertrude Parkinson returned with a plate. 'Busy day today, George?'

'Mm?'

'Oh, put that paper down, please. I was asking what you are doing today.'

'Sorry.' He folded the newspaper and spread the tiniest amount of butter on his toast. 'I'm covering a wedding at St John's this morning, and a meeting of the Housing Committee at the council in the afternoon, unless there's a big fire in the town centre of course. Oh, and I've got to get the 25s and 50s ready.' These were the columns reporting events of interest covered by the *Goole Times* 25 and 50 years ago; dull and tedious, and generally left to trainee journalists such as himself.

'That must be interesting,' said his mother.

'Not really,' he replied, munching the toast. 'Last week I was so bored I made one up about the 1916 Howden Ladies Guild Annual Flower Show and a nanny goat.' He smiled at her.

'George.' Gertrude looked at her son, not sure whether to believe him. 'You're worse than your brother.'

'Today you will be carrying out your first - though hopefully not your last - solo cross country navigation flight.'

Some of the cadets of No 1 Squadron, 2SFTS grinned. One or two even laughed. The instructor stood at the head of the class and cast a stern eye around the lecture hut. 'That is not a joke, gentlemen. Many a Pilot Under Training has been known to fail to return from a solo cross country navigation exercise.'

The cadets settled, picking up on his serious tone.

'You have been well trained as pilots, at great expense to the RAF, and I have every confidence that the vast majority of you will be collecting your wings at the end of this course. But there will be washouts, and next to night flying this exercise will be the toughest task demanded of you to date. You are expected to fly, navigate and control a twin-engine aircraft all by yourselves. Problems will occur, unexpected situations will arise, you will be called on to make instant decisions, but if you have remembered anything that has been drummed into your thick heads over the past few weeks, you will not panic and you will bring your aeroplane back.'

Bill smiled. *This was what he had been looking forward to.*

The instructor continued. 'You will be flying in single control Oxfords – no dual controls today. And you will be working in pairs – cadets only, so there's no cheery instructor to wave his magic wand if you make an idiot of yourself. Your instructors will explain the exercise and pair you up...'

So long as they didn't put him with one of those braying Oxford and Cambridge types who think they know it all...

The instructor referred them to a map on the wall. 'The weather report is good and take-offs start at 0830 – you have got from now until then to pair up, work out your routes and prepare. Do your best. And good luck gentlemen.'

Sixteen chairs scraped back and the cadets looked around at each other. *This was going to be a good day.*

William Newton opened the front door to 24 Devon Gardens and breathed in the early morning air. Away in the distance he could hear the hooters and cranes from the shipyards along the Tyne. His neighbour Mr Heaton was walking down the path towards Lindum Road, trying to stifle a yawn. *Clearly he got as little sleep as I did last night*, William thought. The first air raid siren had sounded at around eleven o'clock, and he and his wife Beatrice had hurried into the garden shelter immediately, still wearing their nightclothes. The last few months had seen heavy raids over Newcastle and only a couple of weeks ago a raider had dropped a bomb on the Wilkinson's shelter in North Shields, with over a hundred people left dead. Not that the numbers were public knowledge, but he had a friend at the *Chronicle* who knew about these things. Anyway, he and Mrs Newton were taking no chances. But they'd no sooner gone back to bed after the All Clear at around one o'clock than a second siren had sounded, which meant traipsing down to the Anderson shelter again, and they didn't get back into bed until gone three.

'Here's your lunch, dear,' said his wife, and she handed him a Thermos flask and a small greaseproof-paper parcel.

'Thank you.' William gave his wife a kiss on the cheek. 'It's a lovely day,' she said. 'You should walk instead of getting the tram. You've got time.'

'No, I can't be late this morning,' William replied. 'The office is running Fire Drills before we open the doors. As if I didn't have enough on my plate.'

'Well, you better hurry up then, hadn't you. Bye.' Beatrice watched her husband close the gate and turn up the path for the Durham Road. Shutting the door, she walked back into the kitchen and leaned against the sink. The cat wound itself between and around her ankles, hoping to get some scraps or perhaps a little milk. It was in these quiet moments, when there was nobody else in the house, and only the cat and the ticking of the clock for company, that she started to think about Robson. It didn't do to worry about him, she knew that, there was nothing she could do to protect him, but all the same it was hard, the *not knowing*. In his last letter he'd said that he expected to finish his course in a few weeks, which would probably mean some home leave before his posting to an OTU, so that was something to look forward to at least. She'd been thinking of buying him a present, a new tie perhaps, or some gloves. Clothes rationing had come in that month, and she was still trying to get her head around how it all worked but she knew it was one coupon for a tie and two for gloves, so she was sure they could manage that.

Beatrice Newton said a little silent prayer for her son, shooed the cat away and collected the breakfast things together.

'Do you two bods know each other?'

Bill Parkinson looked at the man standing next to him. He was clearly a few years older than himself, good looking, dark haired, with intelligent brown eyes and a few inches smaller than Bill, though without his own rugby player's build.

'No, sir.' Each cadet spoke at the same time.

'Well, you do now,' said the instructor. 'LAC Newton, this is LAC Parkinson. You're both from t'north so I'm sure you'll have something in common, even if it is only whippets and football.' Flight Lieutenant Albrighton handed Bill a piece of paper with locations and grid references scribbled on it, and a couple of maps. 'Have you got your pencils, compass, slide rule?'

'Yes sir,' they said together again. Bill thought he detected a faint ironic smile on Newton's lips.

'Good. *These* are your turning points. You have a half-full tank. There's no time limit on your exercise but I expect you back before lunch and I don't want you buzzing off on some jaunt. Radio your position to the aerodromes listed here every twenty minutes or within twenty miles radius of the station. There will be a lot of aeroplanes buzzing around and I don't want to have to spend the rest of the day on the phone to some irate station commander about how two of my sprogs nearly caused an accident, understand?'

'Yes, sir.'

'You're flying T1334. Who's piloting her first?'

The two cadets looked at each other.

'Come on, it's not hard.'

LAC Newton looked at Bill. 'I don't mind... unless you–'

'Oh, for heaven's sake,' said the instructor, exasperated. 'Parkinson, you go first.'

'Yes, sir.'

'Newton, you'll navigate. Check those coordinates, work out your ETAs. And make sure you've got the station frequencies.'

'Yes, sir.'

'Come on then, flying kit and parachutes and I want to see that kite in the air in half an hour.'

They watched as the instructor stalked off to pair up some more cadets. 'Arsehole,' said LAC Newton.

'Hey – watch it,' said Bill. He smiled and extended his hand.

'William Parkinson. Friends call me Bill.'

'Robson Newton,' said the other, shaking hands. 'Where are you from?'

'You won't have heard of it. Goole, near Hull.'

'I know it. Furthest inland port in England.'

'Blimey,' said Bill. 'Have you ever been there?'

'Nope.'

'Well, I can tell where *you're* from, by your accent. You're a Geordie.'

'Well done, bonny lad. Gateshead born and bred. Pleased to meet you.'

Gertrude Parkinson dried the last of the crockery and gazed out of the kitchen window. The garden was coming along nicely now, especially with George's help. He was particularly proud of his broad beans. It was a bit early but maybe there'd be some ready for picking this weekend – she was thinking of making a stew with that piece of scrag end. She would ask George when he got home this evening.

Things were alright at Fountayne Street, on the whole. When William died she had felt completely at a loss for what to do – suddenly widowed, having to move out of the manse on Victoria Street, the boys to get through school – but they had managed, with some help from the church, and they'd found this little house, number 9. At least Margaret had had somewhere settled to live during those last difficult months. Poor girl, she was so brave. And no-one had any idea that within a few years the country would be at war again. Now George was writing for the *Goole Times*, and Billy was in the RAF, learning to fly. She wondered when he'd next be home on leave. Not too long, she told herself, and with a set of wings sewn neatly on his uniform, hopefully.

She folded the tea towel and hung it next to the stove. Yes, on the whole, things were alright...

0845 hours, RAF Brize Norton.

The early morning sun shone brightly as Bill Parkinson and Robson Newton walked around the Oxford, giving the aeroplane a once-over before the flight. Standing a little way off, Flt Lt Albrighton and a corporal mechanic watched as Bill checked the control surfaces and tyres, trying to look like he knew what he was doing. It was a fine morning, the sky was blue, good visibility with a little wind, the grass still wet with dew. The Oxford, T1334, only delivered to 2SFTS from the Airspeed factory in March, was still relatively new and looked to be in good shape, its green and brown camouflaged upper surfaces contrasting sharply with the bright yellow fuselage sides and undersurfaces. Satisfied, with a final run of his hand over the leading edge of the port wing, Billy looked over at the instructor.

'All OK, sir.'

'Good. Jump in, do your cockpit checks and take off when you're ready. We'll see you back here in three hours.'

'Five bob says it's Germany.'

Pilot Officer Stanisław Kowalcze, 28, eased a leg over the bench and placed his tray on the Officers' Mess table, looking round eagerly. None of his crewmates looked up. 'Come on... Bit of fun, eh?'

Aleksander Zirkwitz glanced up from his paper. 'You need to be more exact than that before you see my money, Stan. Where in Germany?'

'Bremen. Any takers?'

The crew of R1017 shook their heads. 'No thanks,' said the navigator, Marian Wojtowicz. 'You must know something we don't, Kowalcze.'

Tadeusz Stefanicki strolled up, catching the last words. 'About what?' he asked, lighting up a cigarette.

'The target for tonight,' said Wojtowicz. 'Kowalcze thinks it's Bremen.'

'And why Bremen?'

'Maybe he owes some fellow in Bremen money,' said Zirkwitz, raising his eyebrows.

'No. Just something in my water,' said Kowalcze.

'*Ugh.*' Wojtowitz made a face.

'You should see the MO about that,' said Zirkwitz. 'He can give you some cream.'

The pilot took a drag on his cigarette and blew smoke out from the side of his mouth. 'Well, I'll take your bet on, Kowalcze. But only if you double it.'

Kowalcze looked at him for a second. 'Done. Thanks, captain.' Each man pulled a handful of coins from his pocket and counted them onto the table. 'Where do you say we're going?'

'Duisburg,' said the pilot.

'*Again?*' said Wojtowizc.

'Why not? Finish the job.'

'I thought we made a pretty good job of it last time,' said Wojtowicz.

Zirkwitz put his paper down. 'You seem confident, sir.'

Stefanicki smiled. 'Something a little bird told me.'

'A little bird in a tight blue uniform?'

'No, a little bird in overalls, with a big moustache. Our dear slob Jakub showed me the petrol chit – they're giving the kites the same amount of petrol they used for Duisburg.'

Kowlacze exploded. 'That's not fair. Inside information.'

'It means nothing,' said Wojtowicz. 'It could be anywhere.'

Stefanicki smiled. 'A bet's a bet. You might as well give me the ten bob now.'

'No chance, captain,' said Kowalcze, pocketing his coins. 'You'll have to wait 'til we get back from Duisburg before you see my money.'

'Diane Ablitt?'

A hand shot up. 'Miss.'

'Angela Avey?'

Another hand. 'Here, miss.'

Class registration at Bottesford Junior School, three miles from Elton village. The class, including three recent evacuees from Sheffield, raised their hands when called by their teacher, Mrs Beryl Morgan.

'Janet Baird?'

'Miss.'

Robert Brown, aged 9, leaned over to his friend Mike Fox, and whispered, 'What you doin' Saturday?'

'I work with me dad Sat'day morning.'

'Susan Bradd?' There was a brief pause. 'Susan Bradd?'

A girl in blond pigtails looked up. 'Yes, miss.'

'Too much talking and not enough listening Susan Bradd.'

Laughter. 'Sorry, miss.'

'Elsie Brown..?'

Robert leant further over. 'After dinner then?'

'Yeah, alright.'

'Robert Brown?'

'*Yes miss, here, miss.*'

Mike dipped his head behind the girl in front and looked at his friend. 'What you wanna do?'

'Bird nestin'. I seen a coot's nest under the canal bridge down Barkestone Lane.'

'I've already got a coot's egg.'

'Well, I haven't and-'

'Robert Brown and Michael Fox!'

The boys sat up straight, arms folded, their faces a picture of innocence.

'Yes, miss?'

'Whatever it is you're talking about I am sure it can wait until playtime.'

'Yes, miss, sorry miss.'

'Jayne Flannery?'

A girl put her hand up. 'She's ill, miss, with earache, miss.' Robert Brown leaned over again. 'Sat'day afternoon then. Bring yer bike.'

'Bit early for your Night Flying Test aren't you sir? I'm not sure the lads are ready yet.' Leaning out of the cockpit window the Chief Mechanic wiped his hands with an oily rag. It was already getting hot under all that Perspex.

Standing between the cowling panels lying beneath the port engine, Tadeusz Stefanicki looked up, shading his eyes against the early morning sun. 'No Chiefy, the Flight Commander wants us to do a spot of close formation flying before tonight's op. I thought we could combine the two.'

'Really?' Chiefy rolled his eyes. 'Well, he might have told me. She won't be ready for another hour at least.'

'How is she? Any problems?' Stefanicki gazed up at the sooty giant.

'Bit of rain got into one of the landing lights, and the cockpit heater's playing up but nothing I can't sort out given a bit of time. We're not miracle workers, sir.'

Tadeusz thought he detected a slight note of irritation in Chiefy's voice. Hardly surprising. Like most mechanics, while the aircraft was on the ground, Chiefy Zajac liked to think SM-K was *his* aeroplane. Air crews came and went but woe betide a pilot if he brought it back with anything broken. 'So long as I can have her by eleven, OK?'

'Eleven?' Chiefy drew in his breath. 'I'll do my best, but I'm not promising.' The mechanic slid the cockpit window shut with a bang, indicating he had things to do and the conversation was over. Stefanicki turned to his second pilot, Kazimierz Mruk. 'Let's hope they have her ready, or Ścibior will have my balls. He was in a foul mood after breakfast. Says we need to keep tighter formation and he wants us to be able to do it with our eyes closed.'

'That doesn't sound like a good idea.' Mruk smiled, sensing his captain's anxiety. 'I'm joking.'

Stefanicki looked grim. 'But Ścibior's not. He's deadly serious. And I'm not going to give him an excuse to drop us, so we'll practice until he's happy.'

'But we're definitely on for tonight?'

'Oh yes.' Stefanicki smiled at last. 'Can't wait. Fancy what passes for a coffee round here?'

'No, I better round the crew up and make sure they know the score.'

Stefanicki walked off towards the NAAFI van, and turned as Mruk called out: 'Any hint about where we're going? Kowalcze seemed to think you'd got some gen.'

'I was pulling his leg,' the captain smiled. 'We'll find out at the briefing.'

'Would madame like these wrapped?'

'Yes, please.'

Beatrice Newton smiled as the girl bent down to find some paper. She was in the Newcastle Co-op Society department store, a skyscraper-like Art Deco building on Newgate Street in the city centre.

'These are lovely gloves,' said the girl as she laid them carefully on the paper. 'The leather is so soft.'

'Yes, I'm glad I found them, they're perfect, I think. And the tie.'

'I'm sure he'll love them,' said the girl.

'Yes,' Beatrice said. She had a strange feeling the girl was looking at her oddly.

'Would madame prefer ribbon or string?'

'Oh, I don't know. Let's say ribbon, while we still have some left.' She laughed, and the girl smiled. A pretty smile, Beatrice thought, and then there was that sly look again.

'Excuse me but... do I know you?'

The girl smiled again. 'I'm sorry. You're Mrs Newton, aren't you? Robson's mother.'

'Yes, I am. Have we er...?'

'I know your son. We were at school together.'

'Oh, I see,' said Beatrice.

'He's in the RAF isn't he?'

'Yes, he's training at the minute, somewhere down south.'

'I know, he told me. I'm hoping to see him soon.'

Beatrice stared at the girl. 'I beg your pardon?'

The girl blushed. 'I'm sorry, Mrs Newton. Robson writes to me, I thought you knew.'

'No, why should I?'

'I suppose not. I just thought he might have said something as we...' She stopped herself, and looked down. 'I'm so sorry, please...'

'No, that's perfectly alright dear... Miss- I'm sorry, what is your name?'

'Audrey. Audrey Knight.'

'I'm sure Robson writes to lots of girls.'

There was a pause as Beatrice watched the girl wind the ribbon around the brown paper parcel and tie a small bow. She had pale delicate fingers, the nails nicely manicured, and was really rather pretty. Beatrice needed some air. The girl snipped the ribbon ends and slid the package across the counter. 'Well, there you are, Mrs Newton. It was nice to meet you. I hope-'

'That's quite alright, dear.' She picked up the parcel, with its pretty ribbon and perfectly tied bow. There was a pause, and the girl thought she saw the lady's fingers tremble. 'On second thoughts, perhaps these aren't right after all. I think I'll leave them, thank you.' The words rushed out in a torrent and before the girl could say anything Beatrice Newton was hurrying down the marble staircase and out into the street where she quickly disappeared into the crowd.

The Oxford rolled across the airfield, bumping slightly on the grass runway, picking up speed. Seated on the left-hand side of the cockpit, Bill Parkinson was aware of stationary aircraft and figures flashing past him, but concentrated on increasing throttle on the starboard engine, fighting the Ox-box's natural tendency to swing in that direction on take-off. The aircraft snaked a little, and it was an effort to keep the tail from swinging round. A gentle easing of the stick brought the tail up, improving Bill's view over the aircraft's nose, which made things a lot easier. Eventually the aircraft reached 70mph and with a firm steady pull back Bill lifted it into the air. He muttered something to himself as he reached over to retract the undercarriage, and with the airspeed indicator creeping past the 100mph mark the Oxford began its climb over the hangars and up into the bright blue sky.

It was a wonderful feeling and one which Bill found hard to put into words. George would have no problem describing it, he thought. Sitting next to him Robson Newton grinned, obviously enjoying the same thrill of leaving the ground. But there was no time for musing on the joys of flight. He had to set a course for his first turning point – Aberystwyth, on the Welsh coast.

In the Watch Office a WAAF stubbed her cigarette out in the ashtray and glanced at the clock. 'Oxford T1334, take-off 0905 hours. Anyone fancy some coffee?'

'Nice take-off,' said Robson, making his calculations over the map. Over the roar of the engines he had to hold his oxygen mask to his mouth to speak on the intercom.

'Thanks,' said Bill. He looked over his left shoulder, down at the patchwork of fields stretching out below. 'I've always wanted to fly. Long as I can remember.'

'Aye man, it's a great feeling. Nothing like it.' There was a pause, each man in his own thoughts. 'So where do you think you'll end up? When you get your wings, I mean.'

'Bomber Command, I hope,' said Bill. 'You?'

'I'm trying for Coastal.'

'Really? Any particular reason?'

'Not really.' Robson felt Bill's eyes on him. 'Well, there is I suppose. I lost a mate last year. Merchant Navy, his ship was torpedoed by a U-Boat.'

Bill was taken aback by the note of anger in the young man's voice. 'Sorry.'

'That's OK man. At first, I thought this war was nothing to do with me. But I couldn't ignore it after that. I thought if I can drop a few depth charges you never know I might just get the Jerry bastard who did for Harry.'

There was a pause as the two men thought about that.

'Anyway,' Robson said eventually. 'Stay on this course and we should make Aberystwyth in about 40 minutes. Put your foot down and we might be able to sneak some fish and chips and a ride on the dodgems...'

In the southeast corner of Syerston airfield, clustered around the parade ground, stood a collection of 'H' shaped buildings, known, unsurprisingly, as the H Blocks. These were the living quarters for the other ranks, each long room on either floor holding twenty beds, with rooms for the corporals by the doors.

There was a rumour flying about that the squadron was on for tonight, but nothing definite yet. Sgt Jerzy Krawczyk, having finished breakfast and with not much else to do, was lying on his iron bed, writing a letter to his girlfriend Joan.

The two had been writing regularly to each other since they met in Blackpool in the summer of 1940. Joan, from Keighley in Yorkshire, was on her annual Feast Week Holiday – the hosiery mill where she worked as a pairer, just like all the other factories and shops in town, had closed down for the week so the workers could enjoy a few days by the sea, or in the hills, anywhere so long as it wasn't Keighley. Joan and her family had gone to Blackpool, as they usually did; her recently-widowed mother having a good relationship with a landlady who had a couple of rooms vacant owing to her RAF lads being posted down south. *The resort was heaving with boys in blue uniforms these days*, Alice Pugh wrote, confirming the booking. Situated on the northwest coast of England, Blackpool was not considered a likely invasion point for Hitler's armies, and quickly became the largest training area in western Europe. The war was good for Blackpool.

Even though the town was full of men and women in uniforms, it still operated on pre-war terms, welcoming holidaymakers with open arms. Compared to the rest of blacked-out, rationed Britain, it seemed a paradise: the dancehalls stayed open, and the theatres showed different plays every night. All the stars, wary perhaps of spending too much time in London, performed in wartime Blackpool: Noel Coward, John Mills, Flora Robson, Robert Donat, Richard Attenborough; in 1940, the Sadlers Wells Ballet brought Margot Fonteyn, Frederick Ashton and Robert Helpmann. So in the last week of July, with her mum, sister Nellie and little brothers Ralph and Jack, Joan Bailey took the train to Blackpool, hoping for good weather, and a few hours later dumped her bags in Mrs Pugh's *Miramar Hotel*. Walking up and down the promenade by day, and dancing at night, for a week at least the family were able to forget the headlines about Hitler and invasion and pretend there wasn't a war on.

One day, somewhere in Blackpool, Jerzy and a Polish pal met Joan and her older sister Nellie, 19. Holiday romances being what they are, and despite the language difficulties, it didn't take long for Jerzy and Joan to pair off, with his friend and Nellie also making a couple. Joan was excited by Jerzy's stories of flying in the air, and he relished her youthful energy, not to mention her good looks. They spent the rest of that glorious day rowing on the boating lake in Stanley Park, Jerzy almost falling in when he got up to change places with his pal and setting the boat rocking crazily. Joan thought she'd die laughing. They walked for hours along the prom, talking about anything and everything, and even got down onto the beach, where they had their pictures taken, and swapped addresses, promising to write, each hoping that the day would never end. But it did, although not before they found time to spend a few minutes alone together... Jerzy had to go back to his billet, and although he promised he'd try to see her again before the week was out, he never made it. Joan was sad when it was time for the Baileys to go back to Keighley, and the boring grind of pairing socks at the mill. 'That's lads for you,' said Nellie, and Joan had to agree. Her delight when she came home from the mill one evening and found her mother waiting on the doorstep with a letter from Blackpool in her hand was a sight to behold. Jerzy had written after all, apologising for not being able to see her again but the RAF had sent him off on a gunnery course. He'd really enjoyed meeting her and wondered if perhaps he could come and visit her on his next leave?

Joan spent the next few weeks on a special project, craftily cadging scraps of fabric and wool and wadding from work, and in the evenings sewing a doll for Jerzy, which she gave him when he visited her. She said it was his lucky charm, and he had to promise to keep it with him every time he flew. And he had, even on the night the Anson he was flying in had crashed over Southampton. 'There you are,' said Joan, when he wrote and told her about it. 'She was protecting you.'

As usual, the letter he was writing today contained little about his day-to-day life on the station, and much more about how he was feeling, about Joan of course, and about the day when he would be able to go back home to Poland. He didn't dare say that she might go with him. He finished the letter, put it in an envelope and sealed it, then wrote Joan's address on the front, and I.T.A.L.Y on the back. She could decide what that meant herself. He was putting the envelope on his bedside cabinet when the billet door swung open and Kazimierz Mruk stood there in full flying kit, breathless.

'What's going on Jerzy? You should be ready.'

'What for?'

'Formation flying practice.'

Jerzy swung his legs over the side of the bed. 'Who-?'

'Flight Commander's orders. Take-off in fifteen minutes or there'll be hell to pay from Ścibior. Come on!' And before Jerzy could reply, Mruk had vanished. Without thinking, Jerzy Krawczyk ran after him.

Koszykowa 40, Warsaw, Poland. Thursday morning.

Halina Krawczyk, 28, older sister of Jerzy, looked out of the window, careful to keep herself out of sight. Down in the street everything was quiet. No people, just some children, sitting on the pavement. A girl, no more than about ten years old, all skin and bone under a dirty cotton dress, held one hand out, while the other was on her forehead, protecting her face or maybe just holding her head up, Halina couldn't tell which. The boys, both younger than the girl, and dressed similarly in rags, seemed to be asleep, despite the steady rain. One was curled up against his sister, the other sprawled along the foot of the wall. They'd been there yesterday, and the day before.

She craned her neck to look up the length of Koszykowa, still fearful of being seen. The Germans were known to shoot at windows just for fun. It seemed to be quiet. Perhaps it was the rain that was keeping everyone indoors. Unless there was something going on nearby and people were keeping their heads down? A round up perhaps..?

Halina waited a few more minutes, feeling her heart beat hard in her chest. She felt faint, had done for months now. They needed bread. Her mother had told her there was a rumour there was going to be bread in the shop on Hoza this morning. Halina knew it wouldn't be there for long, if the rumour was true. A movement caught her eye. From the other end of Koszykowa a middle-aged couple, nicely dressed, were walking down the street from the direction of Poznanska. They seemed to be talking together, and walked past the sleeping children without breaking step, ignoring the outstretched hand and the dead eyes. That decided her. If she was quick, she could make it to Hoza and be back without any trouble.

She grabbed her coat and headscarf from the door and hurried to the stairs.

Flight Lieutenant Stefanicki had to hurry to keep up with Squadron Leader Szczepan Ścibior as he strode towards his aircraft SM-P. The sun was shining brightly now, and in his Irvin suit, heavy boots and gloves on top of his uniform, Stefanicki was already sweating profusely.

'After take-off we fly due east,' barked Ścibior. 'Sharp right turn to pick up the southbound railway line, then another right at Grantham for the castle... once or twice low around the castle to rattle his Lordship's windows then northwest to Elton. The church is our turning point, by the crossroads, with a left turn over the Grantham to Nottingham road as far as Bingham where we change course again for home. Got it?'

'...Yes. I'll be following you, won't I?'

'I want you to stay hard on my port wing no more than a length behind me, so you'll need to be ready to turn when I do – I don't want you straying when I change course. I want you to be able to see the whites of my rear gunner's eyes at all times, understand? Keep *tight*.'

'I'll stick like glue, sir.'

'We'll stay well below the cloud base at 1,000 feet maximum, I want to avoid that haze. And watch your speed – don't drop below 200mph, got it?'

'Yes sir. *Sir* – is there any particular reason why we are practising formation flying?'

'The bombing wasn't tight enough last time we hit Duisburg – the CO wants us to get it right this time.'

'So we *are* going to Duisburg?' said Stefanicki.

'Yes, but you didn't hear it from me. And keep it under your hat.'

In the shadow of his Wellington the Squadron Leader stopped and looked at his countryman. 'Don't worry. I know it's a ball-ache but it'll stand you in good stead for tonight Flight Lieutenant, I promise.'

Stefanicki saluted. 'I know, sir. Thank you.'

Ścibior put a gloved hand on his shoulder. 'Good luck. And smile Tadeusz. It'll be fun.'

Stefanicki watched the Squadron Leader stride over to P for Peter and greet his crew. He'd done this kind of formation flying dozens of times before, here and back in Poland. There was nothing to worry about so long as everyone kept their wits about them. So why was he feeling so nervous? He took a deep breath, smiled at how illogical he was being, turned and walked over to K for King, where his crew waited. They stubbed out their cigarettes as he approached. Sgt Mruk was the first to speak.

'So what's the plan, captain?'

'Piece of cake. We'll be back before lunch.'

The noise in the mill was deafening. The roar and clatter of the enormous knitting frames provided a constant background to Joan Bailey's working days, although as her mum had predicted, she was getting used to it now. When she started the job at 14, she couldn't sleep at night for the whistling in her ears. But her mother had worked in the mill all her life and she was now practically stone-deaf.

Hosiery Pairer, Socks, it said on Joan's clocking-in card, which meant it was her job to sort through boxes of newly-finished socks, matching pairs according to colour, design, material and length. From time to time the piped music that was played on all the shop floors broke through the constant roar of the machinery, and she tried to guess who it was – Bing Crosby, The Andrews Sisters, George Formby..? She thought Artie Shaw was playing now - *Frenesi*, the high notes of the clarinet cutting clearly through the din. *Frenesi* was her current favourite. One of the lads in despatch told her it meant a state of great excitement, and fear, but Joan hadn't understood how you could be both wildly excited and fearful at the same time. Not that there was a lot of either on this job. Just socks.

Sometimes at dinner break they cleared the canteen tables back and you could have a dance, if you wanted. It was mostly the girls and older women who danced, the fellers weren't interested. But she liked it. Except when Mr Evans the foreman insisted on having his four penn'orth.

Here he came now, in that brown work coat of his, checking the girls' work and acting like he owned the place. Joan watched as he examined the pile of socks on Deirdre Morrison's bench, standing just that bit too close to the poor girl for comfort. If only Mrs Evans knew what he was like. Maybe she'd tell her one day. He was at Joan's bench now, picking through the socks like an old woman at the Sally Army bring and buy. Some of the girls tried to avoid making eye contact with Mr Evans, hoping that by looking down at their work pile he would hurry up and move on, but Joan was having none of that – she set her hips and stared at him, like a mother tiger protecting her cubs, daring him to find fault.

Satisfied, the foreman grunted and moved along the work bench, and when he had his back to her Joan stuck her tongue out at him. Across the way, watching this, her sister Nellie laughed silently. Joan gave her a wink and mouthed something. The younger girl gave her an *I don't understand* look. Joan tried again, exaggerating the words, and again Nellie mimed What? Finally Joan slowly mouthed the word, '*Polish.*'

Realising, Nellie laughed, placed her hand on her heart with a simpering look, and returned to her work.

Joan often practised her Polish at work these days, mouthing the words to herself as she sorted socks, trying to get her tongue round all those Ks and Zs. That first day in Blackpool Jerzy had tried to teach her some simple words and phrases, and laughed kindly at her miserable efforts. But she insisted he write them down for her so she could practice until the next time he saw her and she would say them perfectly.

There was 'Czy masz papierosa?' - *Do you have a cigarette?*

and 'Mam na imię Joan i mam osiemnaście lat,' - *My name is Joan and I am eighteen years old*, but her favourite was 'Kocham cię, kochanie,' - *I love you, my darling*, and she mouthed it now, over and over again.

Suddenly Mr Evans came into her eyeline, staring at her as if she had lost her marbles. Joan threw him a cold smile and he walked on, shaking his head. 'Kocham cię, kochanie...' She couldn't wait until she could see Jerzy and say it to him, in his arms.

The other girls thought it was very romantic and exciting going with a flyer. And it was true – she had never been so excited as when she thought about Jerzy and his sweet smile. But sometimes she felt afraid, especially when she thought about the danger he put himself in each night. He didn't talk about it, but she knew. She was scared, and prayed every night for him before she went to sleep.

A state of high excitement and fear. Suddenly she realised what *Frenesi* really meant.

But at least he had that doll with him...

The crew of the Wellington stubbed out their cigarettes and started the difficult job of climbing aboard the bomber, restricted as they were by their cumbersome flying suits, boots and parachutes. One at a time they climbed up the ladder into the entry hatch, just forward of the bomb bay.

'Hey Stan, how about I go up front for this one?' rear gunner Alexey Zirkwitz said to Stanisław Kowalcze.

'What, and me go arse-end Charlie? No thanks.'

'Oh come on, just for this one. We'll go back to normal for the op. What do you say? I'm getting too big for that rear turret.'

Waiting patiently behind them while they bickered like children, Jerzy Krawczyk suddenly felt his blood run cold. *He'd forgotten the doll.* He must have left her in his billet when Mruk dragged him out. He thrust his hand inside his flying jacket, just to be sure, but it was definite – she wasn't there.

He felt his stomach turn over - it was a ritual he never missed. He felt gripped by panic.

'Tell you what, I'll toss you for it.' Zirkwitz was still badgering Kowalcze.

'Alright. Heads you go front turret, tails for arse-end Charlie.' Kowalcze tossed the coin, which landed in the grass. 'Tails. Hard luck Alexey.' Zirkwitz cursed as he headed for the tail and Kowalcze climbed into the Wellington's nose.

Navigator Marian Wojtowicz was waiting behind Jerzy. 'Alright Jurek? Forgotten something?' Jerzy's mind raced – did he have time to run back to his billet and pick the doll up? No. Squadron Leader Ścibior was clearly keen to get up in the air straight away and the captain would do his nut.

'No – it's nothing.' Jerzy wasn't going to tell his mate that he'd forgotten his lucky charm.

'Sure? You don't look too happy.'

'Sure. Just thinking.'

'Yeah, about you and that girl of yours – you do too much thinking – you need to *do* something about it – ask her to marry you before some Yorkshire Johnny gets in there.' Wojtowicz stepped past him, threw in his parachute and disappeared up the ladder.

Jerzy considered. Maybe he was thinking too much – about Joan *and* about the doll. It was only a training flight after all, and not a long one – back in half an hour, the captain said. What could happen? So long as he had his lucky charm with him for the op tonight, everything would be fine, and this weekend he'd have that talk with Joan. Maybe he could wangle a 24-hour leave...

Without another thought, Jerzy Krawczyk heaved his parachute through the hatch door and climbed up into the bomber.

'Aberystwyth coming up.'

'Thank you, navigator.'

Robson Newton smiled at his pilot's confident manner. 'We've made good time. Bang on, I'd say. Look at that.'

The vast grey expanse of the Irish Sea stretched out before them. Aberystwyth was a cluster of grey, slate houses and roofs, with a long curving ribbon of white-fronted hotels where it met the sea. A pier, not a very long one, having been damaged badly in recent storms, reached out into the waves.

'I'll use the pier as a turning point – we should get a good view of the town.' Bill paused, gazing down. 'I came here once on a Sunday School outing. Never thought the next time I saw it I'd be a couple of thousand feet up.'

'Sunday school? You a Methodist then?'

'Yes. My father's – *was* a minister in the church.'

'Me too – Methodist I mean.'

The Oxford banked gently to the right and there was a pause as each man looked down at the coastline.

'Matter of fact, my Grandfather was a preacher round your neck of the woods,' said Bill. 'After he worked in the mines, that is.'

'Down pit, eh? A hard life.'

'He wrote a book about it. Self-taught he was. And he bought his first dictionary in Gateshead. Still on the bookshelf at home. This is back in Victorian times though.'

'Well, you do surprise me,' said Robson. 'You've got coal dust in your veins.'

Bill laughed. 'Not quite. Never been further than the coal hole myself.' He looked down. 'I say, have we got time for those fish and chips?'

'Afraid not, bonny lad. I hope any Ack-Ack boys down there have got their specs on – I wouldn't like them to make a mistake and let fly at us.'

'Don't worry,' Bill grinned. 'I'm feeling lucky today. OK, give me a course for Gainsborough, navigator. Turning right.'

Robson smiled. Today could have been a whole lot worse...

'Engine master cocks on, pressure balance cock off.'

Flight Lieutenant Stefanicki looked at his second pilot. 'She's been standing for a week – better set the pressure balance cock to on.'

'*On*,' said Mruk.
'Throttles?'
'¼ inch open.'
'Mixture controls?'
'Normal...'

From his position in the front turret, Stanisław Kowalcze watched a member of the ground crew clear away the last of the toolboxes from underneath the nose of the bomber. Given the pressure coming from the captain the lads had done well. The mechanic gave him a big grin and Kowalcze replied with a thumbs up. The two men had established a friendship since arriving in England, both coming from the same village, Łętownia, deep in the Carpathians. The village had been burned by the Germans in '39. Although the British tended to frown on it, he was happy to share a drink with his lower-rank friend, and they spent many a night in the bar of The Saracen's Head, remembering the old days.

'...Carburettor intake control?'
'Cold.'
'Cowling gills?'
'Open.'
'And oil cooler shutters..?'
'Closed.' Sgt Mruk breathed out and glanced at his captain.
'Checklist complete, thank you Sergeant.' Stefanicki slid back the cockpit window and gave the ground crew the thumbs up to turn the propellors. Starting with the port engine, the mechanics pushed at the mighty blades, giving them at least two revolutions to clear the oil, before standing back for the start-up. In the cockpit Stefanicki pressed his gloved finger on the port engine starter button.

'Ignition switch on.'
Nothing.
'She's been static for a while,' he shouted. 'Try again!'

The mechanics put their shoulders to the blades and turned the propellor again, giving it more revolutions this time. Stefanicki kept his finger pressed on the starter button until eventually there was a puff of smoke from the exhaust and the engine burst into life. The ground crew stood back as a cloud of blue-black smoke burst from the huge Bristol Pegasus engine and the revs increased to 1,000rpm.

Up in the cockpit, Stefanicki signalled to the ground crew to repeat the procedure with the starboard engine.

'Go home Raque. Hear me? Go on.'

The dog looked away, pretending not to understand. Outside St John's church, George Parkinson leaned his bike against the wall and pulled off his bicycle clips. It was nearly eleven o'clock and the last of the wedding guests were hurrying through the gate into the church. George put on his sternest face. 'The bride'll be here in a minute and I don't want you getting in the way – it's more than my job's worth. Clear off.'

Hurt, the dog turned to go, then looked back, mournfully.

'*Go on.*'

Finally, Raque trotted off down Church Street, in the direction of the docks. George thought that he would give the dog an extra scrap or two tonight to make sure they were still friends, and then saw a wedding car turn the corner from the clock tower.

He squashed his cigarette under his shoe and pulled out his notebook and pencil.

At Syerston, the grass behind Wellington R1017 SM-K was flattened by the propellor wash, and the ground crew stood ready, holding the ropes ready to pull the chocks away. Both engines were now running smoothly on the bomber. 'She sounds fine,' the pilot said to himself, before clicking the intercom on his oxygen mask. 'OK wireless operator, signal K for King ready for take-off.'

In his tiny compartment below and behind the pilot, Sgt Jerzy Krawczyk replied, 'Yes, captain.'

The second pilot was craning his neck to look up at the milky sky. 'I don't like the look of this haze, sir,' said Mruk over the roar of the engines.

'No. What did the Met Officer say about it, navigator?' Wojtowicz's voice was tinny over the intercom. 'Pretty widespread but patchy, captain. And seven tenths cloud. Not very nice, but it should be clear by tonight.'

'Check your intercom navigator,' said the pilot. 'You're a bit quiet.'

'Yes sir, sorry sir.'

'At least it's not raining,' said Alexy Zirkwitz, the rear gunner. Although more than 50 feet away from the cockpit, out on his own, he sounded loud and clear. 'I hate flying in the rain.'

'Here we go. Stop moaning Zirkwitz,' said Mruk.

'You'd moan if you were stuck in this turret,' said Zirkwitz. 'It leaks – I get soaked...'

'Well, it's not raining now,' said Kowalcze.

'Alright, pipe down everybody.' The crew immediately sensed the tension in the pilot's voice. 'Group are obviously determined to see us fly tonight, whatever the weather. Don't worry about the conditions, the flight commander said we'll stay well below the cloud – no higher than 1,000 feet, OK second pilot? Just keep your eyes peeled everybody, understand?'

'Don't worry captain, I won't be taking my eyes off the big bastard in front of us,' laughed Mruk.

Stefanicki smiled. 'You and me both,' he said.

'Navigator to pilot, how's this for level?'

'Perfect navigator,' said the pilot. 'Thank you.'

Jerzy Krawczyk came over the intercom. 'Wireless operator to pilot. P for Peter on the move sir.'

'Thank you.' The engine roar increased in pitch as the pilot brought up the revs. 'Here we go.' He gave a signal to the ground crew, the chocks were pulled away and slowly the Wellington moved towards the runway.

It was just gone eleven o'clock.

Halina Krawczyk had been standing in the queue for nearly two hours and was now thoroughly soaked. There'd been no let-up in the rain but at least once the shutters were opened and the queue started to move she was edging steadily forward all the time. But the longer she waited, and the nearer she got to the front of the queue, the more convinced she was that the bread would run out, or the shopkeeper would close the shutters for fear of a patrol and she'd be left with nothing. By the time she got near the front, she was shivering from her wet clothes, but the few coins in her hand were hot from being gripped so tightly.

Eventually Halina was at the front of the queue, although she still had to use her elbows to stop the man behind her from pushing in. There was no conversation around the purchase; the shopkeeper simply thrust a loaf into her hand and took the money – he didn't even look at her, he was too busy keeping an eye out for Germans. Straight away Halina pushed the loaf inside her sodden coat, pulled it tight around her neck and hurried away towards Poznańska, a surge of relief flooding over her - her mother would be so pleased that she'd managed to get the bread.

She turned the corner out of Hoża into Poznańska and immediately stopped. Twenty yards ahead of her a small crowd was gathered, and to one side was a grey military truck and a smaller *Kubelwagen*. Both had black-and-white German crosses on them, and she could see the smaller death's heads and angular SS badges on the doors. In front of the silent crowd a group of German soldiers, all dressed in black raincoats and carrying machine guns and rifles, were haranguing a middle-aged man. He looked terrified as they pushed him from side to side with their rifle butts or a kick of the boot, but the man kept his eyes firmly fixed on the officer standing calmly nearby, who was smoking a cigarette.

Halina didn't know what to do. If she turned and walked back towards Hoża the soldiers might see her and follow, and that would mean trouble for the shopkeeper. If she stayed, she could be in trouble herself. She decided to walk on, pretending it was nothing to do with her, and hoping the soldiers would ignore her. Trembling, she started forward, head down, holding her coat tightly around her chest. It shouldn't take more than twenty, twenty-five seconds to get to the end of the street. She allowed herself a brief glance up, and saw the men in the crowd removing their hats and bowing their heads as the soldiers walked among them, the Poles avoiding eye contact with the Germans. She also saw the officer, with his high peaked cap and the silver death's head badge, unbutton his leather holster and take his pistol out, the gun hanging loosely in his gloved hand. Halina swallowed, trying not to look terrified, which she was, and quickened her pace, away from the crowd.

Keep going, don't look back.

She heard a few shouts behind her, presumably from the soldiers as she couldn't understand what they were saying.

Don't look back, keep walking.

Then another shout, and this time she understood exactly what was said.

Fraulein! Halt!

Halina stopped and froze. She heard the sound of boots on the cobbles. A soldier was approaching. She dared not turn around. She heard another command, which she didn't understand, but it was repeated, and she turned around slowly, head bowed, eyes fixed firmly on the ground. The boots appeared in her line of vision, and stopped. Her mouth was suddenly very dry, and she felt light-headed again, her heart thumping wildly in her chest. The boots, she noticed, were highly polished, with the raindrops standing proud on the shining black leather. The soldier said something else in German, softer this time, and something made her look up. The soldier was staring at her, his machine gun pointing at her. She quickly looked away from the SS badge on his collar, focussing instead on the hole at the end of the gun barrel. She was aware that everyone in the crowd, and most of the soldiers and the tall officer, were looking at her. The soldier jerked the barrel of the machine gun, indicating to her to open her coat.

Halina froze, unable to move. He jerked the gun again and shouted something. She didn't understand the words, but understood their meaning. Slowly she undid the buttons on her coat and opened it, a little at first, then wider, revealing the loaf of bread tucked under her right arm.

Halina shivered and closed her eyes. She was going to die, here in the street, in the rain. She heard the soldier's boots on the cobbles again, and suddenly sensed the warmth of his breath as he stood much closer to her, almost touching. Then she felt the soldier grab the loaf. After a few seconds Halina opened her eyes. The soldier, she could see, was holding the loaf. Slowly he took a bite out of one end, chewed it roughly, with his mouth open, then stopped and spat the bread out onto the pavement. Halina's heart was beating like a drum, pounding in her ears. She saw the soldier toss the loaf into the gutter, and it made a small splash in the dirty puddle. She watched as the soldier squashed the bread with his boot, grinding it into pieces. She thought her legs were going to give way, but she raised her eyes and fixed them firmly on the German. If she was going to die, she would die with dignity. After a few seconds the soldier smiled and jerked his head, telling her to carry on walking. She didn't wait for a second command, turning and hurrying along the pavement, all the time waiting for the bullet to hit her in her back.

But there was no bullet.

Halina carried on walking, head down, hands at her sides, her eyes suddenly filling with tears, her chest ready to explode. Just before she reached the turning into Koszykowa she heard a shout, and a man's voice, pleading in Polish, then a single shot, incredibly loud, echoing off the walls. She waited for the bullet to smack into her back, between the shoulder blades, but there was nothing. She stopped, quickly looked over her shoulder and saw the man lying on the street, the German officer standing over him. He levelled his pistol, there was another shot and the man's body jumped. Nobody in the crowd moved or said anything. Shaking now, Halina watched as the soldiers walked away, towards their truck, and the officer climbed into his *Kubelwagen*.

As the vehicles pulled away the thought suddenly struck her: what would her mother say when she came home without bread?

'Gainsborough coming up. Even with that crosswind we're not far off my ETA.'

'Maybe I'll just cut the corner and start my turn before we get to it. Make up a bit of time. What do you think?'

'Fine by me. The weather's pretty much as forecast. Should be a straight run back home.'

'Lunch and then your go at flying solo. Looking forward to it?'

'You bet. Not like I've got much to compete with, is it?'

'Thanks. OK, I'm going to start my turn now.'

Bill Parkinson put the Oxford into a wide banking turn to the right, passing over the small villages of North and South Wheatley. As the aircraft came round to the southeast, the sun picked out the glittering line of the river Trent, winding like a ribbon through the wide flat fields of Nottinghamshire.

'We're making good time,' said Robson. 'How's about taking in Lincoln? There's a beautiful cathedral, it'd be something to see it from up here on a day like this.'

'Are you sure? Albrighton'll be livid if we're late.'

'Howay, man. Sod Albrighton. It'll only add a few minutes. We can easily make that up and still be back by lunch. I'll say we were blown off course by that crosswind.'

'Alright.'

'Champion. See that road over the river, the long straight one?'

'Got it...'

'Follow that and we'll see Lincoln in no time. I'll calculate a new course for Brize.'

Tadeusz Stefanicki gripped the control column and flexed his gloved fingers. They'd only been in the air for ten minutes but his arms were already beginning to ache. After a smooth take-off and a circuit around the airfield they had set off towards the east. The job of maintaining a steady position behind and just to the right of P-Peter, the lead Wellington, was hard, and required extreme physical as well as mental effort. Every slight lift or drop of Ścibior's bomber, each miniscule shift of direction as he adjusted his course, had to be compensated for immediately. Flying at this low height and at this speed, even the briefest glance away from the aircraft in front, to check something on the instrument panel, could mean disaster. At one point he saw the rear gunner on the lead bomber give them a wave, and attempted a brief wave back, hoping not to let Mruk see the strain he was under. It didn't help that Tadeusz was still feeling a little fuzzy-headed after last night's post-parade celebrations in the Officers' Mess. If only they hadn't gone on so long...

'Railway line coming up,' said Mruk, looking starboard and shielding his eyes briefly from the glare of the sun. 'Ścibior's turning... *now*.'

Still keeping his eyes glued on the big black shape in front of him, Stefanicki involuntarily gritted his teeth, tensing as he eased the rudder and banked to the right, trying to keep as close as possible to the lead aircraft.

'Isn't it beautiful?'

Bill looked down, marvelling at the huge cathedral. 'Smashing.'

'That was once the tallest building in the world.'

'You're kidding.'

'It's true. It had a central spire but that collapsed the year after Henry the Eighth died.'

'You're like a walking encyclopaedia.'

'Working in insurance you get to appreciate the value of facts.'

As Bill circled the cathedral the late morning sun shone on the warm stone and glinted off the windows. 'Insurance eh?'

he said. 'I was an articled clerk in civvy street – training to be an accountant.'

'Not a patch on this though, eh?' They shared a few moments' silence as the cathedral disappeared behind them. Then Bill said, 'We ought to head south. And keep an eye out for aircraft now – there's one or two bomber stations around here.'

Pilot Officer Kowalcze shifted his elbows and tried to make himself more comfortable. Lying prone in the bomb aimer's position always gave him a stiff neck, but at least on this flight he didn't have flak or tracer shells flying up at him. It was difficult not to feel terribly exposed and vulnerable when your wedding tackle was exposed to everything the Germans could fire at you, with only plywood and linen fabric as protection. Trying to find the target through cloud and smoke helped take your mind off that though. This morning he was looking down at the London to Edinburgh railway line, cutting a long straight scar through the green Nottinghamshire countryside. He always felt it was like looking down on the toy farm his father had made for him back in Łętownia – little cows and horses in the fields, long thin lines of hedgerow, and the odd tractor ploughing the brown earth. He'd heard terrible stories of what the Nazis were doing there now – men and women forced into slave labour at a nearby concentration camp, others beaten in the street... Suddenly a bright white plume came into view – a train, heading north from Grantham. He watched the long line of carriages passing below, the clouds of steam hanging in the air for a few seconds before disappearing, and as quickly as it had appeared, the train was gone. No, there weren't many wartime jobs that could compare to this for beauty and wonder, he thought. The next thing he knew his stomach turned as the bomber banked away to the right, and he remembered why he was here.

'Fancy a flick tonight? There should be something good on in Grantham.'

Sheila Cooper poured some tea from her flask and handed it to her friend. Sitting on the back of the flatbed truck the girls were enjoying a break from the backbreaking work of clearing a ditch in the field between Mansel's Barn and Muston Gorse Covert. Four other Women's Land Army girls, together with a middle-aged labourer from the estate, sat in exhausted silence, with only the odd laugh to be heard above the distant sound of sheep. Behind them the familiar outline of Belvoir Castle rose up on the ridge.

'Don't know if I've got the energy to go out,' said Ruby Dawson. 'Besides, it's bath night. Last week by the time that old bat Maynard had heated up the copper it was past my bedtime. I'm not missing it this week.'

'She does it on purpose. You want to report her.'

'Who to? Farmers are all the same. Mean as hell.' Ruby took a sip of the hot tea and lifted her face to the sun. 'But I can't complain. I did volunteer for this.'

'Well, I've got letters to write I suppose,' said Sheila. There was a pause. The girls had met only a few months ago, posted to Nottinghamshire from their homes in Birmingham and Cheltenham to work for the Land Army, but were already good friends. 'How about a dance on Saturday? I could do with a dance.'

'Yes, I should think so.' Ruby looked around at the sound of engines and saw two aircraft drawing towards them. 'Bombers,' she said, squinting. 'They're low.'

'Wimpys,' said the other.

'How do you know?' asked Ruby.

'You can tell by the tail.' She paused, before adding, 'Geoffrey was on Wellingtons. He sent me a postcard of one.'

'Oh, of course.' Ruby looked at her friend. 'Sorry.'

'That's OK.'

Sheila didn't talk much about Geoffrey, and Ruby had learned not to probe. She had asked a few questions after Sheila got the telephone call but clearly she wanted to keep it to herself. Lucky for her they were only engaged when he lost his legs. Anyway, she'd soon meet another boy...

They watched the bombers as they banked to the right and began a wide circle around the castle. 'Flying awfully close to each other,' said one. A break in the clouds revealed the sun, bright and glaring on this summer morning and the girls both had to shade their eyes as they tracked the aircraft round.

'The pilot's waving to us.'

'Really? Which one?'

'In the second plane. Definitely.'

'You've got better eyes than me.'

Both girls waved back, just in case, and watched the bombers fly away in the direction of Elton, gaining height, getting smaller and quieter until they were hidden by the trees. Ruby knew that Sheila was thinking about Geoffrey.

'Come on, love,' she said. 'Back to work.'

'This windscreen is filthy,' said Mruk, putting away the shammy leather. 'Covered in bugs. I could hardly see anything when we were facing into the sun. I don't know how you managed, sir.'

'I close my eyes and cross my fingers, Sergeant,' Stefanicki replied, not taking his eyes off the bomber in front. 'I find it usually works.'

Mruk grinned. 'I'll give Chiefy a rocket when we get back. I want this Perspex clean enough to eat my dinner off before tonight's op.'

'Least we're heading away from the sun now,' said the pilot. 'What time is it? I'm ready for lunch.'

'Not long now, sir,' the navigator's words came over the intercom. 'We should be back at Syerston in about five minutes.'

Bill opened his eyes. He'd been flying 'hands off' for the last few minutes, having set the trim tabs to keep the Oxford straight and level, allowing him to ease the tightness out of his shoulders and close his eyes for a few moments. 'Is that haze?' he asked.

'Yes,' Robson replied. 'Never really seen it like that before.'

'Better go back to manual.' Bill reset the trim. 'I have control now. Coming down another 500 feet to avoid that haze.'

The navigator was silent. 'You alright?' Bill asked.

The navigator nodded.

'Sure?'

Robson looked out of the side window, his oxygen mask dangling around his neck. Eventually he lifted it to his mouth and spoke. 'I just didn't feel happy with you flying hands off, OK?'

Bill took this in, surprised. 'Why not? I've done it before.'

'Yes, but with an instructor, with dual controls. This is different. Albrighton would have your guts if he found out.'

'Maybe not. He might admire my pluck.' Bill concentrated on looking ahead, but Newton's attitude was annoying him. 'You're not going to tell him, are you?'

Robson didn't answer for a moment, then shook his head.

'Thanks,' said Bill. They flew on for half a minute, then he said, 'OK that's just under 1,000 feet.' He looked straight ahead, his visibility still affected by the haze. 'Sorry, I didn't realise it was a problem...'

'It's not, I just... I didn't expect it, that's all. Forget it.'

They remained silent, Bill flicking his eyes from the view ahead to the instrument panel, then back again. 'This haze is awful.' Finally he said, 'Why do you think Albrighton's always so snappy?'

'No idea,' said Robson. 'Probably something that happened to him in France. He was on Battles wasn't he?'

'Was he? I didn't know. That explains it all then. He's like a bear with a sore head sometimes.'

Robson smiled. 'Having to work with sprogs like us can't help. I wouldn't want his job for anything.'

They laughed, their spat already forgotten.

'Where are we now anyway?' asked Bill.

'Let me see... just approaching a place called Elton. We should be seeing a crossroads and a church about now.'

In his tiny rear turret on board the lead Wellington, SM-P, Flying Officer Zbigniew Siarkowski was hunched over his twin Browning machine guns, looking at the huge bomber flying only a matter of yards away, sticking like glue.

'How's he doing rear gunner?'

'Staying tight, sir. I could wipe his windscreen if I leaned out.'

'Good,' said Ścibior. Siarkowski heard someone else laugh.

'Quiet,' said Ścibior. 'We're not home yet.'

Another voice came over the intercom. 'Navigator to pilot. Elton crossroads coming up. Prepare to turn left.'

'Thank you, navigator.'

'Damned glare.' On the Oxford Bill Parkinson was feeling distinctly uneasy, his former confidence starting to weaken.

'Use your goggles,' said Robson. 'They might help.'

Lifting a hand from the control column, Bill pulled his goggles down.

'Better?'

Bill adjusted them. 'Not really... I'm going down another couple of hundred feet.'

On Wellington SM-P, FO Siarkowski kept his eyes on SM-K as his aircraft banked, the black shape drifting through his gunsight, and wondered idly what it would be like to see a German night fighter that close, moving in for the kill, and whether he would see it before it saw him...

On the Oxford, Robson suddenly sees a black shape emerging from the glare. He calls out, *'Aircraft!'*

'I see him!' says Bill, seeing the Wellington bomber as it turns to their right, revealing its swollen black body and long tapering wings. Lifting his right wing to avoid it he narrowly misses the bomber, noticing the roundel on the fuselage side, and the large grey codes SM-P. That was close, he thinks.

But he doesn't see the other Wellington until it is too late.

On SM-K, still watching the lead bomber as it turns, Stefanicki suddenly sees a small aircraft revealed behind it, coming straight for them.

Jesus!

At the tail end of SM-P, Zbigniew Siarkowski is suddenly jolted back to reality when he hears a confusion of shouts over the intercom. *What the hell's going on*, he thinks.

In the cockpit of K for King, the pilot Tadeusz Stefanicki instinctively throws the Wellington's nose down, trying to avoid a collision... and on the lead Wellington Siarkowski flinches as he sees a bright yellow shape flash past his turret. On SM-K Stefanicki and Mruk duck as their windscreen is filled with yellow and the Oxford flies over the cockpit. Mruk can see the huge black serial numbers on the wings and even the detail of the tail wheel as it passes over them. In the rear turret on P for Peter, FO Siarkowski is the only one who sees what happens next, and although the two aircraft are flying at a closing speed of nearly four hundred miles per hour, everything happens in slow motion for the horrified rear gunner.

The Oxford hits the bomber amidships, the propellors of its starboard engine shattering the Wellington's astrodome in a bright cloud of tiny Perspex fragments. The sun's rays cast a momentary rainbow through the cloud as the trainer ploughs on towards the rear of the bomber. The wooden blades of the Oxford's propellors are shredded as they meet the Wellington's huge black tailfin, which slices into the Oxford's starboard wing before being torn off, spinning up into the air like part of a broken toy, and a second cloud of fragments, bigger pieces this time, metal, fabric, splintered wood and Perspex from the rear turret, explodes violently. Finally, the gunner catches the briefest of glimpses of a face, looking up at him from the cockpit of the stricken Wellington, with an expression which he can only describe as one of surprise.

It all happens in less than two seconds, but the images will remain with Zbigniew Siarkowski until the day he dies.

900 feet below the three aircraft, the Reverend Gerald Marson, newly-appointed Rector of St Michael's and All Angels, Elton, closed the iron gate heavily and walked between the headstones towards the church. St Michael's wasn't a beautiful building – no-one could honestly say that – but it had something about it, and the sleepy village was rather special, despite the almost daily roar of aircraft engines from the nearby aerodromes. He could hear some aircraft overhead now but had already learned not to look up at the sound of every engine. As a contrast to the mining community he had recently left, Elton with its gentle, rolling fields and soft redbrick farm buildings was definitely more than a welcome change. Not that he was feeling totally accepted by his congregation yet. That always took time. But on early summer days like this it was very pleasant just to admire the day, even if -

The silence was suddenly shattered by a huge bang, louder than anything the rector had ever heard before, from up above. He immediately flinched, and instinctively put his hands over his head, as if fearing something might hit him. Turning, he looked up into the bright summer sky, and saw a great black smudge of smoke and a shower of bits and pieces spinning as they fell to earth. Two large objects, clearly aircraft, were hurtling away from each other. The larger one of the two, apparently tailless, was spinning round and round, falling earthwards. The rector could see the large roundels on the fuselage. The other, much smaller in size, and seemingly breaking into several large pieces, was careering over the village in the direction of Sutton. The smaller aircraft was on fire, trailing a plume of oily black smoke, and the engines of both were screaming as they fell, the bomber disappearing beyond the crest of the ridge, and the other behind the roof of the church.

There was a loud explosion. Then another.

'Oh, my word,' he said.

Outside No 1 hangar at RAF Syerston, the small brown terrier, which had been lying in the sun, suddenly lifted its head and looked up.

'Hello, Ciapek. What have you heard, eh?' The corporal mechanic bent down to give the dog a scratch behind the ear but Ciapek was already standing, barking madly. A couple of other men stopped and turned to look.

'Something's upset him. Wonder what it is?'

On board Squadron Leader Ścibior's Wellington there was a state of confusion and horror. Peering out of the cockpit and fuselage windows, the crew saw the burning wreckage of K for King in a field by a road, and further away, another column of smoke was rising from behind the trees.

'Quiet on the intercom!' shouted the pilot, and the babble of voices was silenced. 'Now did anyone see what actually happened? Rear gunner?

Zbigniew Siarkowski, his voice betraying his highly emotional state, tried to explain: *It just came out of nowhere... a trainer, I think... there was nothing they could do... It all happened so fast, it was awful...*

Ścibior banked the bomber to the left. 'Alright, calm down. I'm going round for a look. Keep your eyes peeled everyone, there may be more of them out there. Wireless operator – get onto Syerston and tell them what's happened. Navigator – give him a position.'

'Yes, sir.'

Over the intercom the pilot could hear his rear gunner sobbing uncontrollably.

Several hundred feet below the Wellington, in what was known locally as Barnes' Field, the two horses that had been quietly nibbling away at the grass were now running around the field in a mad panic, their eyes wide, nostrils snorting, tails up. Machine gun ammunition aboard the burning bomber was going off, the bullets cracking and whizzing through the air as they exploded. Up on the rise, beyond the icehouse, where the first farm buildings and houses stood, dogs were barking furiously.

In Goole, Gertrude Parkinson was in the back garden, cutting some sweet peas for the kitchen windowsill. A robin landed at the edge of the veg patch, and for a moment the two looked at each other, Gertrude standing stock still, unconsciously holding her breath. Suddenly there was a scratching and whining from the back door, and the bird flew off. Gertrude turned, the spell broken, and saw the dog Raque, pawing at the back door, desperate to get in. He was either hungry or running away from someone he'd stolen food from – probably the butcher – she thought. She stretched her back and walked to the house, scolding Raque as she went. As soon as she opened the door the dog ran inside and up the stairs, going straight into Bill's bedroom, tearing around the bed and then darting back out onto the landing. Gertrude hardly had time to register what was happening before she heard his paws on the stairs and he shot past her and was away up the street.

'Daft dog,' she thought. 'You will have your mad moments.'

At the same time, less than a mile away, George Parkinson, Bill's twin brother, stood alone at the end of a pew towards the back of St John's church, notebook and pencil in hand. As Mendelssohn's *Wedding March* echoed around the church the newlyweds turned and walked down the aisle. Along with the rest of the small congregation the young reporter noted the happy couple's smiling faces as they walked towards the open church doors and the bright sunlight that streamed in.

Suddenly George shivered. *Someone's walking over your grave*, his mother always used to say when that happened. But that wasn't true, was it?

Wing Commander JKM Drysdale DSO, the British Liaison officer at RAF Syerston, replaced the handset and turned to his colleague.

'There's been some sort of crash near Elton – one of our Wellingtons and a trainer apparently. It doesn't look good. Get the crash teams out there straight away.'

'Do you mean Elston, sir?'

'*Elton* – on the Grantham road.'

'Sorry, sir. In that case should I try Newton and Bottesford too?'

'Newton certainly, Bottesford isn't operational yet but they'll have men and equipment I'm sure.'

'And Group?'

Wing Commander Drysdale thought for a moment. 'Not yet, we don't have the full picture – let me deal with that. Damn, this is just what we needed. Everybody haring around when we're on tonight. I want to make sure this doesn't interfere with tonight's operation, understood? Group wants a Maximum Effort.'

'Yes, sir.'

'Better inform Squadron Leader Kleczyński. And tell the watch office to let me know the second Squadron Leader Ścibior lands – I want to get to the bottom of this.'

Around the village itself, people were coming to terms with the fact that something dreadful had happened. Some rushed out of their houses or looked up from the fields having heard the explosions; others, perhaps standing at the kitchen window, could see the burning wreckage of the Wellington in the field below; those further away simply watched as the two palls of black smoke climbed high into the milky blue sky.

The two land girls, Ruby and Sheila, had noticed the smoke from a long way off, but didn't immediately connect it with the bombers they had seen overhead only a couple of minutes earlier. On the Nottingham to Grantham road, only yards from where the burning Wellington now lay, a handful of cars and lorries had stopped, the drivers getting out and peering over the hedge for a better look, but they couldn't see much for the smoke. Half a dozen .303 rounds whizzed past them, cracking through the air like whips as another ammunition belt caught fire, and they thought it safer to get back into their vehicles and drive off, carefully negotiating the pieces of wreckage scattered across the road.

Near the Becks Plantation a gamekeeper and his dog emerged from the trees to see the burning remains of the Oxford trainer by the track that ran from Sutton Lane. He ran towards the aircraft, hoping he might be able to help any unfortunate occupants, but could get no closer than thirty feet as the flames and acrid choking smoke swirled viciously in the breeze. Fragments of fabric fell like black snow all around him as he stood watching helplessly.

Telephone calls were made by the few villagers lucky enough to have a phone, to the police stations in Bottesford and Grantham, reporting a terrible accident, and PC Kirk, the local policeman, was alerted with a knock on the door. He put down his cup of tea, grabbed his steel helmet from the back of the door and cycled down the road, ringing his bell furiously.

Within 15 minutes the crash teams left from Syerston, Newton and Bottesford; streams of fire tenders, and trucks carrying every available man the stations had been able to round up, and of course ambulances, some men hanging off the sides of the speeding vehicles. The teams from Syerston and Newton sped along the Fosse Way and onto the Grantham Road, and the trucks from Bottesford raced through the village, stopping farm vehicles and carts and causing villagers to stare open-mouthed as the drama unfolded. In their classroom at the Junior School, Robert Brown and Mike Fox heard the bells and sirens of the vehicles from the aerodrome and ran to the windows, desperate to see what all the fuss was. Their teacher Miss Morgan told them to return to their desks and sit down, before stepping out into the corridor to find the headteacher and find out if anybody knew what had happened.

Roughly at the same time that the crash teams hurtled through the gates of RAF Syerston, Squadron Leader Ścibior landed his Wellington. Even before the engines were killed the ground crew ran to the rear turret, which was rotated and the rear door opened so that the distraught gunner could get out. He had to be helped by two of his fellow crewmen to the nearest hut, where he finished a large mug of tea and several cigarettes before he was able to talk about what he had seen. Ścibior meanwhile went straight to the office of Wing Commander Kleczyński, to make his report on the disaster. Also present at the meeting was Wing Commander Drysdale. The Squadron Leader outlined the circumstances of the collision so far as he knew them, and explained that in his opinion, and that of his rear gunner who had witnessed the collision, it appeared to be an accident, with no blame to be apportioned to either crew.

It took just over 20 minutes for the emergency crews to drive the 14½ miles from Syerston to Elton. Although they had been given the approximate locations of the crash sites, the drivers really had no need of them. Just past Bingham, the crews were able to see the columns of smoke winding ominously into the air. The first vehicles to arrive pulled up at Barnes' Field, the men quickly throwing open the gate to allow them into the field where the Wellington was, whilst the others carried on up the hill and through the village to where the Oxford lay burning, about two hundred yards up the track. The gate was padlocked, and someone grabbed a crowbar to force the lock open. Armed guards were stationed at the gates of both fields and told to keep locals away because of the danger of exploding fuel and ammunition, maybe even bombs. Roadblocks were thrown up and diversions posted on all four roads converging on Elton. There was an unmistakeable feeling of panic and confusion in the air.

By this time both aircraft were little more than burning skeletons, and the foam sprayed onto them from the tenders quickly put out the remaining flames. It was depressingly clear to both crash teams that there was no prospect of finding any crew members alive. There was always the faint possibility that a crewman might have been thrown clear of the aircraft, either when it hit the ground or at the point of collision, and so a thorough search of the entire area was organised while the unpleasant job of removing the bodies from the wreckage got underway. However, it didn't take long to ascertain that all eight men had been killed, and the bodies, identified by their ID discs, were covered with blankets and carried on stretchers into the waiting ambulances before being driven to Syerston.

Officers carefully recorded the crash sites, marking each on maps with precise grid references. One officer, not quite knowing how to describe the location of the Oxford, asked a villager the name of the woods just beyond the wreck, and was told 'that's Becks wood.' The officer wrote down Beckswood, and that was the name that appeared on all subsequent reports of the accident.

Once the deaths of the aircrews were confirmed, and it had been established beyond all doubt that the Wellington had not been carrying bombs at the time of the collision, soldiers from the nearby camp at Whatton arrived to guard the crash sites overnight, and the well-oiled process of clearing up the administrative and bureaucratic side of the accident went into gear. With speed being of the essence, uncoded telegrams *en clair* were sent from Syerston to Brize Norton, informing 2SFTS that LAC WW Parkinson and LAC WR Newton had been killed in a mid-air collision, and confirming that the next of kin had not yet been informed. Similar telegrams were sent to the Air Ministry, the Headquarters of Bomber Command at High Wycombe, 1 Group at Hucknall, the Polish Records Office at Blackpool, other offices responsible for dealing with casualties and to 58MU at Newark. Receiving the message at their offices in the former Ossington Coffee House, the officers in charge of the maintenance unit sent their teams of Queen Mary trailers and Coles cranes to Elton that afternoon, with orders to begin the job of recovering the wreckage and clearing the crash sites so that no evidence remained. There were no road signs to direct the crews, having been removed at the start of the war, so men from Syerston had placed special '58MU' signs along the roads, tied to lamp posts or tree trunks, directing the salvage team to the crash sites. They would work until it was too dark to see any more, and continue on Friday morning, after which time the remains of the aircraft, hidden from sight by tarpaulins, would be driven back to the hangar on the north side of Newark. What couldn't be salvaged would be destroyed or melted down for re-use. As the last of 58MU's trucks drove away from Elton, the Damage Officer started to assess the amount of compensation that would be paid to the landowners.

Meanwhile, at RAF Syerston there was still the small matter of an air raid on an enemy target to arrange. Early on Thursday afternoon, briefings were held for the crews of seven aircraft, who were told that their target for tonight was, as Flt Lt Stefanicki had predicted, the railway marshalling yards at Duisburg, in the industrial heartland of Germany's Ruhr. It was to be a Maximum Effort, with aircraft from across No 1 Group taking part. Pilots, navigators, bomb aimers, wireless operators and air gunners noted down routes, aiming points, specifics of bombloads, radio frequencies and codes, and take-off, bombing and return times were confirmed. Out on the busy airfield, after successfully passing their Night Flying Tests the Wellingtons were fuelled up and loaded with bombs, belts of ammunition were fed into trays, machine guns checked, and Perspex canopies and turrets polished. Chiefy Zajac and his crew of mechanics and electricians took half an hour to absorb the news of SM-K's demise, before splitting up and helping the other ground crews. Inevitably underlying all the preparations for the operation against Duisburg was the knowledge that one of their crews had been lost that morning, but efforts were made to ensure that the accident (and by now it had been agreed that it *was* an accident) would not affect the action that night. Nobody wanted doubts or dissent to distract from the focus of carrying out the operation successfully, and living to fight another day. Flying Officer Siarkowski, the unfortunate rear gunner who had witnessed the dreadful collision, was still in a highly emotional state and excused from operational duties until further notice, his place on SM-P to be taken that night by Pilot Officer Stanisław Barzdo.

That evening, as the final preparation for the raid took place, telegrams were sent from Syerston to the Polish Government in Exile, based in London, informing them about the loss of the six Polish airmen, and work started to ensure that where possible, the next of kin back home could be informed by the Polish Resistance. It would be many weeks, and in some cases months, before the news would reach the families in Poland.

At RAF Brize Norton, a cloud of despair settled over 2SFTS as news of the accident filtered through and the cadets discovered that two of their number had been killed. The official entry in the squadron Operations Record Book was brief and to the point: *12.6.41 Nottingham. Crash, Oxford T1334 hit a Wellington u/t pilots Newton and Parkinson of 61 course killed.*

By contrast, the entry in the 305 Squadron Operational Log was more fulsome in its account, describing '*a regrettable flying accident (which) occurred to Wellington No 1017 'K'... engaged in a formation flight with Wellington No 1696 'P'... The accident was seen by the rear gunner of 1696 'P' which was leading the other Wellington in formation. The two pilots took what avoiding action was possible, but owing to the haze had not observed each other's aircraft in time to prevent a collision... Both aircraft crashed from about 900 ft and fell about 700 yds apart, bursting into flames, both crews losing their lives.*'

Also that evening, while the cadets at Brize Norton prepped for their classes in the morning, and the crews at Syerston ate their flying meals before taking off for Germany, telegrams were sent to Goole and to Gateshead...

Raque had been acting strangely all day. After running off from Fountayne Street he had found George as he was leaving the wedding, and refused to leave him while he ate his lunch in the upstairs café at Hackworth's and when he attended the Council Housing Committee meeting later that afternoon. The dog sat patiently outside the Town Hall for two hours, then followed George back to the offices of the *Goole Times*, where he wrote up his columns, and when George finally cycled home that evening, Raque ran on ahead, barking at his master as if urging him to get home as quickly as he could. At the table that night Gertrude mentioned that Raque had been behaving strangely that morning, but nothing more thought of it, and George agreed that the first broad beans should be ready for his mother's weekend stew.

At about the same time there was a knock at the door of 24 Devon Gardens in Gateshead. William Newton answered it, wearing his slippers and with his pipe clenched between his teeth, and a folded copy of the *Chronicle* in his hand. The blackout curtains were already drawn, and he hadn't heard the motorbike parked at the end of the lane. As soon as he saw the uniformed telegram boy on the doorstep, he knew what had happened.

After eating, George helped his mother with clearing away the dishes and washing up, then wandered into the garden to have a smoke and check on his vegetables. Through the open kitchen window he could hear the sound of the programme on the Home Service, a concert of Berlioz and Debussy by the BBC Concert Orchestra. He was still out there, enjoying the evening and watching the first stars come out when he heard a motorbike engine in the street, and not long after, a cry from inside the house. He ran inside to see what the matter was and found his mother sitting on the hallway floor, a piece of paper in her hand. The front door was open and a telegram boy stood awkwardly on the step.

'I'm sorry,' the boy said. George carefully took the telegram and read it, then thanked the boy, gave him a shilling and closed the door. In the kitchen, Raque laid his head on his paws, watching.

In the parlour William Newton gave his wife a cup of tea. Her face was stained with tears, and her hand trembled, rattling the cup in its saucer when she took it.

'Maybe there's been a mistake?' she said quietly. 'These things happen.' William shook his head. There was no question about it. The wording of the telegram had been going round and round in his head since he read it. It said, REGRET TO INFORM YOU THAT YOUR SON 1018127 LAC NEWTON WR KILLED IN FLYING ACCIDENT STOP FURTHER PARTICULARS TO FOLLOW.

Beatrice wiped her eyes with a sodden handkerchief. 'It's my fault,' she cried. 'I'm to blame.'

'No,' said her husband, kneeling down and looking at her. 'It was what he wanted – we couldn't have stopped him, you know that.'

'That's not what I mean,' she said, sniffing.

William looked at her, not understanding. He held her hand. 'What do you mean?' he asked.

'I went into town today, to buy Robson a present for when he got his wings. I found a lovely pair of tan gloves and a blue tie. When I took them to be wrapped the girl at the counter knew me, and said she knew Robson. She said he was writing her letters...'

'Well, I'm sure he writes letters to lots of girls.'

'I know, that's what I said. But it made me feel... angry.'

'Angry? Why?'

She started to cry again. 'Because I didn't know this girl, and she seemed so nice, so pretty and polite. I was angry because this war has taken our son away and I miss him every day. But I realised that Robson had a life all of his own that he didn't tell us about, that I wasn't a part of, and I felt jealous I suppose because I thought he was closer to this girl than he was to me and so I left his present on the counter. It's silly I know but I think it's my fault he's dead, don't you see?'

'No, no...' said her husband, and he reached up and put an arm around her shoulders. 'It's not your fault, love, not at all.'

9-year old Mike Fox knelt beside his bed, saying his prayers, the nails in the bare floorboards pressing into his knees through the thin pyjamas. From downstairs he could hear the muffled sound of the evening news on his parents' wireless. He pictured his dad sitting at the table, braces hanging loose and shirt collar undone, exhausted from a day's labour at Tomlinson's, listening carefully to the reports of battles in faraway places, and his mum by the stove, sewing, with the cat on her knee, but he couldn't make out what the announcer was saying. A few odd words - *Atlantic... North Africa...* and *German* - drifted up the stairs but other than that it just sounded like the usual drone.

'...*foreverandeveramen.*' Finished, Mike leant down and reached under the bed for his shoe box, pulled it out and scrambled into bed. He took the small battery bicycle light from his bedside drawer and turned it on, and as he lifted the lid the soft yellow glow illuminated the contents. Mike's egg collection was impressive. Sitting in small dimples in the cotton wool his mum had given him to line the bottom of the box, he gazed at them, mouthing their names... blackbird, song thrush, mistle thrush, hedge sparrow, house sparrow, robin, wren, skylark, swallow, house martin, pied wagtail, pheasant, peewit, moorhen, coot and his favourite of the lot – a barn owl's egg. Not that it was the most attractive, just a white ping-pong ball of an egg really, but the owl had nearly taken his finger off when he stole it, which made the prize extra special.

He looked up, hearing the familiar rumble of bombers overhead. He inched back the curtain a tiny bit, strained to look up into the night sky, and counted them – one, two, four, five... seven in all, heading down towards Belvoir. Probably from Syerston or Newton. Wellingtons, just like the one that blew up in Barnes' Field, according to his dad.

Mike thought about what Bobby Brown had said that morning, about going down Barkestone Lane to raid the coot's nest under the bridge. It would be far more interesting to see what they could find in Barnes' Field. There could be all sorts lying around – machine gun bullets, maybe some still in their cases, and they could fire them with a nail and a hammer; and maybe some bombs - that would be much more fun. Only when he went past the field at home time there were mean-looking guards all over the place. Not the usual Look Duck and Vanish, but proper soldiers from Whatton camp. There was no chance of getting past them, even at night. And his dad would do his nut if he was dragged home by that sergeant with the revolver in his belt.

He watched until the navigation lights of the last bomber had disappeared from view then let go of the curtain, replaced the lid on his egg collection and shoved the box back under his bed. Perhaps they'll be done clearing the wreckage come the weekend, he thought, lying back on his pillow. He yawned. *I bet Bobby'd rather have some machine gun bullets than a coot's egg any day...*

At a quarter to eleven that night, just before Mike Fox had been sent to bed, the seven aircraft from 305 Squadron took off, joining bombers flying across the North Sea to their targets. The squadron took advantage of the raid on Duisburg to begin the delicate process of dealing with the personal effects of the six comrades who had died over Elton. Known as the Committee of Adjustment, a small group of men, including the adjutant, warrant sergeant, a clerk from the pay office, several orderlies and the station priest entered the rooms and billets of each deceased airman. Quickly and quietly, they stripped the beds of linen, piling it into bags for the station laundry, and fresh folded sheets were placed on the bare mattresses, ready for the next occupant. Lockers, cabinets and drawers were emptied of personal belongings, every pocket and wallet gone through for photographs or any other evidence that might betray an affair, and toilet bags cleared of prophylactics. Anything that might prove embarrassing or upsetting to family and loved ones, tokens of sexual conquest such as stockings or garters, along with magazines and newspapers and incriminating love-letters, were thrown away. Books, clothes and small personal items with little or no value were collected for other crews to divide between themselves, and the rest, including letters (some of them final), photographs, shaving kits, and cufflinks were placed in sealed boxes. Items of flying kit and uniforms were returned to the stores for re-issue, and if all went to plan the operation was over within a few hours; all that remained was to return the personal effects to the dead men's families, along with letters of condolence, which were written by the squadron's commanding officer, Squadron Leader Kleczyński. If the Committee of Adjustment did its job well, by the time the crews returned from the operation over Germany, no trace of the crew of Wellington R1017 would remain, and replacement crews would never suspect that they were sleeping in dead men's beds.

A similar tidying up operation was carried out at RAF Brize Norton, where the other cadets who had taken part in the day's cross-country navigation exercise spoke briefly about their former friends before returning to the business of earning their wings.

Gertrude Parkinson and her only child sat up into the small hours, thinking about Bill. The wireless had been turned off, the curtains drawn. The house was silent, save for the ticking of the clock on the mantlepiece. Each was deep in their own thoughts, trying to make sense of the telegram.

Although he didn't mention it, something had been nagging at George all afternoon, something which he'd kept putting to the back of his mind, because it felt so, well *illogical*. He couldn't quite put his finger on it but had felt that perhaps something *had* happened to Bill. That sudden strange feeling he'd had in church; it wasn't really as if someone was walking over his grave, he'd felt there was more to it than that, but he didn't know what. It had happened a couple of times before, once when they were quite young, and George, who was playing in the garden, had felt a sudden premonition that Bill was in some kind of danger – he'd told his mother who went into the house and found Bill playing with a poker in the fire, having pulled the fire guard away. A similar thing had happened when they were at Ashville, and George, who at the time was working on an essay in a classroom, had felt a blinding pain in his temple, not knowing that at exactly the same time, according to his pals, Bill had cracked his head against a rugby post on the playing field. He'd made nothing of it then, it seemed like a drama spun out of nothing by excitable schoolboys, but the more George thought about today's episode and the fact that the telegram stated Bill had died at 1125, which was just as the wedding service was ending, it seemed as if there might be something in it. And the fact that the two boys had such a close relationship, having lived in the womb and grown up together, made it all the more reasonable that they might have some sort of empathetic communication.

George chose not to tell his mother about what had happened. Like Mrs Newton, Gertrude had hoped there might have been a mistake. She saw that Bill's serial number as it appeared in the telegram was incorrect – that shouldn't happen should it? – and had corrected it with a pencil to prove to herself that she wasn't wrong. But George insisted that this kind of error happened all the time – typists in the office made those mistakes daily...

At last Gertrude said, 'I'm not sure I can take another funeral, George. First your father, then Margaret, and now Billy. It's too much. Too much.'

The woods were silent. Nobody moved or spoke. They hardly breathed.

Tadeusz relaxed his grip on the rifle for just a moment, and lifted his head a little, easing the stiffness out of his shoulders and neck. The partisans had been waiting in the woods for nearly an hour, not daring to move for fear of making a noise. The slightest shift of a man's weight could crack a twig that would echo through the trees and be heard a mile off, Olek said. In the stillness of the moonlit night, without a breath of wind, even whispers would carry a long way.

He looked to his left. About five metres away lay Józefina, her rifle hidden in the undergrowth, the leather strap wound around her wrist. Józefina's aim was deadly, no-one could work out where her talent came from, not even her, but put a gun in Józefina's hand and she could shoot the balls off a fly. A couple of metres to the right knelt Pawel, crouched tight against a tree, his Schmeisser machine gun held still, pointing down to the track. Tadeusz couldn't see the boy's eyes under the peak of his soft cap, but knew that they were fixed on the point where they expected the Germans to appear any minute.

There were another half a dozen fighters positioned in the woods. Intelligence had told them some of the Germans were using this track when returning to their barracks from the town, where they'd been drinking. This far north of Warsaw, in the depths of the forest, the Germans should be more careful, but Tadeusz knew their complacency came from arrogance. Since the invasion they had treated the Poles with utter contempt. Well they'd be taught a lesson tonight...

Tadeusz didn't know the surnames of any of the fighters, and they didn't know his. To them he was just Tadeusz, and he didn't talk about where he came from either. It meant if any were caught they couldn't reveal names under torture, so their families should remain safe. Only their leader, Olek, had that information, and it was kept safely in his head. Tadeusz hadn't seen his family for well over a year now, having fled into the forest to join the Home Army when the Germans marched into Warsaw. There he'd been trained to use a gun and a knife, to throw grenades and attach explosives to railway tracks. They'd taught him how to live off the land, and to steal food when they needed to; he'd learned more about Poland's history, the true intentions of the Soviets towards the Polish nation, and about the struggle. But that was for the future, and Tadeusz could only think about the present.

Maybe the Germans weren't coming tonight. A quiet voice inside his head hoped that was the case; not because he was afraid – he didn't fear death – but because of what he knew would happen if they did manage to kill a few soldiers. The Germans would round up dozens of civilians, as many as fifty civilians for each German killed, and shoot them, in public. It was a horrific, cruel tactic, designed to prevent this kind of operation, but Tadeusz knew they had to carry on if they were going to defeat the Germans. If they didn't take the fight to the Germans, who would? He pushed the uncomfortable thought from his head.

There was a small movement in the trees above, and Tadeusz lifted his eyes to see an owl on a branch, looking down at him. He smiled. The sound of voices, and the tramping of feet, coming from down below, brought his attention back to the job. He placed his cheek against the butt of his Mauser, fixed his eye on the sights, and through the birches saw four men stagger along the track. He looked for a target. *No. Not four men.* Two of them were women, holding tight to the soldiers. And they were all drunk.

Tadeusz tightened his finger on the trigger and waited for the command to fire.

Just before midnight in his office at RAF Brize Norton, the officer in command of 2SFTS, Group Captain Ronald Kershaw, was preparing to write two letters. But he was tired, and it had been a long day, and he told himself he wasn't in the best of moods to do the job just this minute. The writing of the letters of condolence, never an easy task, could wait until the morning. He switched off the anglepoise lamp and closed the office door.

A hundred miles away at RAF Syerston, an unknown Polish officer wrote the following entry in the 305 Squadron War Diary:

RAF Station, Syerston. 12th June 1941.
We report that a tragic accident took place today – Wellington K 1017 together with crew:
F.Lt. Stefanicki Tadeusz
P.O. Kowalcze Stanisław
P.O. Wojtowicz Marian
P.O. Zirkwitz Aleksander
Sgt. Krawczyk Jerzy

Sgt. Mruk Kazimierz
collided mid-air with an Oxford, and as a result both machines went down. All crews were killed.
Rest in Peace![26]

The raid on the marshalling yards was successful, with all seven aircraft from 305 Squadron dropping their bombs and returning safely to land at Syerston at 0425. The exhausted crews were in a strange mood as they climbed out of their aircraft, feeling a mixture of elation after the raid, and sadness about the fate of their friends on board K for King. Pulling their flying helmets and gloves off they mooched around, the talk less excited than usual, the atmosphere subdued. After the debrief some got changed out of their flying kit and went to the mess for a drink or an early breakfast, while others fell into their beds, worn out. Some remained in their overalls and flying jackets, too tired to sleep, and slumped in armchairs smoking cigarettes and going over the events of the last 24 hours in their heads. And some, in need of space perhaps, stood on the balcony of the Watch Office and watched the sun rise on another beautiful summer morning.

They may even have noticed a sentry lift the red and white barrier at the station gate by the Fosse Way, allowing through a horse and cart, driven by a teenage girl, and carrying two dozen churns of fresh milk from her father's farm.

Thirty-Eight

---

[26] Polish Institute and Sikorski Museum, Archive Ref No: LOT.A.V.37/8A

The members of the crew of Wellington R1017 were buried with full military honours at Newark Cemetery on Sunday 15 June, at half-past three in the afternoon. The six coffins, draped with Polish flags and decorated with flowers, were carried on RAF lorries, a guard of honour marching in columns on either side. There was a full of turnout of crews from both 304 and 305 Squadrons.

The funeral service was carried out by the Roman Catholic parish priest of the Holy Trinity church on Parliament Street. Airmen and ground crews stood to attention in the warm summer sun as the coffins were lowered into the graves, flags were lowered and a bugler sounded the Last Post. Led by Squadron Leader Ścibior, the crew of Wellington R1696, which had been flying with R1017 three days earlier, stood respectfully, remembering their friends. 305 Squadron's commanding officer, the newly-promoted Wing Commander Bohdan Kleczyński, saluted the fallen men before turning smartly and marching away, watched by the squadron mascot Ciapek.

The service over, the men of 305 Squadron returned to Syerston, to celebrate their comrades or to be with their own thoughts. The Squadron's log for that day makes no mention of the funerals, noting only that the wind was S to SW 5-10 mph, and recording a few minor personnel changes on the station. The funerals also went unreported in the local paper, the *Newark Advertiser*. Life, and the war, went on.

1941 was to be a hard year for the Polish bomber squadrons – 244 of their men were to die on operations. The night after the funerals the squadron flew again to Duisburg, with all aircraft returning. However, two nights later, on 18 June, Wellington R1696 SM-P would fail to return from an operation over Bremen. Fortunately for him and his crew, Squadron Leader Ścibior was not flying the aircraft that night. The bomber was shot down by a night fighter over the Den Helder peninsula, Holland, and although the pilot Sgt Stanislaus Lewek and three others survived, both gunners were killed. Ścibior himself would be shot down less than two months later during an operation on Frankfurt and Aachen. He survived the attack and was taken prisoner and spent the rest of the war in Stalag 3.[27]

On Monday 16 June, Mr and Mrs W Newton of Deckham, Gateshead, caught the early LNER train from Newcastle to Grantham. They had been issued with railway warrants by the office at RAF Syerston and sat in an awkward silence as they watched the countryside and industrial towns of the north move steadily past their carriage window. Other than them, it seemed that most of the other passengers on the train were servicemen, all smoking, sleeping or playing cards. When they arrived at Grantham several hours later, they were received by an English RAF officer who directed them to a blue staff car and accompanied them the fifteen and a half miles to RAF Syerston. The driver had been given specific orders to go the back way, via Long Bennington, avoiding Elton and Barnes' Field.

The day also began early for the officers, instructors and cadets of 2 Service Flying Training School at RAF Brize Norton. A select number had spent the previous evening polishing belts and buttons and pressing their uniforms, and immediately after breakfast they dressed, paraded and climbed into a convoy of trucks and cars that would take them on the three-hour journey up the Fosse Way to Nottinghamshire. Among them was Ronald Kershaw, Group Captain (Ret.) whose letter of condolence to Mr and Mrs Newton now lay unopened on the doormat in Gateshead. At that moment in Goole, Gertrude Parkinson was sitting down to read another letter from Group Captain Kershaw, written at the same time, commiserating with her on the death of her boy. He was, he

---

[27] Pilot Officer Zbigniew Siarkowski, the air gunner who I believe witnessed the collision between the Wellington and Oxford, survived hostilities, marrying Maria Czerenkiewicz in Basford, Nottingham in 1944 and emigrating with her to Canada after the war. He died in Burlington, Canada in 1979.

wrote, 'a very good lad and a promising pilot with the makings of a splendid NCO.' He also begged her to realise that her son 'died for his country just as though he had been killed in action,' and was sure that her 'loss will seem easier to bear if you think of it in this way.'

That afternoon, Robson Newton's coffin was collected at RAF Syerston, and driven on the back of a lorry, draped in the Union Flag, to Newark Cemetery. The coffin was carried by a bearer party to a plot close to six new graves, covered with fresh earth and with simple white wooden crosses at their head, and lowered into the ground to the sound of the Last Post. A little while later, walking away from the grave, Mrs Newton noticed that the dates on the new graves matched with that on which her son had been killed, and realised for the first time how many men had died that morning. She and her husband were invited back to the Officers' Mess at Syerston, where they were the guests of Wing Commanders Kleczyński and Drysdale, before catching the train to Gateshead. The party from Brize Norton stayed at Syerston, where they spent the night before the second leg of their journey, to Goole.

All weekend George Parkinson had seemed to do nothing but think about his brother's funeral. He had been given a few days' compassionate leave by his editor, which was just as well, because there was no end of things to organise, from putting a death notice in the *Goole Times* to making telephone calls and sending telegrams inviting guests, as well as the matter of arranging cars, flowers and food. At first, he had agreed with his mother that Bill should be buried close to the family in Goole, but as the difficulty of organising everything, from obtaining a plot to arranging the handling of Bill's coffin had grown, he had begun to change his mind. On Monday afternoon Gertrude had shown him a telegram which had just arrived from RAF Syerston, informing her that the cortege would arrive at 1.45pm on Tuesday.

'We need to ensure we leave enough time to conduct the service and get to the cemetery,' she said, thinking out loud. 'But we can't have the sandwiches standing around getting dry,' she added. 'Can you-?'

'Don't worry Mother, I'll sort it out with North Street,' said George. The Methodist church had been a great help, and immediately took a large part of the burden, which allowed George to spend more time with his mother. He thought she seemed to be dealing very well with it, all things considered.

Guests began to arrive on the morning of the 17th, which as for the previous funerals turned out to be warm and sunny. Members of the church, relatives from both sides of the family, Bill's employers at Townends, friends including former pupils from Ashville and the local Auxiliary Fire Service where he volunteered as a messenger, were greeted and taken through to the garden, where they chatted in the sunshine. When the cortege arrived, on time at precisely 1.45, George and his mother were shocked to see the size of the contingent that had travelled up from Syerston. Several RAF staff cars and lorries, stuffed with dozens of men in smart RAF uniforms, formed up in ranks around the hearse containing Bill's coffin, draped in the Union Flag.

Following the funeral service, William Parkinson's coffin was taken the short distance to Goole Cemetery. Neighbours stood in their doorways and front gardens to watch as the columns of officers, NCOs and cadets, with their distinctive white cap flashes, slow-marched along Hook Road. Mourners followed, and traffic stopped as the cortege passed, the drivers getting out and bowing their heads in respect. The short journey took all of 14 minutes.

At the graveside the officers and men stood smartly to attention while the coffin was lowered into the ground. The Last Post sounded, the mournful notes echoing around the flat brown fields alongside the river Ouse, and on command the men turned and marched away.

Bill Parkinson, the last of the eight men who died on June 12, 1941, had been laid to rest.

Thirty-Nine

I step off the 1024 from Doncaster at Goole Station. The train pulls out, revealing the platform opposite, and I look across the line at the bench where my mum and her best friend Lucy sat gabbing one weekend in 1950 while the London train pulled in and then left without them noticing. It is also the platform, I realise, where Bill Parkinson said goodbye to his mother and brother on the day he enlisted, ten years earlier.

I have come to Goole to see for myself some of the places that featured in Bill's story. Although I have made many visits to the town over the years, I need to see it again, through new eyes, placing the characters in the locations where they once lived. I walk down Boothferry Road, once the busy main street running through the town, where George Parkinson worked as a young reporter on the local paper. Now the street is a soulless pedestrianised shopping precinct, and the gorgeous red-brick façade of the *Goole Times* building houses a charity shop. I stand outside 9 Fountayne Street, where the Parkinson's lived (smaller than I had imagined), only a few hundred yards from Frederick St, where my mum and dad bought their first house, which itself is just a stone's throw from Richard Cooper Street, where Mum was born and grew up. The house and street are now gone, replaced by bland modern developments. I do some checking of old maps in the town library, a 1960s building sitting on the site of the old Carlisle Terrace Methodist Church, where Mum and Dad were married, and a little further along that road find Townends, the Chartered Accountants where Bill started his first job and made friends, many of whom later attended his funeral a few months later. I go inside and ask the receptionist if they have any personnel records from the war, but am told they were all thrown out months ago, to make space.

Forking off from Carlisle Street is Victoria Street, and the Manse where Bill's father died one evening while writing a sermon, and behind that the schoolroom of the North Street Methodist Chapel, where he preached, and where his daughter Margaret was assisting with the decorations when he was struck down. The chapel itself seems to have been demolished, replaced by a modern building, and there's a sign outside announcing that this is now the Central Church of the Methodist/United Reformed Church. Looking in past the sign I see a couple of ladies sitting in the porch, talking, and without thinking about it I open the door and ask if this is actually the site of the old chapel. Oh yes, they say, it is, and then I hear the sound of organ music, see the open door to the chapel, and wonder if I've walked in on a service.

But I have only interrupted a bible class, and the minister taking it is sitting quietly to one side, smiling. Joseph introduces himself, and I apologise, explaining what I am doing in town. As soon as I mention that Bill Parkinson's father used to preach here before the war it all comes flooding out. Joan Taun, one of the ladies, knew the family, especially George, and Ann whom he later married, and the rest of the Wilsons, including Enid, who she said used to be her Sunday School Teacher. I immediately assume she must be referring to my auntie Enid, wife of my uncle Roy, my mum's brother, but no, she was meaning my mother, who it turned out used to play the piano for the Sunday School Baby's Class at Carlisle Terrace when she was only 14. Following the demolition of that building to make way for the new library, the two congregations were united and worshipped together at North Street. I explained that I was Enid Wilson's son and Joan also remembered my mother's sisters, including Doreen, who also taught at Sunday School, and her brothers Roy and Fred, who later played in the Salvation Army band.[28] I remembered Mum telling me about how she had begged her mother to pay for dance lessons when she was little, but was told that she could have piano lessons instead. 'One day you'll be too old to dance but you'll never be too old to play the piano,' my grandmother told her. And so soon she was playing piano for the Sunday School, which she continued to do in later life, playing hymns for the local old people's home when we moved to Bingham.

'Is your mother still alive?' Joan asks, and I reply that she's 94 now and doing very well. 'Please remember me to her,' she says, 'although she'll remember me as Joan Richardson. I was only a little girl then,' and I promise that I will.

Joan asks me what I'm doing in Goole, and I say something vague about revisiting a few of the old places. However, I am really in Goole for another reason.

---

[28] I actually bumped into my Auntie Enid later that afternoon, when I saw her in the café opposite the train station. I had to hurry to catch my train so only had time for a few words but we spoke properly a couple of days later on the phone. She and her son Simon also gave me invaluable help in trying to track down the Mr and Mrs Bean who attended Bill's funeral.

Forty

William Wharton Parkinson's grave can be found in Section D of the West Plot, Goole Cemetery, Grave number 3239. It is a quiet spot, on the edge of the cemetery, beneath some trees and with views of the flat Yorkshire landscape and the railway swing bridge over the Ouse. Curiously, he lies not next to his father William and sister Margaret, or his mother Gertrude, as I had expected, but alongside another serviceman, a young artilleryman who died in 1940.

Instead of the simple wooden cross that was placed there on the day of his funeral in 1941, there is now a white Commonwealth War Grave headstone, bearing the inscription:

> 1067083 LDG AIRCRAFTMAN
> WW PARKINSON
> U/T PILOT
> ROYAL AIR FORCE
> 12TH JUNE 1941 AGE 19

In addition to the formal details of name, rank and age, there is also a simple but moving epitaph:

> TO LIVE IN THE HEARTS
> OF THOSE WE LOVE
> IS NOT TO DIE

I'm not familiar with the quotation but discover later that it comes from the poem *Hallowed Ground* by the Scottish poet Thomas Campbell (1777-1844). As well as being a popular romantic poet he was a passionate and outspoken supporter of Poland, which in the early 1830s was suffering at the hands of Imperial Russia. Campbell co-founded the Literary Association of the Friends of Poland, whose cause he championed in his poem *The Pleasures of Hope*. News of the capture of Warsaw by the Russians in 1831 affected him personally and he wrote in one of his letters 'Poland preys on my heart night and day.'

In the bare branches spreading over William Parkinson's grave, a robin sings. I say a final short prayer and turn away to go home.

Forty-One

January 2023.

The phone rings, startling me out of sleep. I'm not sure where I am. It is dark. Fumbling for the phone, I look at the time through aching eyes – not quite 5.30am. I see it's my brother Tim calling, and in the same moment I suddenly remember where I am – in a hotel room in Leeds, where I am working. I better answer it.

Tim is straight to the point. Mum has been rushed into hospital in Nottingham and he's there, waiting for news. It doesn't look good. Can I get down?

I call the 2nd AD, apologising for waking her and explaining that I won't be coming into the studio today. She says she'll let production know and tells me not to worry about the shoot, hoping everything's alright with my mum. In no time at all I dress, brush my teeth, stuff my clothes and books into my bag, check out of the hotel and am driving down the M1. Negotiating the early morning traffic, I remember that the last time I did anything like this was when my father had his second heart attack – a phone call in the middle of the night, this time from Mum, in a dreadful state, a panicked drive down south, fearing the worst and arriving at the hospital to find Dad in a coma. I took Mum home to get some rest and was driving her in to see him the following morning when my brother called to say that Dad had gone.

I was never able to say goodbye to Dad, and he was lying dead on a trolley when I told him for the first time that I loved him. Mum held it together, only shedding a tear when the minister came round from the chapel to comfort her. She was more concerned about making sure she had a smart coat and hat to wear to Dad's funeral, so I took her to the shops and we bought what she needed.

Thankfully however, Mum isn't in such an extreme situation as Dad was. It seems she may have had some sort of a ministroke – she is hallucinating, very confused and in great pain with her hip, but nothing is broken and the medics can't quite diagnose the problem. She remains in hospital for three weeks, still delirious and getting physically weaker by the day as the doctors fight the infection. Sepsis is raging through her system - she thinks she is in chapel one minute, hearing hymns from her childhood which she sings out loud, and back in the present the next, extremely frightened because she doesn't know what is happening to her. In rare moments of lucidity my brothers and I talk to her about the future – if and when she is finally discharged, going home doesn't seem to be an option, so many changes would need to be made. Mum agrees that going into a home, at least temporarily for respite and while we assess the situation, would be the best idea. We find a care home nearby named (ironically, as it has been obsessing me for over a year) the *Fosse Way View*. Tim says he'll eat his hat if she sets foot in there, having previously refused to even consider the place because it didn't have a view of the Fosse Way and said it should be called the *A52 Nottingham to Grantham Road View* instead. But it's a nice place, with good people working in it, and Mum is happy to give it a try. A short while later she is discharged from hospital and taken into Fosse Way View, and Tim posts a photograph of himself eating his hat.

Mum settles into her new home, uncomfortable at first, asking how long she will be there, but she knows she is vulnerable now and needs to regain her strength; the staff are wonderful with her, she discovers she has some old friends from the village as neighbours in the home, and as she slowly becomes used to the unexpected change in her life we can see her returning to her old self.

The year continues as it started when only a few weeks later I am involved in a car crash, serious enough to make me stop driving, and as I can't work at my day job for a while I spend a lot more time with Mum. We talk about how she feels now, and the future, but she is happier talking about the past. I bring in photos and letters relating to Bill's story, and she remembers more episodes from her younger days. But although I try to move forward with the book, typing with one finger, it's proving hard going. The Fosseway Writers are all working on short stories which they are going to publish in a collection in time for the Newark Book Festival in July.[29] I want to be included, but haven't written anything yet, having lived with the story of the crash for nearly a year now, and promising myself that it must come first, worried about failing to make good on my promises. One day, without really thinking about it I start writing a wartime story about a young air gunner arriving at an RAF station not unlike Syerston on his first posting after passing through gunnery school, and the letters he writes to his parents. A parallel story emerges of a senior officer, a lonely man brought out of retirement to help run the RAF administrative machine, who has responsibility for running the Committee of Adjustment, including writing letters of consolation to the bereaved families of lost aircrew. You can probably guess how it ends.

The story goes forward for inclusion in the collection, and having enjoyed writing it, I start thinking about writing a few more, describing life on the anonymous station as seen from the point of view of other members of the squadron – pilots, ground crew, WAAFs and so on. I've lived and breathed this world for so long now it is not difficult to write a fictional version of it. I begin to think I might even be able to put together my own collection of stories. One night in the pub I chat to Martin about it, and we remember the conversation we'd had last year when I fantasised about writing about Lancasters, thinking that if it had the bomber's name in its title there would be a ready audience out there. I'd forgotten all about the idea because I was determined to write this book about Bill, but if I made the stories about Syerston when the

---

[29] Writings On The Walls, Fosseway Writers, 2023

Lancs were there, after 305 Squadron and their Wellingtons left for Lindholme, it could work... I have already promised Martin that I would have *What Happened* ready for publication in the summer, but a collection of fictional stories feels much more doable, and gives me another excuse for distancing myself from the problem of what to do with Bill's story. It's not that I haven't written any of the book – I have pages and pages. But I can't quite see how they make a complete story, and depressed by Mum's situation and my car accident I don't seem to have the energy to focus on it. What I don't see at the time is that I have been dwelling on death for months now, albeit deaths that occurred over eighty years ago, and it's all been getting to me. My brain is just desperate for a break.

So I write the stories, and *L For Lanc* is published, selling well. I am surprised and encouraged. My broken wrist is healing nicely, and I am able to return to my day job. Maybe now I can get on and finish the book...

After Mum has been in the home for half a year it is clear she won't be able to return to the independent life she was used to. She's increasingly frail and finds it daunting to face everyday issues. After discussions with the home and Mum we agree that she should stay in Fosse Way View, and as a result I spend all my spare time over the next couple of months sorting through the house before it is sold. Almost before I know it the 'FOR SALE' sign has come down, and the house is cleared. After several weeks of frenetic clearing and sorting, I take the opportunity (my last) to stand in my old bedroom and remember. This was where I spent my teenage years, making those models of Lancasters and Ju88s, displaying them on shelves and the pegboard my dad put up, hanging them from the ceiling and imagining being a bomber pilot as the beam from my torch sought them out in the dark skies over Berlin. Downstairs I stood for the last time in the living room, bare and empty now, thinking about when I first saw *The Dam Busters* on the telly, showed my finished models to my parents, and many years later, introduced them to the woman I was going to marry, and brought my young sons to see their grandparents. It was all gone now. I locked the door for the last time.

In May 2022, with no planning or real expectation, I set out to see if I could find out what happened to William Parkinson during the war. Soon I discovered that his death involved the deaths of seven other young men, and found stories about many more people, then and now, whose lives were (and still are) affected by that accident in the skies over Nottinghamshire. I have been thinking and writing a lot about death these past two years, dwelling on the deaths of those eight men, and by association the many thousands of men, women and children who died as a result of RAF bombing raids (flyers and civilians), German action in Poland and other occupied countries, and Putin's ongoing aggression in the Ukraine. More recently I have had to confront the possibility of death in the present, thinking about my mother and also myself. It's no surprise perhaps that the obsessions which trying to write this book created became the reasons why I couldn't finish it, although I wasn't necessarily aware of the irony at the time. I just tried to get on with it until it proved impossible, and I thought it was going to remain incomplete, unfinished, another failure. That was when I looked for help and found a wonderful doctor who took the time to listen to me. Talking therapy, and the support of family and friends helped me to recognise the things that were causing me so much anxiety. With their help I was able to re-emerge into the daylight, and soon I found the strength to continue and eventually finish this book. I am now having positive conversations with the residents of Elton village about placing a memorial in St Michael's church, commemorating the men who died that day, and if not completely healed, I think relations with my sons are on the way to recovery. That bottle of Bollinger, however, remains unopened...

What have I learned, having finished the book? I feel satisfied that I have discovered so much about William Parkinson and what happened on June 12th, 1941, although I couldn't answer all the questions that were raised by my research, and inevitably some teasing threads are left dangling. I never discovered whether that silver bracelet inscribed *Toby Dec 1939* belonged to any of the dead airmen, and I will forever wish I could turn back the clock so that Robert Brown didn't lose the St Christopher he found in Barnes' Field along with those bullets from the Wellington. What stories those objects might have told. Sadly, last autumn I heard from Robert that his dear friend Mike Fox had moved into a care home as his health deteriorated, which affected Robert badly. And then just a week ago I heard from Robert's daughter that Robert himself had been admitted into a care home in Grantham. She also told me that Mike had died a few months ago, which I didn't know.

In writing this book, where actual historical fact eluded me, I have resorted to fiction, based on research and the actual lived experience of people who were there. Perhaps some distant relatives of Robson Newton will read it and make contact, or the grandchildren of Joan Bailey will recognise the story of a wartime romance and get in touch, helping me to fill in more gaps. But with the help of my Auntie Enid and the *Goole Times* I did discover that the Mr and Mrs Bean who attended Bill's funeral were local Methodists, John and Minnie, who worshipped with the Beulah congregation on Moorland Road, although Sandra Spence, their granddaughter, is sure they were not related to my branch of the family. I wish I had been able to trace more relatives of the men on board the Wellington, but I am happy that I was able to meet Paula Pietrzak and learn so much about Jerzy Krawczyk's life. I don't think I will ever know if the doll that now sits on Marianna Machnikowski's shelf was with Jerzy when he died, or who made it, or who it was finally intended for. But I know what I think.

Most of all, I still don't know exactly what happened to make those two aeroplanes crash into each other over Elton, why they met in that place, at that height, at that time, when they were flying in such a huge, wide-open summer sky. These are things we may never learn, and I have to accept that. Some things just happen.

But I feel that, unintentionally perhaps, I have learned a few more things about myself. I already knew that like all human beings I have an inbuilt need to create (and enjoy) stories, to help make order out of chaos and sense out of confusion, but I wasn't fully aware of how much that affected my life. I have learned that there are things around me – places, buildings, objects and of course people, that I may have grown up with, ignored or taken for granted, which can suddenly show another side of themselves and reveal links to a hitherto unknown past. I have learned lessons about loss and guilt, and the value of life. I can see now where I have gone wrong, and maybe even begun to understand why. Hopefully I have a better idea about how to avoid making the same mistakes in the future. I have learned that I need to accept the good and the bad in life, and in me, however difficult that is.

I visit Mum as often as I can in her new home. She still has episodes when she becomes distressed and confused about where she is, and where Dad is, but mostly she's happy to see me and my brothers and talk about the old days. She has friends, her health and a nice view over the gardens. Importantly, I have learned from the mistake I made with my dad and am careful to tell Mum I love her each time I see her.

And I am becoming used to the very strong sense that from time to time there are ghosts over my shoulder, the ghosts of this story, watching and listening. They don't frighten me. I hope they are pleased with my story.

Acknowledgements

I would like to thank all the people and organisations who have given me so much assistance and advice, and without whose generous support this book would not have been possible: Fiona and Mike Reid and family; Robert Brown and Mike Fox; Tony Young, Gillian and Barrie Roberts and Adam Fisher; David Flint; Megan Bowden; Paula and Piotr Pietrzak and family; Magda and Marianna Machnikowska and family; Ian Shaw; Brian Gunn, John Johnson and Angela Copley; Chris Kemp, and Erin and Chris Page; Magda Brown; Tim Chamberlain; Shaun Noble, Piotr Hodyra and Wojciech Zmyślony; Lechosław Musiałkowski and Robert Pęczkowski; Joan Taun and Reverend Joseph Khwallah, Minister of the Central Methodist Church, Goole; Enid and Simon Wilson; Sandra Spence; Dr Pavneet Kaur of Ashville College, Harrogate; Tim and Pam Powell and members of EOTH Parish Meeting and PCC, and the residents of Elton-On-The-Hill, and Dr. Mo Elshazly.

Grateful thanks are also due to the staff and volunteers at Newark Air Museum; Andrew Dennis of the RAF Museum, Hendon and the staff and volunteers at RAF Museum, Cosford; the RAF Air Historical Branch, RAF Northolt; Metheringham Airfield Visitors Centre; the Lincolnshire Aircraft Recovery Group and the Lincolnshire Aviation Heritage Centre, East Kirkby; Ingham Heritage Group and the Polish Bomber Squadrons Centre, RAF Ingham; The National Archives at Kew; Lee Barton, Photographic Section, RAF Cranwell; The British Library; Jane Rogers, Editor, *Goole Times*; The British Newspaper Archive; Dan Ellin and the staff and volunteers at the International Bomber Command

Centre, Lincoln; Dr Andrzej Suchcitz, Keeper of Archives at the Polish Institute and Sikorski Museum, London; Squadron Leader Mark Williams and staff at 2 Flying Training School, RAF Syerston; Ben Dunnell and *The Aeroplane* Magazine/Key Publishing; Alamy Stock; Newark-Upon-Trent Cemetery; Access Models, Newark; the Fosseway Writers and Anthony and Lucy Foxwell and the staff of the LetsXcape Together Event & Boardgame Café, Newark, and finally the staff of the Fosse Way View Care Home, Bingham.

Special thanks to Martin Costello of Another Small Press for his encouragement and patience, to my brothers Johnny and Tim and their families, to my sons Gabriel and Daniel, and last but not least, my mother Enid Bean, who started the ball rolling.

If I have omitted to mention any person or organisation, or incorrectly captioned any photographs, please accept my sincere apologies.

Adrian Bean.

Bibliography

Publications:

Andrews, CF. *The Vickers Wellington 1&11 (Profile 125).* Profile Publications 1966.

Beck, Pip. *Keeping Watch, A WAAF in Bomber Command.* Goodall/Crecy 1989.

Bowman, Martin W. *The Wellington Bomber Story.* The History Press 2011.

Bowyer, Chaz. *The Wellington Bomber.* William Kimber 1986.

Calder, Angus. *The People's War.* Cape 1969.

Brooks, Robin J. *Nottinghamshire & Derbyshire Airfields in the Second World War.* Countryside Books 2003.

Cormack, Andrew, (illus. Volstad, Ron). *The Royal Air Force 1939-45 (Men At Arms 225).* Osprey 1990.

Cousins, Rodney. *Newark Inns & Public Houses.* Nottinghamshire County Council Leisure Services 1991.

Cynk, Jerzy B. *The PZL P23 Karas (Profile 104).* Profile Publications 1966.

Cynk, Jerzy B. *The PZL P37 Los (Profile 258).* Profile Publications 1973.

Davies, Norman. *Rising '44, The Battle for Warsaw.* Pan 2004.

Desbois, Father Patrick. *In Broad Daylight, The Secret Procedures behind the Holocaust by Bullets.* Arcade 2021.

Delve, Ken. *Vickers-Armstrong Wellington*. Crowood Press Aviation Series 1998.

Fahey, John. *Britain 1939 – 1945: The Economic Cost of Strategic Bombing.* University of Sydney 2004

Falconer, Jonathan. *Filming The Dam Busters.* Sutton 2005.

Ernest K Gann. *Fate is the Hunter.* Cassell 2011.

Garbutt, M and Goulding, B. *Lancaster.* Ian Allan 1971.

Hamlin, John F. *The Oxford, Consul and Envoy File.* Air-Britain 2001

Hastings, Max. *Bomber Command.* Michael Joseph 1979.

Herbert, Flt Lt JW (Janusz Meissner). *G For Genevieve.* Roy 1944

Herbert, Flt Lt JW (Janusz Meissner). *L FOR LUCY.* Riverside Press 1945.

HMSO. *Bomber Command.* HMSO 1941.

HMSO. *Pilot's Notes for Oxford 1 and 11.* HMSO 1944.

HMSO. *Pilot's Notes for Wellington.* HMSO 1944.

Kennedy, Paul. *Engineers of Victory.* Penguin 2014.

Lewis, Bruce. *Aircrew.* Cassell Military Classics 2000.

Mallory, Robert. *Newark in the Second World War.* Nottingham County Council/Newark and Sherwood District Council 1995

Machnikowska, Marianna. *The Story of a Doll. GAPA Aircraft History Magazine, Issue No 23.* August 2017

Marsh, Mike. *Goole At War Vol 1.* Chronicle Publications 2001.

Morris, Richard. *Guy Gibson.* Viking 1994.

Murray, Iain R. *Vickers Wellington Owners Workshop Manual.* Haynes Publishing 2012.

Musiałkowski, Lechosław. *Bomber Aircraft of 305 Squadron.* Mushroom Model Publications 2014.

Parkinson, George. *True Stories of Durham Pit-Life.* Kelly 1912.

Passmore, Richard. *Blenheim Boy.* Thomas Harmsworth 1981

Rawlings, John DR. *The Airspeed Oxford (Profile 227).* Profile Publications 1971.

Sweetman, John. *Bomber Crew.* Abacus 2005.

Shute, Neville. *Pastoral.* Pan 1964.

Shute, Neville. *Slide Rule.* Vintage 2009.

Spiller HJ. *Ticket to Freedom.* William Kimber 1988.

Taylor, James and Davidson, Martin. *Bomber Crew.* Hodder and Stoughton 2005.

Ward, Chris and Korcz, Grzegorz. *301 304 305 Polish Squadrons.* Bomber Command Books 2022.

Ward-Jackson, CH. *No Bombs At All.* Sylvan Press 1944.

Wilson, Kevin. *Men Of Air.* Phoenix 2008.

Websites:

Aircraft Q Failed To Return
https://rafww2butler.wordpress.com/

BAE Systems/Vickers Wellington
https://www.baesystems.com/en-uk/heritage/vickers-wellington

Blue Squadron – graves, cemeteries, monuments, memorials of Polish Airmen
https://niebieskaeskadra.pl/

British Newspaper Archive
https://www.britishnewspaperarchive.co.uk/

Commonwealth War Graves Commission
https://www.cwgc.org/

Find A Grave
https://www.findagrave.com/

International Bomber Command Centre
https://internationalbcc.co.uk/

Krysztek's List
https://listakrzystka.pl/

Lincolnshire Aircraft Recovery Group
https://www.lincsaviation.co.uk>about>aircraft-recovery

Lincolnshire Aviation Heritage Centre
https://www.lincsaviation.co.uk

Metheringham Airfield Visitor Centre
https://www.metheringhamairfield.co.uk/

National Archives
https://www.nationalarchives.gov.uk/

Newark Air Museum
http://www.newarkairmuseum.org/

Polish Air Force in WW11
https://www.polishairforce.pl/

Polish Airmen's Association UK
http://www.polishairmensassociation.org.uk/index.html

Polish Institute and Sikorski Museum
https://pism.org.uk/

Polish Bomber Squadrons Centre
https://www.rafingham.co.uk/

Royal Air Force Commands
https://forum.rafcommands.com/

RAF Air Historical Branch
https://www.raf.mod.uk/what-we-do/our-history/air-historical-branch/

RAF Brize Norton
https://www.raf.mod.uk/our-organisation/stations/raf-brize-norton/

RAF Museum Cosford
https://www.rafmuseum.org.uk/midlands/

RAF Museum Hendon
https://www.rafmuseum.org.uk/london/

RAF Syerston
https://www.raf.mod.uk/our-organisation/stations/raf-syerston/

305 Squadron Living History Group
https://www.305squadron.com/

Also by
Adrian Bean

L FOR LANC

While researching for the biography that would become *What Happened*, Adrian Bean met a former WAAF who had been stationed at Syerston in 1942. She was extremely helpful in providing background to life on a wartime bomber station, and shortly before her death, gave him a boxful of documents, including a number of anonymously written short stories about life in a Lancaster squadron, telling him that 'they were his to do what he wanted with'.

Although set on a bomber station during the darkest days of the war, these stories focus not on heroic derring-do in the flak-torn skies over Germany, but on day-to-day life. From the poignant tragedy of 'The Committee Of Adjustment' to the satire of 'A Different Angle', and the chilling 'The End Of The Tour' to the dark introspection of 'Ubendum Wemendum', this short but powerful collection of stories conveys life on a wartime bomber station as experienced by the ordinary men and women, aircrew, groundcrew and 'desk-flyers' who lived it.

£7.99

Laura Lee Dove

NAILING JELLY TO THE CEILING

Life is full of possibilities, we're told. We are encouraged to reach out and grasp them. But what happens when life seems to present us with an overload of impossibilities? For some of us, all we can do is try to cling on as we slowly and painfully lose our grasp on life itself. There are some things we just cannot control. Nailing Jelly To The Ceiling searingly illustrates this truth, whether you believe it or not. It is a deeply personal, brutally honest account of painful events that impacted the author's life over a long period of time.

Mental health is a complex, diverse subject and despite positive anti-stigma campaigning and acceptance discourse prevalent in modern culture, often remains an unwelcome topic for discussion. The reality of living with mental illness is not easily put into words, but Laura Lee Dove has achieved precisely that, nurturing understanding and support for both those who suffer as well as those who don't.

£9.99

Martin Costello

ALL THE THINGS I WROTE BEFORE I WROTE THE THING I ALWAYS WANTED TO WRITE

Eight picaresque ballads of life in the East Midlands - and sometimes on the seashore - by mild mannered anarchist & writer Martin Costello.

The elder boys carried the old sofa to the end of the pier, and the family set it up looking outward across the water so that they might catch an early sight of the ferry. They took turns on the watch through the long late afternoon, the children happily amusing themselves on the pier, under the pier, behind the sofa, in the mud, in the shallows, in the empty car park, on the roof of the ticket hut, up and down the ferry lane, along the grassy dunes of the strand, on the smooth round rocks of the tide wall and around the skirts of the mother Bidna to her passing amusement and then impatience and then amusement again. As evening threatened, a dog-walker from the lane helpfully called out that there would be no ferries that day, on account of the coming storm.

The story the author had always been trying to write is not included in this collection but happily is now complete after 22 years of editing.

£7.99

ANOTHER SMALL PRESS

A selection of titles available from www.anothersmallpress.net

Roger Stennett

CLOUD CUCKOO LAND

Roger Stennett is a Welsh poet, dramatist, screenwriter, audio and animation writer who has written thousands of poems since the 2020 global pandemic struck. Cloud Cuckoo Land represents the distillation of some 4,000 works into a selection of 100.

In a Classical Greek comic play by Aristophanes called 'The Birds', cuckoos were challenged to build a city in the sky amongst the clouds, to prove how powerful and godlike they were. Such a bizarre undertaking was clearly unreasonable and impractical, and ever since that time the phrase has been regarded as shorthand for impossible plans, unrealistic schemes and crazy dreams.

Classicist Roger Stennett remains undeterred.

Covering a wide range of themes and approaches including love poems, nature poems, historical poems, theatrical poems and poems of childhood, every page turn is an encounter with a new joy, an old friend, a common foe or a familiar sense of the cycles of lived experience.

£12.99

Printed and bound by CPI Group (UK) Ltd, Croydon, CR0 4YY
12/08/2024
01025371-0002